POLITICAL CONFLICT AND ECONOMIC
CHANGE IN NIGERIA

Written under the auspices of the
Center of International Studies
Princeton University

Also by Henry Bienen:

*Tanzania: Party Transformation and
Economic Development* (1967 and 1970)
Violence and Social Change (1968)
*Kenya: The Politics of Participation
and Control* (1974)

Editor and coauthor of:

*The Military Intervenes: Case Studies
in Political Development* (1968)
The Military and Modernization (1970)

With David Morell:

Political Participation under Military Regimes (1976)

With V. P. Diejomaoh:

*The Political Economy of Income
Distribution in Nigeria* (1981)

POLITICAL CONFLICT AND ECONOMIC CHANGE IN NIGERIA

HENRY BIENEN

Professor of Politics and International Affairs,
Woodrow Wilson School, Princeton University

FRANK CASS

First published 1985 in Great Britain by
FRANK CASS & CO. LTD.
Gainsborough House, Gainsborough Road,
London, E11 1RS, England

and in the United States of America by
FRANK CASS & CO. LTD.
c/o Biblio Distribution Centre
81 Adams Drive, P.O. Box 327, Totowa, N.J. 07511

British Library Cataloguing in Publication Data

Bienen, Henry
   Political conflict and economic change in
   Nigeria.
   1. Nigeria — Social conditions — 1960–
   I. Title
   966.9'05   HN831.A8

   ISBN 0-7146-3266-X

Typeset by Williams Graphics, Abergele, Clwyd
Printed and bound in Great Britain by
A. Wheaton & Co. Ltd., Exeter

To
Leigh Buchanan Bienen,
my wife and traveling
companion

Contents

List of Tables

List of Figures

Acknowledgments

Political Conflict and Economic Change in Nigeria is based on articles and essays written between 1978 and 1983. These articles and essays have been edited but they have not been revised.

Chapter 1 is new; chapter 2, 'Oil Revenues and Policy Choice in Nigeria', was published as World Bank Staff Working Paper number 592, The World Bank, Washington, DC, 1983, and is reprinted with permission from the World Bank. Chapter 3, 'The Politics of Income Distribution: Institutions, Ethnicity and Class', is reprinted from my chapter of the same title, in Henry Bienen and Vremudia P. Diejomaoh (editors), *The Political Economy of Income Distribution in Nigeria* (New York, Holmes and Meier, 1981), pp. 127–72, reprinted with permission from Holmes and Meier. Chapter 4, 'Religion and Economic Change in Nigeria', was first published in James Finn (editor), *Global Economics and Religion* (New Brunswick, Transaction Books, 1983) pp. 201–28, reprinted with permission of the Council on Religion and International Affairs. Chapter 5, 'The 1979 Nigerian Elections', is from *Competitive Elections in Developing Countries*, edited by Ergun Ozbudun and Myron Weiner, forthcoming, by permission of the American Enterprise Institute and Duke University Press. I am grateful to all the publishers for their permission to reprint these essays.

I have benefited from the comments of many people. James Finn and colleagues at the Council on Religion and International Affairs gave thoughtful criticisms of my paper on religion and economic change. Myron Weiner and Ergun Ozbudun were helpful editors for my paper on the 1979 elections in Nigeria. My colleagues at Princeton and in Nigeria and the United Kingdom who participated in the project of the Research Program in Development Studies of Princeton University on income distribution in Nigeria were most helpful in commenting on my own work for that joint endeavor. I want to especially thank my co-editor Vremudia Diejomaoh for all his help on the project and for all his effort in Nigeria.

I am in debt to the universitites of Ibadan and Lagos for providing hospitality and intellectual and administrative homes for various undertakings over the last decade. Ambassador Donal Easum, now President of the African–American Institute, was always helpful to me in Nigeria. At Princeton University, my colleagues Robert Tignor and Mark Gersovitz have been friendly critics of various papers on Nigeria. Indeed, chapter 2 on oil revenues and policy choice relies on some work that Mark Gersovitz and I did together. This chapter also benefited from comments by Alan Gelb and Geoffrey Lamb of the World Bank and from Joan Nelson of the Overseas Development Council.

The Woodrow Wilson School has provided excellent administrative and secretarial support over the last years and Dean Donald Stokes has supported the research task of his faculty. While I was Director of the Research Program in Development Studies, and continuing to the present, Jerri Kavanagh has provided assistance on budgets, office management and my own work. To her I am especially grateful.

I dedicated my first book on Tanzania to my wife in 1967. It is time to say thanks in this way again to Leigh Buchanan Bienen.

Henry Bienen

CHAPTER ONE

Introduction

In the early morning hours of 31 December 1984, the Nigerian military once again removed an elected head of state. A coup carried out by senior military officers ended the Second Republic which had been ushered in by elections at the end of 1979. The 1979 elections had been won by Alhaji Shehu Shagari. He had come to the Nigerian presidency under a cloud since there was a dispute as to whether he had fulfilled the constitutional provisions of the Second Republic. For a Nigerian president to be duly elected, the constitution required that he win a plurality of the vote and that he win at least 25 per cent of the vote in two-thirds of Nigeria's 19 states. Shehu Shagari won 25 per cent of the vote in 12 states and about 20 per cent in a thirteenth state. The election would have been thrown into an electoral college if Shagari's election had not been sustained by a Special Electoral Tribunal and the courts all the way to the Supreme Court. The leaders of the armed forces, during the final days of their regime, made clear that they preferred that the presidency be decided by the votes that had taken place and not through an uncertain and stretched out process of an electoral college.

Thus for many Nigerians, and certainly for the leading opposition party, the Unity Party of Nigeria (UNP), led by Chief Obafemi Awolowo, the very installation of the new president lacked legitimacy and was seen as having been decided not by a constitutional and electoral process but, in the end, by a military leadership which preferred Shagari and his National Party of Nigeria (NPN). Since the Unity Party controlled five states by virtue of having won gubernatorial elections, and since the other parties that had contended in the 1979 elections, the Peoples Redemption Party (PRP), the Nigerian Peoples Party (NPP) and the Great Nigerian Peoples Party (GNPP) all won governorships and national and state legislative seats, they had a stake in maintaining civilian rule and the federal system of states. It was better not to rock the boat as that might bring back the armed forces. Instead, jockeying for coalitions in the national and state legislatures began immediately and all parties and leaders had an eye on the national elections of 1983.

During the four years of civilian rule, Nigeria's economy reeled under a drastic fall in oil revenues. Grandiose plans to industrialize were put forward and the regime committed itself to large-scale steel complexes and to building a new capital city at Abuja. Defense spending remained high. And, as oil revenues poured in and domestic demand for foodstuffs increased, Nigeria no longer exported substantial amounts of groundnuts or palm products. At the same time, it became an ever increasing importer of food grains. Plans, which were predicated on oil revenues to be produced by pumping over two million barrels a day at close to forty dollars a barrel, faced the reality of OPEC limits on Nigerian production to one and a third million barrels per day by 1983 and an oil price of under thirty dollars a barrel. During the years 1979–83, Nigeria often produced at under one million barrels per day because its oil was priced high in world markets. Its revenues, in real terms, were less than a third of anticipated funds. And, Nigeria had lost its agricultural export base. Furthermore, Nigeria, which had once vowed not to enter international money markets again as a borrower, became a country which owed probably more than 20 billion dollars in private and public debt. Its accounts were so chaotic that the only way to tell how much Nigeria really owed was to ask its creditors and then sum the results. The Central Bank, Ministry of Finance and the International Bank for Settlements all differed on Nigerian debt figures. While not a huge debtor by Brazilian, Mexican or Argentinian standards, Nigeria was listed as a serious debt problem by the end of 1983, as it fell into arrears on suppliers' credits on which its imports depended.

The Nigerian economic crisis was not unique in developing countries. But Nigeria's economic situation was exacerbated, and the Shagari regime's legitimacy further eroded, by the rampant corruption which occurred. Corruption was nothing new in Africa or in Nigeria. But the scale of corruption was staggering. Controls were weak; the possibilities for skimming, through contracts given for the new capital city and for industrial enterprises, were immense. An overvalued exchange rate and a system of licensing foreign exchange provided many opportunities for illegal profits by means of foreign exchange manipulation and smuggling. Although President Shagari had a reputation for personal rectitude, NPN leaders were considered tremendously corrupt, as were many governors in states led by the opposition parties as well as by the NPN.

During the years of the Second Republic a number of events called into question the regime's stability. Nigeria was buffeted by large-scale violence in a number of northern cities perpetrated by followers of a sect led by Muhammadu Marwa Maitatsine. The military was forced to step in when police actions were insufficient to put down uprisings by sect members. Also, the Nigerian government expelled on short notice perhaps a million non-Nigerians, mostly Ghanaians, in January and February 1983. While this was a popular move in Nigeria, it tarnished the country's reputation. And, during the four years of civilian rule, a number of state legislatures could barely function; some governors faced impeachment. Party rivalry was heated and bitter.

Thus, by the time national elections were held again in the summer of 1983, Nigeria's economic and political situation was extremely fraught. Prior to the December 1983 military takeover, rumors of impending military coups were numerous. There was doubt as to whether or not the 1983 elections would be held, and there were intense controversies over how the elections would be conducted. Party strife existed over voter registration and balloting procedures right up to the elections themselves. Controversy did not abate during and after the elections.

Shehu Shagari won the presidency by much larger numbers in 1983 than in 1979. His plurality was less than a million over Chief Awolowo in 1979; in 1983 he won by over four million going from about one-third to over 47 per cent of the vote. In the 1979 gubernatorial elections, the NPN won seven out of nineteen states. In 1983, the electoral results showed the NPN winning thirteen states, including Ondo and Oyo states in the Yoruba heartland of the UPN. On hearing the results, violence broke out in those states and it was difficult for the NPN governors to take up their seats. Later, the courts overturned the Ondo outcome and also overturned legislative elections, including some that had first gone against the NPN. The major result was to call into question the veracity of the electoral process.[1] Most people thought that Shagari had won the presidency but by nothing like the size of the victory he was given. If the 1979 regime came in with questions about its legitimacy, the 1983 elections were a disaster for civilian government itself. The results were so unreliable that any electoral analysis of the kind undertaken in the chapter on the 1979 elections would really make little sense.[2]

It was the timing of the coup, perhaps, more than the fact that it took place which was surprising. Once the Shagari regime had survived its own electoral process, the president moved to assure Nigerians that a new team would be appointed, that corruption would be curtailed and that, while austerity policies had to be adopted, better economic management would occur. In fact, the president's budget speech, delivered just before the coup, did call for austerity measures although it avoided announcing a devaluation of the naira. And, Shagari did bring in mostly a new Cabinet and set of presidential advisers; his new team was received well since many of them were individuals of good reputation.

Since the coup had to be planned before the budget speech, it could not have been any specific measures in that speech which triggered the military's takeover. And, later, the new military leader, Major General Muhammed Buhari, as Head of the Federal military government, would announce his own austerity measures. Since the Nigerian military had become so restive, there is reason to believe that the senior officers who assumed power had in mind to pre-empt a junior officer coup. However, it would have been difficult given the size of the Nigerian armed forces and the coherence of chain of command to have carried out a junior officer coup. Nonetheless, the movement of senior officers warded off this possibility, for a time at least. And, subsequently, General Buhari himself has spent a considerable amount of effort visiting troop commands.

The new military regime came to power with little opposition. One brigadier general was killed by the military bodyguards of President Shagari. In most of the states of the Federation, the military regime was hailed with popular approval. Indeed, there does not seem to have been a pattern of regional variation to the warmth with which the military was accepted. Opposition areas were keen, but so were many areas of the north where the NPN had been strong. Since so many of the officers were northerners, and also Moslems, it is perhaps striking that ethnic issues have not surfaced so far in reaction to the leadership's ethnic composition. If political issues and civil–military relations have not been couched in ethnic terms, as they were at least for the 1966 coups, it is perhaps an indication of the reconstruction of the armed forces which took place during the 1970s and their relative insulation from the ethnic tensions that persist in Nigeria.

Nor can it be said that the armed forces have taken political positions which are clearly derived from social class stances. The armed forces have not seen themselves as the surrogates for the middle and professional classes. Nor have they represented either working class or peasant interests. And, while they have announced their intention to curb corruption and indiscipline in Nigerian society and to put Nigeria's economic house in order, they have not articulated populist programs as Rawlings did in Ghana and as Sankara has done in Upper Volta.[3] It is not that the Nigerian military completely stands apart from the social forces of Nigerian society. The armed forces are part and parcel of that society. They do, however, have their own corporate identity from which they define their own interests and which has insulated them from the direct pressures which emanate from Nigeria's social cleavages.

If the Buhari regime should fail, and if the senior officer corp is discredited as a group, splits will widen in the armed forces and pressures within will increase from below. Alliances might be formed between junior officers and noncommissioned officers and elements of the urban working class, students and party politicians on the left. But even then, a populist coup would entail real and probably bloody social struggle in Nigeria. Classes are weakly defined in Nigeria and elites are fragmented by ethnic-language group membership, place of origin and institutional identity. It would be difficult to create alliances among students, workers and poor farmers, just as it is difficult to create cohesive political groupings based on high income or high status in Nigeria.

The aims of the chapters which follow are to explore the nature of social cleavage in Nigeria and the political effects and economic policies that can be traced to the behavior of social, economic and institutional groups. All the chapters, whether dealing with how Nigeria used its oil revenues (chapter 2); income distribution (chapter 3); religion and economic change (chapter 4); and the elections of 1979 (chapter 5), explore distributional issues, the role of the military and civil-military relations, and the maintaining of economic choices and political pressures.

These are all large and complex issues for students of African (or any) politics. Nigeria is hardly a typical African country — if there is any such thing — in which to explore these issues. The Nigerian population of perhaps 90 million[4] is much larger than that of most African countries. It has many more cities over 250,000 than most other African countries. Its revenues from oil are matched only by Libya and Algeria on the African continent. Because of its size and oil revenues, Nigeria's GDP is also large in African terms. Yet Nigeria is a poor country, its *per capita* income put by the World Bank at $870 per annum (1981), ranking it about fifty-fourth poorest out of 125 countries or at the low end of the middle-income countries.[5] Nigeria has many features of poor African economies and societies. Its population grows at about 2.5 per cent per annum, at least. Its labor force was still 54 per cent engaged in agriculture in 1980, although this is a drop from 71 per cent in 1960. Industry's share of the labor force has grown from 10 to 19 per cent in 1960–80, while the service sector has grown from 19 to 27 per cent during this time. The large service sector growth reflects the burgeoning informal sector which in turn is a function of Nigeria's high rate of urbanization of 4.8 per cent in 1970–81. Nigeria's annual agricultural growth declined between 1970–81 even while GDP was growing 4.5 per cent per annum.[6]

Nigeria, then, is larger than other African countries and its oil revenues give it resources that are not available to most of the countries on the continent. While these revenues fueled inflationary fires and led to a worsening of maldistribution of income, they also gave the government more power to intervene in the economy than was available in most African countries. Taxes were raised and collected from millions of producers. Now, well over 80 per cent of government revenues are derived from taxes, rents, royalties on oil companies, and from the direct operations of the Nigerian National Petroleum Company. The extension of the scope of the central government's authority and the development of stronger central institutions have been evident in many ways. In 1967 Nigeria moved from a federation of four regions to one of twelve states. In 1976 the number of states was increased to nineteen. These changes were a response to complex ethnic-regional tensions in Nigeria and were designed to defuse ethnicity and regionalism. But it was also true that the creation of states meant more control for the center and less power for state units that were no longer so huge.

However, while Nigeria operates under a federal system which is itself unique in Africa, and the federal nature has obtained under military as well as civilian regimes, Nigeria does share many features in common with other African countries. Poverty, decline of the rural economy and rapid urbanization, a weak industrial base, an overvalued currency, foreign exchange rationing and high levels of corruption have characterized Nigeria's economy as well as many

African ones. Complex relationships between military and civilian elites have existed under both military and civilian regimes. Civil–military relations remain fluid and cannot be understood by recourse to conventional analyses based on class and ethnic variables.

Nigeria's new military regime in the mid-1980s faces the unresolved political and social problems of the 1970s. These include the relationships between states and between them and the Federal government, relationships which in turn lead to debates about revenue allocation formulas and the question of new states. Also still open is the pace of the construction of the new capital city at Abuja. The role of civilian and political organizations under a military regime once again is at the forefront. Rural to urban migration and the distributional issues attendant upon rapid urbanization in an oil-based economy remain. The fact of plural identities and whether or not organizations are based on class, ethnic and/or territorial groups continue to be contentious issues. These political and social problems must be treated in the context of an economy which relies on oil for its revenues and which is heavily indebted to commercial banks, trade suppliers and public institutions, and where corruption is rampant. The second half of the 1980s will be a difficult period indeed for Africa's giant.

NOTES

1. See Larry Diamond, 'A Tarnished Victory for the NPN?' *Africa Report*, November–December, 1983.
2. Or undertaken in Haroun Adamu and Alaba Ogunsanwo, *Nigeria: The Making of the Presidential System, 1979 General Elections*, Kano, Triumph Publishing Co. Ltd., 1983.
3. For statements by various leaders and spokesmen of the 1983 coup see 'The Return of the Military', a *Daily Times* (Lagos) Publication, edited by Enyina Iroha, no date. This compilation from various sources, mostly dated January, 1984.
4. *The World Development Report* of 1983 puts the population of Nigeria at 87.6 million. But since there has not been an accepted census in Nigeria for many years, population estimates vary widely. *World Development Report, 1983*, Washington, Oxford University Press, 1983, table 1, p. 148.
5. *Ibid.*
6. *Ibid.*, tables 2, 19, 21, 22, on p. 110, 150, 184, 188.

CHAPTER TWO

Oil Revenues and Policy Choice in Nigeria

INTRODUCTION

The purpose of this chapter is to explore political factors in Nigeria's use of oil revenues and to try to account for governmental objectives through an analysis of political processes and institutions and the interactions of elites and socio-economic groups during a period of exceptionally great resource availability. The focus is on Nigeria after the sharp rise of oil prices in 1973 and through the period of military rule which ended in October 1979. The return to civilian rule after 13 years and the first few years of the civilian regime occurred during a period of fluctuating oil prices. Moreover, after 1979, Nigeria operated with a new constitution which meant presidential rule, changed relations between civilians and military personnel, and an evolving federal system in which the tasks of government as between national and the state level are different from those that obtained during the military period. The post-1979 story is, therefore, some-what different with respect to the themes elaborated for the 1970s: (1) centralization of authority; (2) the growth of the central state apparatus; (3) and its expanded economic and political roles; (4) the contraction of the agricultural sector; (5) the expansion of services provided by the state; (6) the push to indigenize the Nigerian economy. Post-1979 developments are outlined only in brief.

The Nigerian story is one of very great pressures to deliver services to large numbers of people. Only the government could have done this in Nigeria. The expansion of the government sector was service based, but government also tried to increase human capital especially through education programs. Service based public expansion has had a great influence on the Nigerian economy. It has affected, in particular, sectoral patterns on the supply side. Why was this option chosen to dispose of oil rents? This chapter tries to explain the politics of revenue use in Nigeria by describing the specific pressures and constellations of interests that were accommodated or deflected.

THE BACKGROUND

A brief historical analysis is necessary in order to understand the political pressures, institutions, and groups which were consequential in Nigeria's use of oil revenues in the 1970s. It would be expected that profound shifts in political balances might occur in a society in which the mineral sector's share of GDP went from around 1 per cent in 1960 to above 27 per cent in 1977 and then remained above 25 per cent in 1979; where petroleum exports were well over 90 per cent of total exports in 1979 whereas petroleum extraction began only in 1958. Oil exports rose quickly after 1964 and by then accounted for one-third of exports. Oil exports accounted for at least four-fifths of total government revenue in the years after 1973–4.[1]

Large new oil revenues not only provided government with the financial resources to undertake new programs and projects and to expand oil programs, but they affected the very institutions which were to make policy and the nature of centralization of authority and decision making in Nigeria.

The Nigeria that benefited from new oil revenues in 1973 had already undergone major changes in its political system since independence in 1960. Electoral politics had preceeded formal independence as elections were held for the Federal House of Representatives and for regional parliaments in the 1950s. A dominant party had emerged in each of Nigeria's three and then four regions. The North, East and Western Regions were dominated respectively by Hausa-Fulani, Ibo and Yoruba leadership, although only the Western Region was homogenous by ethnic-language group. Indeed, about half of Nigeria's population was neither Hausa-Fulani, Ibo, nor Yoruba.

By 1965, ethnic tensions between the regions were great. Electoral politics broke down over the 1963 census, and over ethnic-regional conflict which involved struggle over appointments to civil service and military positions, over investment in infrastructure, plants and social services in different parts of the Federation, over revenue allocation formulas between the Federal government and the regions, and over the intervention of northern power into the Western Region. Part of the constitutional and political bargain that had been struck between the regions and the large ethnic groups that dominated them was agreement that each region would abstain from political intervention in the affairs of the others. Factionalism among the Yoruba in the Western Region created openings for the national government, dominated by the north, to influence factional outcomes in the Western Region.[2] By late 1965, Nigeria's politcs were increasingly violent. Peaceful elections could not be carried out everywhere in the Federation.

Nigeria's first military coup occurred in January 1966. This coup was perceived widely as an Ibo sponsored coup, although its originators were largely officers who were not ethnically motivated but who were interested in freeing Nigeria from what they understood to be the thrall of ethnic strife and corruption. The first coup was followed some six months later by a second coup, dominated by northern and Middle Belt officers and noncommissioned officers. During the period between the two coups, ethnic violence had broken out against Ibos in northern and western cities. Following the second coup, and the breakdown of negotiations between military leaders representing the center and the regions, Nigeria's Ibo area constituting itself as the Republic of Biafra, tried to secede. A civil war was fought, with perhaps the loss of life from famine, battle and disease of two million people. The Nigerian Federation was preserved and Biafra surrendered in early 1970.

Oil had been relevant to the onset of the Civil War. The governments of the Northern and Western Regions had favored the principle of derivation prior to 1960 when groundnuts and cocoa were the major sources of export revenue. But when petroleum was found in the east and the delta areas of what became the Midwestern Region, the Northern and Western Regions reversed their arguments and the Eastern Region became the proponent of derivation as a major component of a revenue allocation formula.[3]

But the revenue allocation changes that became effective in 1966, while giving more to the regions at the expense of federally retained revenue, worked to the disadvantage of the Eastern Region. That region hoped that secession would give it control of oil revenues and make financially secure a relatively poor part of Nigeria, a part that had exported educated people to Lagos and people to the north as traders and civil servants. The Achilles heel of the Eastern Region, however, was that onshore oil and oil facilities were not in areas that were indigenous to Ibo speaking people. And while the towns of Port Harcourt and Bonny, which had grown with oil, had large numbers of Ibo speakers, Biafra lost control of its ports and oil facilities early in the war. Ibos fled those cities. Foreign corporations who had either put funds into escrow accounts or even had paid some revenues into the Eastern Region's accounts, now paid into the Federal government's accounts. The East was starved of funds, blockaded, and eventually literally starved of foodstuffs.

Early in the Civil War, the military government replaced the four regions with twelve states. This was aimed at achieving the support of minority peoples in the northern and south eastern parts of Nigeria who wanted to be free from the domination of large ethnic groups. The military government, cutting the gordian knot which the civilians had been unable to do, also set the stage for a centralization of government in Nigeria by expanding the number of states, so diluting regional power. While the Civil War caused the output of oil to decline in 1967 and 1968, by 1969 output had risen from the 1966 figure of 152.4 million barrels per year to 197.2. By 1973, output was up to 750.4 million barrels per year and the average export price of oil was $4.80 per barrel. One year later, oil production was at 823.3 mby and the price was $14.69 per barrel. The military government now also had a vast increase in revenues.

Oil revenues, together with the creation of more states, worked to further the centralization of decision making, reinforcing the commitment of the military government. The military had been made extremely conscious of Nigeria's fragility and its vulnerability to outside powers during the Civil War. For defense and national security purposes, it was committed to a Federal Republic which would not be a collection of large regions. While certain military leaders had considered secession (and by no means all of those were Ibos), after the war, the military was a centralizing force. Its own chain of command and its hierarchical procedures accentuated its commitment to centralization. In this, the military was joined by its civil service partners to whom much power was delegated for policy formulation and articulation as well as implementation at national and state levels.

By the time that Biafra was defeated, the Nigerian military had expanded rapidly from an army of around 10,000 in 1966 to over 200,000 in 1970. The ethnic composition of this military had altered too. About 20 per cent were Yoruba whereas in 1966 relatively few soldiers, apart from some officers, were Yoruba. Technical officers, such as signal corp and logistics personnel had been largely Ibos and they were out of the Nigerian army. A significant number of high level officers, such as General Yakubu Gowon, the military Head of State, were from smaller ethnic groups in the Middle Belt areas between the north and south. Most of these officers were not individuals with deep associations with the banned political parties. Nor were they people whose policy views were established and well known. This large army was to be an important claimant for resources, and its leaders were to make critical decisions about the use of new oil revenues.

Of course, the military did not rule Nigeria by itself, anymore than armed forces alone ruled most African states. Even with its expanded size, the military did not often reach down to the grassroots. It continued to rely on federal and state civil servants, who held their positions from the civilian regime, for both policy formulation and implementation. Officers did not want to become deeply involved in representative politcs; nor did they feel competent to exclusively dominate policy discussions on economic issues although they had the final say on decisions brought to them by civil servants. The civil servants' own roles and power expanded. And some civilian politicians from the old parties were brought back into executive positions after 1967 at both federal and state levels in order to link the military to the populace.

Officers and civil servants had a number of things in common. Their own powers and status increased with the expansion of state and parastatal organizations. Their sense of corporate and professional well-being was and is tied up with the expansion of state power. Thus, the first order of motivation of civil service and military rulers in Nigeria stemmed from the identity of public officials' interests and the expansion of the state. Control of the economy was to be a major aim of the military government. The increase in oil revenues led military and civil service to believe that growth objectives and their concern for an independent economy, that is, one controlled by Nigerians, could be pursued at the same time.

The history of independent Nigeria had been one in which regions and ethnic groups struggled for shares of national revenue obtained first from sale of commodity exports, especially groundnuts and cocoa, and then from small but growing oil sales. Each major group had its own elite. Vertical stratification was more important than that based on individual wealth, occupation or class. Major controversies also occurred over the siting of cement plants, refineries, and other major industrial or infrastructural investments. No civilian government had been able to deal successfully with the demands for new states by ethnic minorities; nor had any civilian government been able to obtain consensus around a formula for distributing revenues accrued at the center. The military's response was to create more states, strengthen control over revenue and resource dispersal and use the large new revenues to further growth objectives.

POLICY GOALS

The macro- and micro-economic policies that were intended in Nigeria have been spelled out in a series of five-year plans and in the descriptions of economists.[4] The sectoral characteristics of Nigeria and its pattern of public expenditures have been analyzed, sometimes, in the comparative perspective of other capital importing oil exporters by the World Bank and others.[5] Thus, I want to spend as little time as possible redescribing public expenditures and to try to account for the patterns. A brief account of the stated policy goals of Nigerian governments is necessary, however.

Nigeria had been receiving increasing prices for its oil between 1971 and 1973, but in October 1973 the price per barrel was about $3.00 and the rise had been about 22 per cent. By April 1974, the price was above $11.00 per barrel and oil production had risen from less than 2 million barrels per day to 2.34 bpd in mid-1974. Nigerian government oil revenues almost quintupled in nine months, the rise coming from higher prices, greater production and an increase in the government's share of the oil revenues from higher taxes and royalties and ownership.[6] Thus, the Nigerian government had in mid-1974 much larger revenues than it had anticipated and a very large surplus in 1974–5. The overall surplus in the balance of payments went up about 20 times from the small naira 153 million that had existed in 1973. Nigeria had vast new revenues to accomplish social, political and economic objectives. What were those objectives?

GROWTH

The first major statement on economic policy by a Nigerian military regime was made prior to the second coup of July 1966. In June 1966 the *Guidelines for the Second National Development Plan* was published. The main objectives of the Second Plan period were stated to be a high overall rate of economic growth, rapid industrialization of the economy, increased production of food for domestic consumption without relaxing efforts in the export sector and a drastic reduction in the unemployment problem. Other objectives included increased diversification of the economy, a more equitable distribution of incomes among persons and maintenance of a reasonable measure of stability through use of appropriate instruments of policy. The *Guidelines* made clear that growth was the priority, should the goals prove inconsistent. This emphasis on growth as the prime goal was to continue through the 1970s.

Because the Civil War raged between 1967 and 1970, the tasks of government were prosecution of the war and then reconstruction of the country. War damage was significant in the old Eastern Region of Nigeria where many towns were badly damaged. But neither Nigeria's small industrial base nor its oil industry had been hurt in a major way. When the *Second Five-Year Plan* itself was developed for 1970–4, it was in a context of economic optimism, even before the oil boom had really become pronounced.

The Second Plan called for avoiding uncertainty and instability, and for building on national unity after the war and on the economic base provided by oil. Plans for growth were ambitious. While the goals of the Second Plan included 'a just and egalitarian society' and a 'land of bright and full opportunities for all citizens', its real thrust was to implement economic growth and nationalism although, in practice, there were many compromises with foreign interests in this period.

INDIGENIZATION

Perhaps the most striking goal of the Nigerian military government of the mid-1970s was indigenization of the economy. There was heated debate within the government and outside it about the meaning of indigenization and how it was to be carried out.

While Nigeria's indigenization decrees were put forward by the Gowon and Obasanjo military regimes in 1972 and 1977, there had been a long history of indigenization pressures predating the military regime and even predating Nigeria's independence.[7]

Nigerians had long been conscious of foreigners' presence in their economy. The Tax Relief Act of 1958 required transnational corporations seeking 'pioneer' company status to increase Nigerian ownership and personnel and to use Nigerian materials. Immigration laws established quotas for expatriates in order to increase Nigerian managerial participation.

In the petroleum sector specifically, Nigeria had been following

Venezuela's and then the Arab countries' pressures on foreign oil companies. In 1959, through the Petroleum Profits Tax Ordinance, the government had instituted a 50–50 profit sharing arrangement with foreign concerns. In 1966, government reduced the rate at which companies were allowed to depreciate capitalized investment by one-half. In 1967, OPEC terms were imposed in Nigeria. In 1969, a Petroleum Decree established the state's option to own shares in commercial oil operations. In 1971, the Nigerian National Oil Company (NNOC) was created and between 1972–5, in accordance with other indigenization measures, government increased its share of ownership and altered terms of compensation and buy back arrangements in its favor.[8] The initial terms of the NNOC participation in foreign companies up to 1974 has been estimated at 1.3 billion dollars cost to Nigeria; receipts to government from oil revenues and NNOC's shares and revenues from royalties were more than a multiple of ten over that cost.[9] In terms of direct revenue use, indigenization was not costly.

The First Plan (1962–8) and the Second Plan (1970–4) had stressed increased national control over the economy. It was, however, the Nigerian Enterprise Promotion Decree of 1972 which set out broad objectives and means to increase Nigerian control of the economy. This decree meant different things to different participators in Nigeria. During the late 1960s and early 1970s, Nigerian planners were committed to acquiring and controlling productive assets, especially strategic national resources. This was to be done by the government alone or in partnership with private concerns. Nigerian planners, military officials and high level civil servants were well aware of the inefficiency and corruption of Nigerian statutory corporations and state owned companies. Nonetheless, they pushed ahead for control of the oil sector and other mining areas. The decree, promulgated in 1972, came before the first large oil price increases and itself was a continuation, not the start, of measures to control and Nigerianize the economy.

From the point of view of military and civil service policy makers, indigenization was designed to increase Nigeria's control over its own resources and to expand the state sector. It was not intended as a mere handing over of foreign owned equity to the private sector. At the same time, the military regime was not completely unresponsive to pressures from Nigerian private businessmen.[10] Civil servants and military officers had business connections. Moreover, while some civil servants and military officers wanted to move ahead and nationalize large sectors of the Nigerian economy, most, including those in the highest positions, were committed to maintaining the private sector as an important participator.

Nigerian private businessmen, for their part, have been much more interested in participation and in windfall profits than in control over foreign enterprises. Yet both those in the state sector and private businessmen have shared the goal of growth and they have been cautious in the indigenization programs. Officers and civil servants have been conscious that Nigeria continues to have severe lacks in required technical and managerial skills. Nigerian governments have never been willing to cripple the economy, as Uganda under Idi Amin did with expulsion of Asians, or as Zaire did for a time when the government handed over foreign businesses to Zairians and also tried to run large mining firms and market their output through state enterprises, all with disastrous effects. Nor have Nigerian businesses pressed for complete indigenization; they have been conscious that their own profits would be harmed by a too rapid Nigerianization of the economy.

Thus, Nigerian indigenization has been phased, relatively slow in implementation, and government has adjusted measures from time to time. True, once indigenous businesses received a protected position in commercial and low technology activities through the first, 1972 decree, they pressured for an extension of the decree and a larger share of foreign enterprises.[11] But businessmen who had been left out of the 1972 decree or men who were newly come to prospects after the start of the oil boom wanted a share of the proceeds more than they wanted control, while control was the goal of state officials, both civil and military. Indeed, the growth of the state sector left some businessmen nervous. For while individuals could play a middleman role between parastatals and foreign enterprises, many wanted the state to limit its reach in order to provide more scope for their own equity participation.

More generally, the Nigerian governments of the 1970s wanted growth through partnership with private investors. Nigerian governments did not attack Nigerian private capitalists. Some have argued that the indigenization program itself was designed to lessen private investment in the economy and to begin to socialize wealth. The framers of the indigenization policies have denied this. Nor is there any evidence in the various plans that a far-reaching socialization of

Nigeria was intended through direct nationalization.[12] If anything, the military governments wanted to expand both the public and private sectors. Indigenization would help accomplish both goals. The military regimes did not see the public and private sectors as two arms of a balance, going up and down at each others' expense.

The military governments did claim to want to broaden the social base of capital ownership in the economy, to reduce the high degree of concentration of stock shareholding and to enable more Nigerians to share in the increasing profits being generated. The means to achieve these goals were said to be a new national leadership that would be honest and dedicated, and an investment policy that would be consistent with national goals.

DISTRIBUTION

While the Second Plan stated an increased emphasis on the welfare of the common man and on a more equitable income distribution, and successive plans and policy statements gave priority to a better income distribution, there was no intended direct assault on equity problems either by mobilizing popular participation from below or by implementing radical changes from above. As argued in chapter 3, such an assault would have been difficult to mount in Nigeria given the conditions of economic and political life. Government did not face a landed aristocracy whose land it could expropriate throughout the country. Government was not willing to take over the private business that did exist in trade and industry and to risk a sharp fall in growth.

The role that Nigerian military and civil service leaders and technical planners saw for government was one where government would guide investment through incentives, and where the government would increase the services it was delivering. The aim was to increase welfare through service expansion and better delivery. Government would help create more entrepreneurial know-how, and indigenization would expand opportunities. The responsibility of the private sector was to develop better habits of saving and thrift so as to raise economic levels in the country.[13]

Even when General Gowon was replaced by General Mohammed in 1975, and the latter employed a rhetoric of populism and stressed the need for a more equitable distribution of welfare, he also embraced the Third National Development Plan. However, depending on what part of the Third Plan one reads, the conclusion might be drawn that growth was the most important consideration, or that the highest priority was to effect a more equitable distribution of income, or that control of inflation was most critical.[14]

The concern for price stability and for controlling inflation was a function of new developments in the Nigerian economy. As we shall see, the oil boom after 1973 helped fuel a rapid rise in prices. With an inelastic food supply and imports limited by erratic trade policy and problems in ports, transportation and storage, prices rose rapidly. I will return to the mechanics of the inflation issue below. Here I want to add that trade unions, while still relatively weak, were growing in power in the 1970s. The government's own spending policies which were expanding services and infrastructure, but not increasing production in the short run, were also putting pressure on prices to move upwards. Thus price stability was becoming a major issue throughout the country but especially in the rapidly growing urban areas.

The Third Plan articulated a strategy for internalizing rapid growth of the oil sector by using the increases from oil revenues. The strategy that was actually adopted was to try to create an infrastructure for self-sustaining growth and to directly deliver welfare benefits. The Third Plan period represented continuity with the second; there was to be no direct assault on equity problems. The extent of service delivery was to be much greater since larger revenues existed. Indeed, neither the earlier and continuing indigenization programs nor the new direct spending increases in the Third Plan period should be seen as an attempt to restructure the internal economy beyond shifting control of some sectors from foreign to domestic hands.

The government had political space for its revenue programs and its overall economic strategies. I will argue below that the most pressing interest groups were the elites of the state themselves – military and civil service personnel. Major competition over revenue allocation was between ethnic and geographically-based groups, not between class interests or occupational categories.[15] Nigerians had struggled both before and after independence over revenue allocation formulas. While the distribution of income among households or factors of production might be intractable to policy, the allocation of revenue among constituent parts of the Federation was not. Nigeria had operated with various formulas established by revenue allocation commissions from the 1940s on. (The Okigbo Commission on Revenue Allocation convened by the military government to propose a new revenue formula to obtain under civilian rule was the eigth since 1946.)

The components of the formulas were population, regions, and later, states' *per se*, needs, ability to use funds and derivation. Oil, of course, raised the stakes over particular formulas for revenue allocation between the states and between the Federal government and the states.

REVENUE ALLOCATION AND THE STATE

Revenue allocation goes to the heart of the federal system's stability. It also affects what the states can do on their own. While there are Central Bank restrictions on the ability to borrow abroad, and while states are not supposed to freelance on attracting investments and trade from abroad, state governments have shown much initiative on these matters both under civilian and military regimes. At present, the Federal government will guarantee loans only for those states that in the government's judgement can pay, yet some states did borrow externally without government approval.

Revenue allocation formulas are crucial to allocative patterns in Nigeria because states and the Federal government may well have different responsibilities and priorities, and states differ among themselves on their priorities. Political pressures vary from state to state, and the nature of civilian power is variable with regard to constituency base, ethnic and social groups. The *per capita* spending levels in each state have varied and still vary enormously.

Indeed, almost all observers of Nigeria agree that interregional income differentials have been more important than interpersonal ones and that income differentials *per se* have been less contentious in Nigerian political life than disparities in endowments of schools, roads, health services and the like. Regional inequality in income *per capita* has been low, relative to most other regional disparities measured. Creating states and altering the formula for distributing federal revenues led to benefits and losses for particular ethnic groups. For example, in the early 1970s many high civil servants and military officers would have been glad to get rid of derivation of oil revenues as a factor in allocating funds. The oil producing states resisted this. Indeed, here the oil states, Rivers and Bendel especially, which were small population states with non-Hausa, non-Ibo and non-Yoruba majorities, broke ranks with the military government. Nonetheless, in 1970 the distributable pool of revenues to go to states without concern for derivation was enlarged by increasing the proportion of mining royalties paid into it and adding shares of the proceeds from port duties and some excises. Also in 1970, allocation of federal loans to states was done on the basis of half according to population and half shared equally among states. This formula gave added inducement to the creation of more states. One year later, royalties from the extraction of offshore oil were claimed by the Federal government for its own retention.

Under the Nigerian federal system, some responsibilities have been federal only, some have been concurrent, and some have been vested only in the states. These responsibilities have changed over time and not always by constitutional alteration. Thus, even prior to the constitutional changes that took place at the end of 1979, the relationship of the states to the Federal government altered during the 1970s. As noted, the number of states expanded from four regions to twelve states in 1967 and then nineteen in 1976. The Federal government during this period increasingly took over the marketing board functions of the states; the states' taxing powers were limited and as tables 1 and 2 make clear, the Federal government's allocations to the states became an even larger share of their spending. Table 2 shows also that loans and non-statutory allocations became important to the states after 1976. Federal lending to the states went up well over 1000 per cent between 1969 and 1977 and federal development spending in the states also rose remarkably from 91.6 million naira to above five billion naira during this period.

However, while the states employ about twice as many civil servants as the Federal government, state administration is often very weak. Control over state budgeting is not strong; revenue collection is often inefficient. While we do not have much data on detailed state spending activities, there is good reason to suspect that the states have been at least as responsive to popular wishes as the Federal government in their spending patterns but have been less financially responsible in their overall budget and revenue processes. (For state revenue and spending see table 1. For federal spending see table 2.)

The spending responsibilities of the states changed over time too. When the massive Universal Primary Education system was launched in 1976–7, the Federal government funded it. It was estimated that it could cost the government ₦17 million by 1982. By 1978 it was already costing four times that amount. Demand for education proved to be larger than estimated. Primary education enrollment went from 3.5 million in 1970 to 9.5 at the start of UPE in 1976 and leapt to 13 million by 1980. However, with the advent of civilian government,

TABLE 1
REVENUE AND EXPENDITURE OF STATE GOVERNMENTS 1972/73–1976/77
(₦ Thousand)

ITEMS	Actual 1972–73	Actual 1973–74	Actual 1974–75	Provisional 1975–76	Estimate 1976–77
Independent Revenue	127,153	179,493	215,384	293,200	353,100
Statutory Allocation	322,300	323,700	833,700	1,846,600	1,422,000
Total Revenue	449,453	503,193	1,049,084	2,189,800	1,755,100
Recurrent Expenditure excluding Transfers to Development Fund	402,864	513,344	688,543	1,515,600	1,494,800
Recurrent Surplus	−46,589	−10,151	+360,541	+624,200	+250,300
Capital Expenditure	299,376	440,177	883,266	707,771	2,560,908
Overall Surplus/Deficit	−252,787	−450,328	−522,725	−83,571	−2,280,608

Source: Central Planning Office and World Bank.

TABLE 2 :
Federal Government's Outlays, 1969–1976
(millions of ₦)

	Recurrent Spending	Allocations to States Statutory	Non-statutory	Loans on-Lent to States	Develop-ment Spending	Total Federal Outlays
1969	287.2	138.2	—	31.2	91.6	548.2
1970	638.3	267.6	—	20.4	200.6	1,126.9
1971	492.8	330.8	—	27.6	146.2	997.4
1972	681.4	331.0	—	155.4	295.9	1,463.7
1973	644.4	307.3	11.8	130.6	435.1	1,529.2
1974	873.6	643.0	0.5	325.9	1,223.5	3,066.5
1975	1,685.9	1,039.9	9.1	310.5	3,207.7	6,253.1
1976	2,170.4	1,142.8	502.2	200.6	4,041.3	8,057.3
1977	2,315.9	1,202.7	300.6	437.7	5,004.6	9,261.5

SOURCE: Central Bank of Nigeria, *Annual Reports.* As found in Rimmer, P. 64.
Note: Figures of recurrent spending are net of transfers to the states and the Development
Fund; development spending excludes on-lending to states.

constitutional responsibility for primary education was vested in local governments. Thus for the 1981–5 Fourth Plan period, unlike the Third Five-Year Plan period, there were no projects for primary education to be funded at the national level.

Of course, politicians and civil servants, businessmen and university personnel all have their vested interests in the creation of states. Not only was statehood an element in the formula for distributing revenues to population groups, but creating new state capitals meant investment in services and infrastructure. New universities were created; new state civil services had to be staffed. The creation of states spoke to the expressed needs of the elite who are defined in both status and ethnic terms, while it also diluted the power of large ethnic groups.

None of the above is meant to argue that income distinctions have not been important in Nigeria. I am arguing (and will do so more fully in chapter 3) that the perception of distinctions and the formulation of political issues have been more in terms of inter-state, inter-ethnic and federal-state relations than in terms of class relationships. There is no doubt that equity issues had a greater salience after General Mohammed came to power in 1975. But there was not strong pressure

from below to move the system to deal frontally with equity issues
– either conceived as rural–urban distribution or in class terms.

RURAL AND URBAN CONCERNS

The *Third Five Year Plan* published in 1975 had emphasized not only
an increase in income but a more even distribution. It stressed that
delivery of welfare through subsidized public services would be a
primary mechanism for bringing about more even distribution. *The
Guidelines to the Third Plan*, published in September 1973, argued
that a community of 20,000 was the size above which basic amenities
should be delivered. While reduction in disparities between rural and
urban areas was an aspect of balanced development, it was one not
easily reconciled with the desire to use social services and public
utilities for the relief of poverty when delivery of those services and
utilities was to go to communities above 20,000. There could be no
rapid and frontal assault on rural–urban imblances with these
provisions as criteria for service delivery.

We will explore what government did in agriculture in the 1970s
and why it did so. Government's spending on agriculture in the 1970s,
despite the talk about campaigns such as Operation Feed the Nation
and other so-called crash programs in agriculture, has not been
significant. Government claimed that it wanted to reduce the disparities in rural and urban incomes in order to have balanced development and to increase the welfare of rural inhabitants. But since the
policy choices were to relieve poverty by means of social service
expansion and increase in access to public utilities, no impact would
be easy to make in the rural areas where service delivery was more
difficult and more expensive. More attention was given to urban
poverty through massive intervention by the Federal government in
the urban housing market via construction of housing for low income
groups than was given to rural areas through the provision of over-
head capital to smaller communities or through direct investment in
agriculture. Insofar as large inputs went to the rural areas, they arrived
through primary education expansion and transportation investments.
This was not irrational given the administrative and political problems
faced by the Nigerian government and even given the preference of
many rural inhabitants for investments in education so as to allow them
to 'exit'. Many Nigerians were migrating out of rural areas and saw
their future in the urban areas. What many wanted was education

and skills which would allow them to compete in labor markets outside of agriculture. Thus, in rural areas expenditures on education have been popular although there are widespread concerns about the quality of the education that is provided. The public, teachers and politicians have all pressured for more funds to be spent on education. The size of tuition and fees for secondary schools has been an important issue in Nigerian politics. The proliferation of states had led to strong pressures to have a university in each state. Technical colleges were upgraded to university status. By the time of the 1981 budget, the planned capital expenditure for the universities for the Five-Year Plan period was ₦1.25 billion which was more than the capital allocation to other educational levels combined. In sum, more effective pressure groups have existed for education than for agriculture in Nigeria.

THE PATTERN OF EXPENDITURES IN NIGERIA

It is important to recognize that spending targets in Nigeria were often established without systematic analysis of the relationship of goals to each other. Individuals who participated in the planning process, both expatriates and Nigerians, have described how as money started to flow in, spending on education or on transportation was increased without a careful analysis of the impact of spending on inflation, or of the public sector's capacity to implement the targets.[16] True, planners realized that there might well be problems in executive capacity and administrative implementation for achieving spending levels set by *The Guidelines to the Third Plan*, published in 1973 even before the huge surge in oil revenues that occurred in 1974. The *Guidelines* stipulated that there would be a ₦10.7 billion total investment during the 1975–8 Plan period. The public sector was to account for about 40 per cent. In March 1975, the Third Plan, promulgated by General Gowon after the surge in oil revenues, projected total investment at ₦30 billion, in which the public sector share, allowing for 'slippages' resulting from executive capacity, would be about two-thirds of investment.[17] A revision in 1976 increased the public sector spending for investment to ₦26.5 billion.[18]

The spirit at the top of the Nigerian government was expansive. Government felt that it had the resources both to increase present welfare and to lay the groundwork for a modern and powerful

Nigeria. The Third Plan noted that oil was a wasting asset and, thus, that productive capacity of the non-oil economy had to be developed. Yet political pressures to spend money rapidly were very intense. The Gowon regime had determined not to move quickly back to civilian rule. It tried to build support by investing rapidly and by handing out wage increases to public sector employees. The large new oil revenues were, therefore, funneled disproportionately to the urban sector where political pressures were strongest and where government *could* give money out quickly.

The data tells a consistent story.

(1) There was an extremely rapid rise of the Federal government's outlays and a huge jump from 1973 to 1975 (table 2).

(2) There was a large increase in central government allocations and loans made to the states (table 2). The increase in loans even precedes the rise in oil revenues. The states become ever more dependent on federal allocations.

(3) The bulk of oil revenues were saved and invested domestically and government investment rose very rapidly as a share of total investment from 1973/4–1977/8 (tables 3–4).

(4) Government recurrent expenditure for education rose tremendously. By 1976–7 when Universal Primary Education programs were in swing, education was the largest single item in the recurrent budget, although education's share was to decline thereafter (table 5). Nonstatutory transfers were largely for education. Defense spending declined after the Civil War in percentage terms of recurrent budget (table 6) but continued to increase absolutely in capital expenditures, although not as a share of total government capital expenditures (tables 7–8). Defense spending shifted to barracks building and new weapons and the army slowly was pared down in size.

(6) Transportation and communication continued to be very large items in the capital budgets throughout the oil boom period and agriculture continued to have a small and even a declining share of total Federal government spending in the mid-1970s (tables 6–8).

(7) Not only was agriculture budgeted for relatively small amounts, but from 1975 to 1978 agriculture had consistent shortfalls in actual investments compared to those allocated to it by the Third Plan (table 9).

(8) Despite the fact that General Mohammed raised producers' prices for agricultural commodities when he came to power in 1975 (table 10),

TABLE 3:
Annual Average Rates of Growth and Percentage Distribution of
Expenditure Categories of Nigerian GDP at Current Prices,
1970/71–1977/78

	Annual Average % Rate of Growth 1970/71–1977/78
Private consumption expenditure	11.9
Gross fixed capital formation	36.9
Government consumption expenditure	32.8
GDP at market prices	20.3

Percentage Ratio of GDP

	1970/71	*1971/72*	*1972/73*	*1973/74*	*1974/75*	*1975/76*	*1976/77*	*1977/78*
1. PCE	74.8	72.2	68.4	66.9	50.9	52.4	40.7	44.9
2. GFCF	14.8	17.8	18.2	16.7	17.6	31.1	34.6	36.6
3. GCE	10.0	8.7	10.4	9.1	7.3	13.5	20.4	19.9
Total	99.6	98.7	97.0	92.7	75.8	97.0	95.7	101.4

Source: Calculated from IMF, *International Financial Statistics*, February 1978 and February 1980. As found in Rimmer, p. 53.

agricultural production lagged severely (table 11) and we see a real growth in agriculture of about two per cent per annum (table 12) which is accounted for by additional land and labor inputs into agriculture.

(10) With agricultural production not expanding rapidly enough to meet rising demand, food prices rose rapidly (table 13). Indeed, the official prices for foodstuffs understate the rises. Government continued to complain about black market prices for foodstuffs in urban areas. Imports were liberalized to prevent even higher prices. Wheat and flour imports grew from 400,000 tons in 1975 to 1.3 million tons in 1978 while rice imports, spurred on by progressive tariff reductions, grew even faster from 1974 to 1978 (See figure 1.). Infrastructural and marketing bottlenecks limited the ability to use imported food to hold down costs, however. Food prices increased more than those of non-food items between 1973 and 1978. (See table 13, the consumer price index.) Nigeria's highly elastic demand for food, stagnant domestic supply, and marketing difficulties all exerted upwards pressure on food prices.

TABLE 4

GROSS DOMESTIC EXPENDITURE AND ITS DISTRIBUTION AT CONSTANT (1977/78) PRICES

(₦ Million)

	1973/74 Value	1973/74 Share (%)	1974/75 Value	1974/75 Share (%)	1975/76 Value	1975/76 Share (%)	1976/77 Value	1976/77 Share (%)	1977/78 Value	1977/78 Share (%)	1978/79 Value	1978/79 Share (%)	Growth Rate 1973/74– 1977/78 (%)
Exports of Goods and Non-Factor Services	8,626	34.4	8,324	30.6	6,887	24.6	7,692	24.5	7,553	23.3	8,091	23.8	−3.4
Imports of Goods and Non-Factor Services	2,654	−10.6	3,548	−13.0	5,488	−19.6	7,168	−22.9	8,703	−26.9	7,976	−23.5	36.0
Gross Domestic Investment	3,793	15.2	4,320	15.9	6,940	24.8	9,327	29.8	9,922	30.7	10,696	31.6	30.9
Government	472	1.9	1,513	5.6	4,675	16.7	6,075	19.4	6,464	20.0	6,502	19.2	97.9
Others	3,321	13.3	2,807	10.3	2,265	8.1	3,252	10.4	3,458	10.7	4,194	12.4	2.3
Government Consumption	1,877	7.5	2,334	8.6	3,194	11.4	3,133	10.0	3,826	11.8	3,157	9.3	18.8
Private Consumption*	13,417	53.5	15,763	58.0	16,479	58.8	18,350	58.6	19,761	61.1	19,962	58.8	9.7
GDP at Market Prices	**25,059**	**100.0**	**27,193**	**100.0**	**28,012**	**100.0**	**31,334**	**100.0**	**32,359**	**100.0**	**33,930**	**100.0**	**6.7**

*Residual

Source: World Bank Estimates

TABLE 5: CURRENT EXPENDITURES OF THE FEDERAL GOVERNMENT, 1973/74–80

(million Naira)

	Actual						Estimates		
In Current Prices	1973/74	1974/75	1975/76	1976/77	1977/78	1978/79 Revised	1979/80 Approved	1979/80 Final	1980 (12 month)
General Services	570	709	1,136	995	1,312	1,212	1,219	1,266	2,169
Defense	329	340	780	582	696	596	520	522	621
Others	241	369	356	413	616	616	699	744	1,548
Community and Social Services	36	163	377	742	397	419	486	530	932
Education	13	129	295	601	261	268	326	369	606
Health	20	29	70	93	100	81	97	97	155
Others	3	5	12	48	36	70	63	64	171
Economic Services	60	100	152	138	222	191	243	244	401
Agriculture	17	30	40	23	37	20	34	34	33
Construction	31	51	81	81	89	92	106	106	210
Transport and Communication	9	15	23	27	37	29	44	44	58
Science and Technology	–	–	–	–	40	31	33	33	64
Others	3	4	8	7	19	19	26	27	36
Non-Statutory Transfers to the States	12	1	485	26	560	535	593	651	595
Interest on Public Debt	78	87	70	139	207	235	199	199	590
Total Current Expenditures	755	1,058	2,220	2,040	2,697	2,592	2,741	2,890	4,687
In Constant 1973/74 Prices									
Current Expenditures net of Interest	677	971	2,150	1,901	2,490	2,357	2,541	2,691	–
Government Consumption Deflator	100	108	135	159	192	224	258	258	–
Current Expenditures in 1973/74 Prices	677	897	1,597	1,197	1,294	1,051	985	1,043	–

Source: Federal Ministry of Finance and World Bank

TABLE 6: CURRENT EXPENDITURES OF THE FEDERAL GOVERNMENT, 1973/74-80

(percent)

	1973/74	1974/75	1975/76	1976/77	1977/78	1978/79	1979/80 Approved	1979/80 Final	1980
			Actual				Estimated		
General Services	75.4	66.9	51.0	47.9	48.6	43.2	44.5	44.9	46.3
Defense	43.5	32.1	35.0	28.0	25.8	22.1	19.0	17.7	13.3
Others	31.9	34.8	16.0	19.9	22.8	21.1	25.5	27.2	33.0
Community and Social Services	4.8	15.4	16.9	35.7	14.7	15.6	17.7	18.0	19.9
Education	1.7	12.4	13.2	28.9	9.7	10.0	11.9	12.5	12.9
Health	2.7	2.7	3.2	4.5	3.7	3.0	3.5	3.3	3.3
Other	0.4	0.5	0.5	2.3	1.3	2.6	2.3	2.2	3.7
Economic Services	7.9	9.4	6.8	6.6	8.2	7.1	8.9	8.3	8.6
Agriculture	2.2	2.8	1.8	1.1	1.4	0.7	1.2	1.2	0.7
Construction	4.1	4.8	3.6	3.9	3.3	3.4	3.6	3.6	4.5
Transport and Communication	1.2	1.4	1.0	1.3	1.4	1.1	1.6	1.5	1.2
Science and Technology	-	-	-	-	1.5	1.2	1.2	1.1	1.4
Other	0.4	0.4	0.4	0.3	0.6	0.7	1.0	0.9	0.8
Non-Statutory Transfers to the States	1.6	0.1	21.8	3.1	20.8	25.4	21.6	22.1	12.6
Interest on Public Debt	10.3	8.2	3.1	6.7	7.7	8.7	7.3	6.7	12.6
TOTAL	100.0	100.0	100.0	100.0	100.0	100.0	100.0	100.0	100.0

Source: Federal Ministry of Finance and World Bank.

PCEN-B*

TABLE 7

CAPITAL EXPENDITURES OF THE FEDERAL GOVERNMENT, 1973/74-80

(N Million)

	1973/4	1974/5	1975/6	1976/7	1977/8	1978/9 Budget	1978/9 (Revised)	1979/80 Approved	1979/80 1st Supp.	1979/80 2nd Supp.	1980 (9 months)	1980 (12 months)
General Services	**199**	**308**	**1,085**	**1,059**	**1,126**	**1,113**	**779**	**1,038**	**1,110**	**2,110**	**1,126**	**1,502**
Defense	91	193	455	455	563	709	496	602	644	644	500	667
Others	108	115	698	704	563	404	283	436	466	1,466	626	837
Community Services	**10**	**245**	**221**	**505**	**567**	**516**	**437**	**471**	**471**	**498**	**1,038**	**1,383**
Housing	9	195	167	263	202	121	121	84	84	84	453	603
Water Resources	1/	48	27	221	276	246	172	360	360	360	538	717
Others	1/	2	27	21	89	149	144	27	27	54	47	63
Social Services	**40**	**192**	**791**	**621**	**349**	**351**	**246**	**471**	**629**	**629**	**805**	**1,073**
Education	30	179	750	568	294	301	211	391	533	533	695	926
Health	10	13	41	53	55	50	35	80	96	96	110	147
Economic Services	**276**	**672**	**1,555**	**2,672**	**3,469**	**3,017**	**2,407**	**4,456**	**5,328**	**5,539**	**4,486**	**5,981**
Agriculture	41	103	174	90	142	128	90	220	322	322	327	436
Power	21	92	113	160	207	509	509	540	540	540	400	533
Manufacturing, Mining and Quarrying	61	133	320	621	1,418	1,049	734	2,131	2,600	2,600	1,997	2,663
Transport and Communication	154	342	948	1,801	1,702	1,331	1,124	1,565	1,866	2,077	1,762	2,349
Transfers	**242**	**439**	**479**	**475**	**428**	**641**	**457**	**815**	**815**	**815**	**536**	**715**
External Financial Obligation	5	268	172	58	4	204	143	175	175	175	168	224
Loans On-Lent to States	237	165	307	417	424	437	314	640	640	640	368	491
Total	**767**	**1,850**	**4,131**	**5,332**	**5,939**	**5,638**	**4,376**	**7,251**	**8,353**	**9,591**	**7,991**	**10,654**
Less Amount Reserved*								−1,124	−1,271	−2,271†	−1,164	−1,552
Total	**767**	**1,850**	**4,131**	**5,332**	**5,939**	**5,638**	**4,376**	**6,127**	**7,082**	**7,320**	**6,827**	**9,102**

* Each year part of the appropriation for projects that are domestically financed is held in reserve. The reserved amount cannot be spent unless actual revenue collections exceed the budget estimates.

† Includes N1.0 billion that was appropriated for the capital contingency fund in the second supplementary estimate but not spent before the end of the fiscal year.

Source: Federal Ministry of Finance and World Bank.

TABLE 8 : CAPITAL EXPENDITURES OF THE FEDERAL GOVERNMENT 1973/4 - 80

	1973/74	1974/75	1975/76	1976/77	1977/78	1978/79	1979/80 Approved	1979-80 Final	1980 (12 Months)
General Services	26.0	16.6	26.3	19.9	19.0	17.8	14.3	22.0	14.1
Defense	11.9	10.4	9.4	8.5	9.5	11.3	8.3	6.7	6.3
Others	14.1	6.2	16.9	13.2	9.5	6.5	6.0	15.3	7.8
Community Services	1.3	13.2	5.4	9.5	9.5	10.0	6.5	5.2	13.0
Housing	1.3	10.5	4.0	4.9	3.4	2.8	1.2	0.9	5.7
Water Resources	a/	2.6	0.7	4.2	4.6	3.9	5.0	3.8	6.7
Others	a/	0.1	0.7	0.4	1.5	3.3	0.3	0.5	0.6
Social Services	5.2	10.4	19.2	11.6	5.9	5.6	6.5	6.6	10.1
Education	3.9	9.7	18.2	10.6	5.0	4.8	5.4	5.6	8.7
Health	1.3	0.7	1.0	1.0	0.9	0.8	1.1	1.0	1.4
Economic Services	36.0	36.3	37.6	50.1	58.4	56.2	61.5	57.8	56.1
Agriculture	5.3	5.6	4.2	1.7	2.4	2.1	3.0	3.4	4.1
Power	2.7	5.0	2.7	3.0	3.5	11.6	7.5	5.6	5.0
Manufacturing, Mining and Quarrying	8.0	7.2	7.8	11.6	23.9	16.8	29.4	27.1	25.0
Transportation & Communication	20.0	18.5	22.9	33.8	28.6	25.7	21.6	21.6	22.0
Transfers	31.5	23.4	11.6	8.9	7.2	10.4	11.2	8.5	6.7
External Financial Obligation	0.6	14.5	4.2	1.1	0.1	3.3	2.4	1.8	2.1
Loans On-lent to States	30.9	8.9	7.4	7.8	7.1	7.1	8.8	6.7	4.6
Total	100.0	100.0	100.0	100.0	100.0	100.0	100.0	100.0	100.0
Less Amount Reserved	-	-					-15.5	-23.7	-14.6
Total	100.0	100.0	100.0	100.0	100.0	100.0	84.5	76.3	85.4

a/ Negligible amount.

Source: Federal Ministry of Finance and World Bank.

Table 9: Distribution of Federal Capital Expenditures for
Selected Categories

	Second Plan Allocation	Actual Investment (1970-74)[1]	Third Plan Allocation	Actual Investment (1975-78)
	(Percent of Total)		(Percent of Total)	
Agriculture	6	5.2	6.5	2.5
Manufacturing	-	-	19.0	14.0
Power	8.1	8.4	5.0	3.0
Transport*	37.7	29.3	27.5	28.1
Education	8.8	8.9	7.5	10.9

Source: For Third Plan, "Agricultural Investment: The Opportunities and Realities for U.S. Agribusiness Companies" Prepared for OICD/USDA by Agribusiness Associates, January, 1981, p. 167.
For Second Plan, calculated from World Bank Nigeria Economic Memorandum, 1976 and the Third National Development Plan.

[1] The Second Plan was originally intended to cover 1970/71-1973/74, but was extended to include 1974/75. I have used estimates and actual expenditures for the original Plan period.

*Transport for Second Plan Period is Transport and Communication.

(11) With large wage rises given through the Udoji wage recommendations of 1974 and constant pressures for wage increases in the urban areas, and with inelastic supply and policies and bottlenecks which restricted imports, Nigeria had significant inflationary problems (table 14).

(12) Government was able to finance the control of the petroleum industry and the establishment of a Nigerian National Oil Company (later renamed and reorganized as the Nigerian National Petroleum Company) by increasing its share of the oil take. Furthermore, large new revenues made it possible for government to embark on some nationalizations and on a broader indigenization program while being able to compensate foreign enterprises.

(13) By 1974–5 the military government had determined to build a new federal capital at Abuja, near the middle of the country. There was no provision in the Third Plan for costs.[19] In June 1977, the Federal Capital Development Authority commissioned a master plan for the new federal capital city. When this plan was published, again, no cost figures were included.[20] However, technical and special reports on the new capital did include planners' estimates of costs.

Table 10:   PRICE INDICES OF AGRICULTURAL PRODUCTS, 1974/75-1977/78

(1973/74 = 100)

	1974/75	1975/76	1976/77	1977/78
Yam	162	242	347	394
Cassava	102	119	155	182
Millet	153	175	283	361
Maize	108	152	213	198
Guinea Corn	135	183	273	302
Rice	132	159	174	174
Beniseed	149	149	186	..
Cocoyam	196	264	303	375
Melon	140	160	150	163
Groundnuts	124	158	218	191
Cocoa	158	166	178	330
Palm Kernel	180	80	89	126
Rubber	110	84	111	117

Note: The indices were calculated on the basis of farmgate price data collected by F.O.S. in the rural areas. Except cocoa, palm kernel and rubber for which the calculations were based on international price data.

Source: Federal Office of Statistics.

It was recognized that substantial demands would be placed on Nigeria's resources. The direct capital costs were estimated to be between 10.2 and 14.7 billion naira, distributed over a 20-year period, with a likely cost of about ₦12 billion chosen.[21] The military leaders themselves pushed for a new capital and in the mid-1970s believed that they did not face strong financial constraints.

(14) Finally, in a spirit of determination to make Nigeria a regional if not a world power, and with expectations for continued buoyant oil revenues, the military regime committed the country to two steel complexes and three rolling mills. The commitment to go ahead with an integrated iron and steel industry after a number of feasibility studies indicated it was not an economical proposition was based on the desire to be 'self-reliant' and was, like Abuja, a result of the possibilities opened up for Nigeria's leaders by oil revenues. The budgetary impacts of these new commitments were to be felt by the end of the 1970s and early 1980s.

TABLE 11: AGRICULTURAL PRODUCTION IN NIGERIA

Year	Total Food Output Index	Food Output Per Capita Index	Cocoa Output (1000 metric ton)
1962	88	111	179
1963	96	117	220
1964	95	112	298
1965	96	111	184
1966	86	97	264
1967	86	93	238
1968	89	93	192
1969	100	103	223
1970	102	102	305
1971	98	95	257
1972	100	94	244
1973	94	86	215
1974	103	91	207
1975	107	91	220
1976	109	90	165
1977	109	88	202
1978	111	87	160
1979	114	86	180

Source: FAO Production Yearbooks (Rome, various Years)

Notes: Columns 1 and 2 are index numbers with 1969-71 = 100.

TABLE 12:   INDICES OF AGRICULTURE VALUE ADDED IN CONSTANT PRICES, 1973/74-1978/79
(1973/74 = 100)

	1973/74	1974/75	1975/76	1976/77	1977/78	1978/79
Crops	100.0	107.5	103.9	107.7	107.7	109.6
Livestock	100.0	100.0	100.0	101.0	102.8	103.4
Forestry a/	100.0	110.5	112.5	112.5	112.5	112.5
Fishing b/	100.0	101.7	98.8	106.7	108.2	111.4

a/ Based on total production of major varieties of wood as estimated by
FAO for Nigeria.
b/ Based on domestic fish production data provided by the Federal Department
of Fisheries.

Source: Federal Office of Statistics and World Bank.

We must put a little more meat on the bones of this story. *Why*
did the patterns of public spending unfold as they did?

ACCOUNTING FOR THE PATTERNS

So far, we have seen that government investment grew at a much
higher rate than government consumption, private consumption and
investment (table 3). The concern of Nigeria's rulers in the 1970s was
to expand, grow and to indigenize the economy. Even with massive
new oil revenues, Nigeria remained a very poor country in terms of
per capita income. Its infrastructure was underdeveloped, and in terms
of education and life expectancy it ranked far below the norm for
countries at its income level. Investments in transport and education
could easily be justified. Oil provided an opportunity for getting
control over the economy and for trying to establish new growth
patterns. Nigeria's leaders did not face tremendous pressures from
below to redistribute income. Politically, Nigeria's rulers knew that
people cared more about raising standards of living than they did
about making relative comparisons among individuals. This recognition
and the reality of the weakness of class-based politics gave leaders
a great deal of political space.

In the next chapter we will see that it is very hard to speak generally
about relationships between class and ethnicity, and it would be
misleading to generalize the salience of class and ethnic issues over
time and place in Nigeria. The very meaning of wealth and equity vary
within and between communal and occupational groups. *Per capita*

TABLE 13: COMPOSITE CONSUMER PRICE INDEX RURAL AND URBAN CENTERS

(Base: Average 1975 - 100)

	1973[a]	1974[a]	1975	1976	1977	1978	1979	1980
All Items	66.3	75.2	100.0	123.9	143.0	166.7	186.3	204.8
Food	60.8	70.4	100.0	122.0	146.0	171.9	185.7	199.9
Drinks	71.4	72.3	100.0	131.8	140.0	154.0	175.8	195.7[b]
Tobacco and Kola	91.3	97.4	100.0	142.7	183.1	186.0	202.9	229.2
Accommodation, Fuel & Light	91.8	93.8	100.0	108.6	127.3	131.4	166.9	177.3
Clothing	70.6	83.0	100.0	128.1	141.4	176.3	219.1	270.2
Transport	70.3	91.8	100.0	116.1	141.1	158.4	195.5	197.3
Other Purchases	64.9	73.2	100.0	120.9	136.9	147.1	156.0	181.5
Other Services	74.3	80.4	100.0	118.0	143.0	166.7	177.7	235.2
Rate of Inflation (%)	6.1	13.4	33.0	23.9	15.4	16.5	11.8	9.9

a/ Consumer price index in urban centers for lower income group.

b/ Estimate. Based on weighted average ratio between food and drink for January through June 1980.

Source: Federal Office of Statistics and World Bank

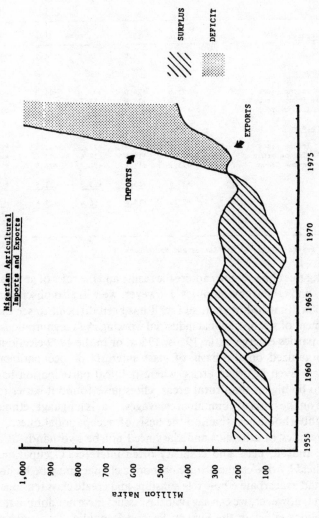

FIGURE I:

**Nigerian Agricultural
Imports and Exports**

IMPORTS

EXPORTS

SURPLUS

DEFICIT

Million Naira

1,000
900
800
700
600
500
400
300
200
100

1955   1960   1965   1970   1975

Source: "Agricultural Investment: The Opportunities and Realities for U.S. Agribusiness Companies," prepared for OICD/USDA by Agribusiness Associates, p. 51.

TABLE 14:   ANNUAL RATE OF INFLATION (%) 1976-80

(Base year = 1975)

Category	1976	1977	1978	1979	1980
Urban	+24.3	+14.0	+24.3	+11.1	+11.4
Wage Earners					
Lower Income Group	+25.6	+14.0	+21.7	+11.8	+10.0
Middle Income Group	+32.1	+12.9	+13.7	+10.6	+12.7
Upper Income Group	+18.2	+14.0	+25.2	+14.7	+11.9
Self Employed					
Lower Income Group	+23.0	+13.9	+27.3	+10.4	+12.1
Middle Income Group	+24.8	+12.5	+18.6	+13.2	+11.7
Upper Income Group	+25.9	+11.1	+20.7	+16.5	+14.3
Rural	+23.8	+15.6	+15.5	+11.9	+ 9.7
TOTAL	+23.9	+15.4	+16.4	+11.8	+ 9.9

Source: Federal Office of Statistics and World Bank.

income figures alone do not capture the reality and the roles of groups, families, and ethnic communities. However, we will also observe in the chapters that follow that, so far, it has been difficult to see the development of strong national industrial working class organizations. Nor did parties emerge in the 1950s, 1960s, or in the 1979 elections which organized on the basis of class interests or occupational categories. Even in urban areas, where political participation has tended to be higher than rural areas, elites have found it easier to organize on the basis of communal cleavages, that is language, ethnic and neighborhood ties, than on the basis of occupational ones.

The politics of ethnicity and class need not be two hands of a balance. Indeed, class and ethnicity often intersect. Occupations may be held by one ethnic group; economic changes may be highly uneven and exacerbate ethnic relationships and create class tensions. In Nigeria, however, we can say that class issues have not dominated party politics either in the First or Second Republic. This reflects the complexity of Nigerian society in ethnic/communal terms as well as in occupational/class terms. The size of the industrial working class in Nigeria has remained relatively small. The informal sector is hard to organize. Trade unions have been internally split and, while perhaps growing stronger and capable of short-run disruptions, do not constitute as yet a solid organization base for political leaders.

Thus, it should be no surprise that there has been no clear movement from ethnic to class identifications and that ethnicity has remained an important organizing tool and concept for party politics in Nigeria. It is true that during the military period communal politics became less overt and the 19 states became less significant bases of power than were the old regions. The social composition and occupational structure of society have changed since 1960. Occupational differentiation has proceeded; the industrial working class is growing in size although it is still a small part of the urban employed. The commercial and business sectors have expanded along with the strengthening of parastatal and public sector organizations. That is, the private business sector and the middle class in private employment grew along with the growth of the public sector in the 1970s.

Nonetheless, power and status in Nigeria did not and do not rest principally on private economic resources. Control of the institutions of state has been critical for the elite. And communal stratifications have been critical factors for those members of the elite who were contending for power. It is for these reasons that the pressures on high level decision makers were from civil servants, the military and from ethnic groups.

We now come directly to try to account for the important policy initiatives that were undertaken in the 1970s. I have already suggested that workers did not exert strong pressures from below. We will see that the rural sector was unable to exert pressures except sporadically. The elites of the state, both military and civil service, had their own policy objectives and biases, but they were also constrained by the administrative frameworks and by the capabilities which existed in Nigeria. Moreover, past policies and the structure of development up to the boom in oil revenues had to be taken into account after 1974.

Civil servants and military officers had interests of their own to take care of and they had policy inclinations which were expressed through macro-economic strategies and which were reflected in spending priorities. As self-interested individuals and as interested groups, public officials pushed very hard for large increases in their salaries, and these were granted after a two-year inquiry of the Public Service Review Commission (the Udoji Commission), which submitted its report in September 1974. Many salaries were doubled retroactive to April 1974. The Udoji Commission in the first instance had provided recommendations for administrative grade (higher) civil servants. But pressures from the general grades in the civil service led to widespread salary increases. At the end of 1974, a decision was taken by the Gowon government to double many civil service salaries and to make the increases retroactive to April 1974. Salaries towards the bottom of the civil service were increased by 130 per cent. As other organized workers clamored to keep up, the Udoji wage accords had the impact of fueling inflation in Nigeria. It has been estimated that the Udoji awards increased the public sector wage bill by 50–60 per cent.[22] The cost of the Udoji increases was estimated at Naira 366 million.[23] This amounted to 23.4 per cent of the total Federal government expenditures of the preceding year.

Commentators have seen the Udoji wage increases as the Gowon regime's attempt to encourage acquiesence to its retention of power by giving a pivotal sector of the population a sizeable share of oil wealth.[24] For just as the Udoji awards were announced, General Gowon also said that the country was not ready to return to civilian rule. However, aside from the desire to strengthen support from its immediate constituency, public sector civilian and military officials, the Nigerian government was in a hurry to spend money. It wanted to avoid being burdened with the charge that it was not spending when Nigeria was poor. Wage increases were a way of spending money rapidly. Government also committed funds hastily to new domestic investment with little planning. This led to waste and corruption and many individuals profited tremendously. Planners who were involved in formulating plans for government spending have related how orders came down to simply multiply spending levels on transport and education. By 1975–6, programs were being implemented and expenditures reached more than six times the pre-oil boom of only three years before.[25]

There was a backlash effect against the Gowon government. After Murtala Mohammed took over in July 1975, thousands of civil servants were dismissed for corruption and inefficiency and a significant number of military officers were purged also. By the time of General Mohammed's assassination, as many as 11,000 civil servants were reported to have been removed. Mohammed became popular as a 'clean government' leader and one who used the rhetoric of populism to build support.

INFLATION: THE POLICY RESPONSE

It can be asked if the Gowon government had foreseen the inflationary consequences of its own spending. The government might have thought that wage increases would be sopped up through a rise in private consumption, but since imports were restricted, and domestic food supply was inelastic in the short-run, prices could be expected to rise to choke off excess demand and in the process to reduce the public's spending power.

What is clear is that the inflationary pressures of the pre-1974 period from government spending, and the pent up demand and reconstruction needs from the Civil War were accelerated by government spending policies after the first oil shock. The government did try to reduce inflation by subsidization of public sector enterprises. Utility prices were kept low (table 18). However, these policies led to growing public sector deficits. There was a large jump in the money supply after 1974. Oil receipts were monetized; the money supply rose and the banks were also rendered very liquid as the government, sliding into deficit, became a net creditor to the banking system.[26]

In fact, government had tried to increase agricultural production by giving producers higher prices. In early 1973, General Gowon had transferred the power to fix producers' prices from state marketing boards to the Federal government. Export duties and the states' produce sales taxes on crops that the board dealt with were replaced by a single federal tax of 10 per cent *ad valorem*. In 1974 this tax was removed. When General Mohammed came to power in mid-1974, he increased producers' prices for agricultural commodities. Between 1974–6 producers' prices doubled for many agricultural commodities. Government undoubtedly hoped that it would attain larger agricultural production increases than occurred.

Did government consciously try to transfer revenues to the public sector through an inflation tax? After 1974, seigniorage transfers to government amounted to the equivalent of 15 per cent of private sector savings.[27] Government knew that it had limited ability to transfer revenues to the public sector through taxing incomes in the urban sector. Although it did impose uniform tax rates throughout the Federal Republic in 1975 (retroactive to April 1974), personal income tax enforcement remained low in Nigeria. Moreover, as just noted, government was in the mid-1970s removing taxes from agricultural producers. There is some reason to believe that policy makers saw inflation as an easier way of pulling domestic resources out of the private sector than through taxation. Of course, these views were not publicly articulated in Nigeria.

TRADE POLICY

Trade and the balance of payments became issues in Nigeria's macro-economic policies especially after 1976. As Obadan and Ihmodu have argued, during the military regimes policies were aimed at managing the external trade sector by depleting reserves in periods of deficits and accumulating reserves in periods of surplus.[28] Nigeria's leaders were reluctant to borrow in international money markets, although they were to do so when oil prices fell in 1978. After 1973, when a devaluation of the naira occurred, small adjustments to the exchange rate were made in an *ad hoc* manner as oil revenues rose or fell, until 1979 when a 14 per cent revaluation occurred. Nigerian governments operated largely through tariffs and direct controls such as import regulations and licensing. Foreign exchange controls have been used too. Government has frequently changed controls, travel allowances and restrictions on income transfers. This had led to uncertainty for domestic marketing, overseas investors and lenders. Government also used its taxing powers to increase revenues via customs duties and export taxes. Government did not, however, try to handle balance of payments problems through cutting back on its macro-spending policies until 1978. However, earlier in 1976, when very large deficits occurred in balance of payments, concern over external trade balances became a major policy issue. As figure 1 makes clear, agricultural imports were becoming significant after 1975, and as table 15 shows, imports were rising steadily and Nigeria's balance of payments situation worsened in 1975 and 1976. Nigeria ran severe deficits in trade in 1978. In response, government did cut back on spending projections in that year.[29] Prior to 1978, government still opted for growth, and, while it imposed stricter direct and exchange control measures at various times, it was increasing its expenditures. One result was smuggling and exchange control violations. Another was rising prices, particularly of food and consumer goods.

TABLE 15:

Balance of Payments
(Millions of U.S. Dollars)

	1974	1975	1976	1977	1978	1979	1900
Merchandise Exports fob	9698	8329	10,122	12,431	10,509	16,740	23,422
Merchandise Imports fob	-2480	-5484	-7,478	-9722	-11,686	-11,803	-15,940
Other Goods, Ser. &Income Cred.	350	801	802	918	1175	1294	1977
Other Goods, Ser. & Income Deb.	-2572	-3477	-3647	-4461	-3512	-4167	-5958
Private Unrequited Transfers	-91	-112	-162	-178	-253	-350	-410
Official Unrequited Transfers	-7	-15	6	-5	-19	-30	-168
Direct Investment	257	418	339	441	213	304	595
Other Long-Term Capital	-88	-209	-367	-18	1401	1,020	990
Other Short-Term Capital	-23	-22	-39	-138	152	10	49
Net Errors & Omissions	70	-42	46	-50	-101	187	05
Counterpart to SDR Allocation	-	-	-	-	-	48	49
Counterpart to Valuation Change	152	203	-27	-121	-223	417	-4
Payments Arrears	-216	-	-	-	-	-	-
Change in Reserves (-for increase)	-5050	16	405	948	2344	-3662	-4607

Source: International Monetary Fund, International Financial Statistics
February 1982.

DISTRIBUTIONAL CONSEQUENCES

Government did realize that rising prices and the impact of oil revenues affected various groups differentially. Even though trade unions have not been strong organizations in Nigeria, they could try to protect unionized workers. Between 1963 and 1974, labor's share in industrial value added never exceeded 26 per cent. Labour did poorly in Nigeria during the initial period of military intervention and the subsequent civil war, but much of the ground lost by labor between 1965 and 1970 was regained between 1970 and 1974. A freeze was imposed on wages, and the Trade Disputes Decree of 1968 had made some types of strike actions illegal. Still, Nigeria continued to have strikes and work stoppages even under restrictive legislation during military rule, although it is clear that times of crises impaired labor's ability to increase its share of total value. Nonetheless, it is important to note that total industrial wages rose more than fivefold from 1963 to 1974. Subsequently, organized labor was better able to protect itself during the period of inflation in Nigeria by getting catch-up wage increases through wage commission recommendations, as compared to the informal sector and the rural sector.

Rhetorically, the Gowon government was committed to developing an incomes policy and to achieving better social equity as well as price stability. As noted, price stability was not achieved. In 1975, the money supply increased by nearly three-quarters and prices rose by 43 per cent. Following the 1976 budget, there was an attempt to keep the money supply in check and wages were frozen for a time. But the Nigerian pattern of freezing wages followed by wage jumps continued.

Discussions of income distribution are notoriously difficult, but while the picture is somewhat mixed for Nigeria in the 1970s, we can say that oil worsened the maldistribution of Nigeria's income.[30] Income inequality appears to have increased in the 1960s and early 1970s with respect to overall interpersonal income distribution measures, and with respect to rural–urban differentials. From 1963 until 1970 there was a narrowing of interindustry earnings differentials. But since then that trend has reversed. There was a stability of the industrial wage hierarchy among industries. However, the income gaps between Nigerians with disparate levels of education were reduced between the 1960s and 1970s.

During the period 1963–74, the average earnings of non-Nigerians as a percentage of all employees' average earnings fell. Also, during this period, there was a movement toward compressing earnings between professional, managerial and clerical employees. The higher the average earnings of a group, the lower the percentage increases in its earnings. The bulk of income shares lost by professional and managerial personnel went to manual workers. Clerical personnel held their shares. Within the Nigerian civil service, wide differentials obtain between grades, but they have been narrowing. Indeed, between 1954 and 1975 a Federal government permanent secretary's wage was reduced from 36 to 17 times that of an unskilled labourer. This is still more than five times the gap in Britain, and, if fringe benefits were included, the Nigerian gap would appear to be even wider.

For the period after 1975, we have even more severe problems with data on Nigerian income distribution than we have for the pre-1975 period; thus, it is difficult to measure the impact of oil on income distribution profiles throughout the 1970s. Diejomaoh has captured aspects of income distribution by looking at *per capita* production in rural and urban areas and by measuring labor productivities in different sectors of the economy (tables 16–17).

The magnitude of sectoral differentials in Nigeria up to 1970 was similar to many developing countries with respect to labor productivity and rural–urban income inequalities. The Kuznets ratio (labor productivity in the industrial and service sectors divided by labor productivity in agriculture) increased from 2.0 and 2.4 for Nigeria in 1966 and 1970 to 6.2 in 1975. The last figure is outside the range of higher values for most of the least developed countries. The sharp increase in inequality between sectors from 1970 to 1975 was due largely to increases in oil production and prices during this period. As Diejomaoh and Anusionwu argued, the sharp rise in industrial productivity is, in fact, largely due to windfall gains arising from oil price increases rather than to technological change or manpower development.[31] (Of course government received most of the oil income, not the factors of production.) They calculated K-ratios without including the mining sector which is almost all oil production and found that they would have been:

> 1966: 1.8 instead of 2.0
> 1970: 2.0 instead of 2.5
> 1975: 3.0 instead of 6.2

This trend of increasing differentials in labor productivity would probably have persisted without oil but the magnitudes almost

TABLE 16:
Distribution of GDP and Population Between Urban and Rural Areas, 1963–1975

Years	Total Population (thousands)	Rural Population		Urban Population	
		Numbers (thousands)	% of Total Population	Numbers (thousands)	% of Total Population
1963	55,672	44,943	80.7	10,729	19.3
1966	59,959	47,653	79.5	12,306	20.5
1970	66,939	51,842	77.8	14,796	22.2
1973	71,260	54,333	76.2	16,927	23.8
1975	74,878	56,354	75.3	18,524	24.7

Years	Total GDP at Current Factor cost (₦ millions)	Rural Population		Urban Population		Rural Per Capita Product as % Urban Per Capita Product	Urban Per Capita Product as % Rural Per Capita Product
		Agricultural Product (₦ millions)	Per Capita Product (₦)	Nonagricultural Product (₦ millions)	Per Capita Product (₦)		
1962/63	2,630.8	1,609.6	35.8	1,021.2	95.2	37.7	265.9
1966/67	3,210.0	1,784.4	37.4	1,425.6	115.8	32.3	309.6
1970/71	5,281.1	2,576.4	49.7	2,704.7	182.8	27.2	375.4
1973/74	8,452.7	3,122.9	57.5	5,329.8	314.9	18.3	547.7
1975/76	15,718.2	3,854.4	68.4	11,863.6	640.4	10.7	936.3

SOURCES: Computed from data from the Federal Office of Statistics, Central Planning Office, (Washington, D.C.: The World Bank, 1979). As in V. P. Diejomaoh and E. C. Anusionwu, "The Structure of Inequality in Nigeria: A Macro Analysis," in Bienen and Diejomaoh, The Political Economy of Income Distribution in Nigeria, p. 99.

TABLE 17

LABOR PRODUCTIVITY IN AGRICULTURE, INDUSTRY AND SERVICES
AT CURRENT FACTOR COST 1966–75
(output per worker in naira)

	agriculture	industry	services	non-agriculture				
	(A)	(I)	(S)	I + S	I/A	S/A	I/S	(I+S)/A
1966	₦109.9	₦269.2	₦192.5	₦222.3	2.5	1.8	1.4	2.0
1970	₦153.5	₦415.7	₦336.5	₦371.4	2.7	2.2	1.2	2.4
1975	₦203.5	₦1,463.4	₦611.8	₦1,056.7	7.2	3.1	2.4	6.2

Sources: Computed from data from *Second* and *Third National Development Plans* and *First Progress Report on Third National Development Plan 1975–80* (Lagos: Central Planning Board). As found in Diejomaoh and Anusionwu, *op. cit.*, p.97.

certainly would have been less.[32] As younger people, both men and women, migrated to cities and towns, went to work in public construction or were taken out of production through the spread of education, labor productivity in agriculture actually declined in real terms.[33]

When we look at income differentials between urban and rural sectors (table 16) we see an increasing ratio of urban to rural incomes. For interpersonal income distribution, no comprehensive nationwide survey has ever been carried out in Nigeria that would enable us to have great confidence in estimating degrees of inequality. There are many fragmentary studies of interpersonal income inequalities. Surveying these works and doing their own calculations, Diejomaoh and Anusionwu concluded that there was a sharp trend towards inequality within the modern sector from 1970 to the mid-1970s, after a moderate degree of inequality in the 1960s. They put the Gini coefficient in the modern sector at .55 in 1970 and at .7 in 1975−6. The magnitude of interpersonal income inequality in the rural sector has been low with Gini indices probably around .3.[34] For the urban sector as a whole, the bottom layer comprises the self-employed in the informal sector. In 1975, in urban Nigeria, the low income self-employed had an average monthly income which amounted to 62 per cent of the average income of the lowest paid wage earners. Large income inequalities appear in Nigeria as the modern sector is compared to the rural and urban informal sector. Growth of the former relative to the latter sectors, therefore, increases the degree of overall inequality.

Diejomaoh and Anusionwu estimate that interpersonal income distribution nationwide moved from around a Gini index of about 0.5 in 1960 to about 0.6 in 1970, and perhaps above 0.7 in 1975–6. A decline in inequality may have occurred after 1976 through a sluggish performance in the modern sector, especially in the oil sector in 1978, and with a rise in agricultural production of about 3 per cent in 1976–7. With the renewed boom in oil prices in 1979–80, income inequality probably was on the increase once again because government funneled its oil revenues into the urban sector.

For a number of reasons, policies aimed at income distribution have focussed on incomes within the urban sector rather than on urban–rural redistribution or within-rural redistributions. Politically, urban–rural redistributions would be difficult to carry out. Fundamentally, the government would have had to radically revise its policies to alter the trend of increasing rural–urban inequallity. It did not do so in the 1970s although it took the aforementioned measures to improve rural incomes by ending certain taxes on producers and by raising producers' prices from 1973 values (table 10). While we do not have good data which would enable us to calculate well the terms of trade between rural and urban sectors, table 18 gives us a rough measure by showing us sectoral price indices.

This table suggests that agriculture did not improve its terms of trade position. However, table 13, the consumer price index, does show that food prices increased rapidly. The discrepancy between price increases in food shown on table 13 and the sectoral price increases for agriculture (table 18) can in part be accounted for by increases in trade margins. However, table 10 also shows significant rise in farmgate prices for basic foodstuffs such as yams, cassava, millet and guinea corn. Thus, there are some discrepancies that appear in the data. There is a range of uncertainty expressed in the different tables. It is clear that Nigeria did increase its food imports significantly (figure 1). While this helped to keep farmgate prices of rice and other foods down, the Nigerians did not develop a 'cheap food' policy as did the Iranians. While imports did compensate, to some extent, for falling *per capita* food production (table 11), the system of import licenses which controlled food imports gave high profits to distributors and kept food imports lower than unregulated markets would have produced. Probably, relative prices for agriculture did not change much from 1973 to 1979.

In 1977, the state marketing boards were replaced by a national

TABLE 18:

Sectoral Price Indices

Sector	73/74	74/75	75/76	76/77	77/78	78/79	79/80
Agriculture Forestry & Fishing	100	111	133	136	136	137	138
Mining & Quarrying	100	178	192	214	235	215	239
Manufacturing	100	106	134	139	153	168	182
Utilities	100	102	98	100	102	104	105
Construction	100	88	93	127	126	133	141
Transport & Communication	100	109	124	130	164	150	158
Trade	100	140	156	179	176	169	173
Privately Provided Services	100	103	106	109	112	116	117
Government Services	100	103	170	171	172	173	174
GDP Deflator	100	129	145	159	164	159	168

Source: Guidelines for the Fourth National Development Plan, 1981-85. Figures were calculated by dividing nominal quantities by real quantities.

Notes: 1973/74 = 100

board for each commodity. The move to put the power for setting agricultural prices in the hands of the Federal government through the creation of national boards was another example of the transfer of power from states to the center. Revenues, it was felt, no longer had to be raised by taxing producers with lower than export prices, because oil was filling revenue needs. Moreover, for many agricultural commodities, there was no longer any surpluses above consumption for the home market. Cocoa was an exception, but for most of Nigeria's traditional agricultural exports the rise in domestic consumption and in some cases stagnating or even falling production ended the possibility of exports (table 11).

The development and expenditure policies of the Federal government show that most investments were made in the urban areas; insofar as investments went to rural areas they were in transportation and education. Nigerian agriculture depended, in the short-run, on increases in its traditional inputs − labor and unirrigated land. Arable land has increased from 21.4 million hectares in 1961−5 to 23 million hectares in 1978. Virtually none of this land is irrigated. In 1960 the economically active population in agriculture was 13.1 million (70.8 per cent of the total). In 1978 it was 14.5 million (55.1 per cent). In line with the increase in productive factors, agricultural value added grew in constant prices by about 10−15 per cent this period. (The base year 1962 or 1963 gives different results and data is poor in any case.) Labor and land are virtually the only inputs used in Nigerian agriculture. Production is almost exclusively by small farms using rudimentary techniques. Commercial fertilizer use of all kinds averaged only to 3.4 kg/per hectare of arable land in 1977; the corresponding figure for all of Africa is 13.0 kg/per hectare and for the world is 69.0 kg/per hectare. Only the simplest of farm tools are used on most Nigerian farms. The picture is that of a technologically stagnant environment unable to meet the food demands of rapid urbanization. Labor was drawn off the land into construction and service projects funded by the exploding public investment program, without agriculture benefiting from increased productivity out of public spending.

There have been a number of factors which have led to the relative neglect of agriculture in government spending. While the Nigerian population still had a very clear majority occupied in agriculture, the political power of those in the agricultural sector was, as in most African countries, dispersed and unorganized. During military regimes, elections did not count and the rulers did not have to go to the people on a record of investment and expenditure which was low for agriculture. Even in the 1950s and 1960s when governments were elected and when groundnut and cocoa exports were important for export revenues, farmers were not powerful political or economic interest groups in Nigeria. Cocoa farmers in the Yoruba areas where cocoa is grown never functioned as a well organized and powerful pressure group to the extent that planters were able to function in the Ivory Coast. Indeed, in the 1950s and early 1960s, much of the cost of delivering welfare and promoting development in Nigeria was financed through withholding earnings from commodity producers by paying them below the world market prices and then by directly taxing them.[35] This pattern occurred in Ghana also.

Overall, Nigerian policy makers have not faced strong pressures from below to make large new inputs into the rural areas. Policy makers were thus relatively free to be more concerned with urban problems and to follow their own predilections. They believed that urban inequality and urban poverty could be attacked through service delivery. Nigerian policy makers have felt that investments in agriculture were difficult to make. This applies especially where small and middle size farmers are to be the recipients of investments in agricultural extension, new seeds and other inputs, marketing facilities, etc. Thus, in the 1970s government, insofar as it did push in the agricultural sector, went for programs like the National Accelerated Food Production Program which was not backed by real investments or for 'self-awareness programs', for example, Operation Feed the Nation, and for investment in pilot farm schemes and agri-business. The hope frequently has been that overseas investors through their technical skills and capital would provide an impetus to agricultural growth. There has been a feeling in the past among high policy makers that investments in agriculture made in the small-holder sector would take too long to pay off, if they paid off at all. This abandonment of the smallholder in the 1970s before any major commitment to the sector had been made has been not unique to Nigeria in Africa.

Nigeria has also had many bottlenecks in administration. As we have seen, public sector investment programs fell short of estimates due to constraints in the implementation process. This was especially true for agriculture where expenditures increasingly fell short of projected amounts as the 1970s progressed (table 9). Government had a hard time getting funds out to the rural areas. In part, there was a problem in finding good projects to fund. In part, the administrative networks to develop projects and implement them were very weak in the rural areas. It was simply easier to contract for the building of roads and ports and to invest in plants.

Agricultural capital expenditures were in the hands of the state government as well as being the responsibility of the Federal government. In the Second Plan, the capital expenditures of the states for agriculture were budgeted at about twice those for planned investment of the Federal government. In the Third Plan period, the states had a somewhat larger planned investment in agriculture than the Federal government. Although the administrative capacity of some states was very low, and the states had shortfalls between planned investments and expenditures, shortfalls for the states in agriculture do not seem to have been invariably worse as compared to shortfalls in other sectors. Perhaps this was because agricultural producers could exert more effective pressure at the state level compared to their abilities at the national level.

In sum, while all observers have been conscious of lower average incomes in rural areas and of relatively small amounts of investment (both public and private) in the rural sector, political pressures, the availability of data and a sense of what can be done have all worked to keep the focus of attention on the urban sector.

THE MILITARY'S CLAIMS ON RESOURCES

I have noted that the military and civil service can themselves be considered important interest groups in Nigeria. The Nigerian military had general orientations towards growth and economic nationalism that have been described. It was narrowly concerned to build barracks and to improve the terms of service for officers and men. Indeed, these concerns were made explicit by General Gowon early in his regime when he announced what the military government needed to accomplish before it could hand over to civilians. Moreover, there was military reconstruction to be done after the Civil War. The army that had expanded from 10,000 in 1966 to well over 200,000 in 1971 had to be re-equipped and supplied. Defense in Nigeria has usually been the largest item in the recurrent expenditure budget (tables 5 and 6) and it has been a large and significant although declining share of the capital budget (tables 7 and 8). Defense recurrent expenditures, however, did not rise precipitously after the oil boom because they had already risen rapidly from 1966 to 1972/3 because of the military expansion of the Civil War. In 1971 and 1972 Nigeria was already spending over 300 million naira a year on defense. Capital expenditures did more than double from 1972/3 to 1973/4 as the oil boom made purchases of equipment possible.

Expenditures on the military have declined as a share of total government expenditure.[36] But Nigeria's defense expenditures as a share of GDP have remained near 5 per cent. Defense spending in Nigeria seems more related to perceived needs from the Civil War period and subsequently to a concern with Nigeria's regional defense posture than to the possibilities opened up by oil revenues. That is, defense, more than any other expenditure item, seems relatively unrelated to oil revenues. Indeed, defense went up as a share of capital spending in President Shagari's civilian budget of 1981. One could argue that this was a consequence of a civilian need to keep the armed forces happy. But it is also true that Nigeria in the late 1970s and early 1980s began to acquire costly sophisticated weapons such as new battle tanks, C 130 transport aircraft and Roland missiles. Nigeria is determined to acquire new fighter aircraft; the navy wants to upgrade its ships. Plans are also underway to become more self-sufficient in arms and ₦19 million was set aside in the 1981 budget for the Defense Industries Corporation.

While the prospects for large-scale warfare between Nigeria and its neighbors are remote, Nigeria has security concerns *vis-a-vis* Libya, Chad and Cameroon. It feels compelled to take a hard line against South Africa. Thus, Nigeria's considerable defense effort is geared both to internal security, conflicts with neighbors and to some extent to creating a modern armed force that might confront South Africa in the future. Spending on defense may be costly in development terms and Nigerian political leaders have not been unanimously enthusiastic about defense levels. But the perceptions of the need to meet the armed forces' own concerns and demands, the support of strong anti-South African positions and the generally shared view of Nigeria as the Black African power has meant that there has been no bitter debate over defense spending. The civilian regime was certainly not going to curtail defense spending given the history of coups in Nigeria and the desire to keep the armed forces in the barracks.

Indeed, when the armed forces finally moved to bring down the Second Republic at the very end of 1983, it was not because of issues pertaining to defense spending or the military's prerogatives. Rather, large-scale corruption, electoral fraud during the 1983 elections and the collapse of the oil-based economy after a period of stagnant or declining oil revenues triggered the coup. The armed forces were not able to make specific objections to the pattern of spending by the civilian regime. A number of initiatives started by the military were maintained and their funding was expanded under Shehu Shagari's National Party of Nigeria regime.

SPENDING PATTERNS OF THE CIVILIAN REGIME: AGRICULTURE, EDUCATION, REVENUE ALLOCATION AND DEFENSE

The context for the NPN regime's spending was: its own victory was incomplete and it did not control a majority in the legislature and only controlled the executives of seven of the nineteen states; it came to power after a period when Nigeria's revenues suffered shortfalls in 1978 as oil prices softened and Nigeria maintained high prices and a consequent loss of markets. While prices more than recovered in 1979 they fell sharply and seesawed in 1981 and 1982. While the first part of 1981 was buoyant for Nigeria, the 1981 budget was based on revenues deriving from sales of 1.9 mbd at $36 per barrel. Actual earnings fell far short of projections from April 1981 on. The Fourth National Plan had envisioned a production rate of 2.19 mbd at $36 per barrel. By February 1981, revenues were already below estimated figures (table 19).

Nigeria had been one of the OPEC hawks. When world oil prices softened in 1978, Nigeria had been very reluctant to lower its own price. Government had been criticized internally and from abroad for lack of understanding of international oil markets and for facing much larger than anticipated production cuts. When oil prices shot up again, Nigeria's decision to leave oil in the ground did not look so poor.

In 1981, Nigeria's oil production fell much more than anticipated. At the start of the year, it was running at 2.2 mbd. It was down to 700,000 bd in July 1981 and below that in August. By November 1981, the Nigerians were cutting prices significantly by means of direct cuts and through credit terms; production rose rapidly in December 1981. Nigeria was in a weak position to keep production low in late 1981 because she had so many domestic commitments.

TABLE 19:

NIGERIA OIL PRODUCTION AND GOVERNMENT REVENUE

	Production rate Thousand b/d	Net exports Thousand b/d	Net government revenue $ million
1980 (year)	2.060	1.860	23.405
1981 January	2.092	1.892	2.306
February	1.943	1.743	1.918
March	1.868	1.668	2.033
April	1.623	1.423	1.678
May	1.293	1.093	1.332
June	1.351	1.151	1.357
Half-year	1.683	1.481	10.624
July	770	570	695
August	708	508	609

Notes: These estimates are calculated independently as follows: prevailing
government selling price for Bonny Light 37% API less production costs
for NNPC's share of production; prevailing posted prices using standard
royalty and tax rates for onshore fields of 20 percent and 85 percent
respectively for the companies' share of production. 1980 figures
calculated from the weighted average government selling price for
the year of $35.72 barrel. The figure for net exports assumes
200,000 b/d of domestic consumption. (Actual exports are higher --
1.979m b/d in 1980 according to Central Bank figures -- but some
refined products and small volumes of crude are imported.)

Source: West Africa, November 9, 1981, No. 3354 p. 2621.

The Shagari regime was determined to press ahead with the new
capital at Abuja. The determination to create a new federal capital
city both accentuated the realignment away from the old regions and
was meant to symbolize the new Nigeria. A new capital had been
talked about in Nigeria for many years. There have been political,
ethnic, cultural and economic reasons for wanting to move the capital
to the center of the country, away from the coast and the colonial
associations and away from the domination of Yorubaland.

When President Shehu Shagari presented the first civilian budget
in almost 15 years in March 1980, the federal capital was allocated
only ₦118 million. When he presented his second budget for 1981
in November 1980, he acknowledged that the cost of the federal
capital territory had been estimated by the Revenue Allocation
Commission to be at ₦553 million per year between 1981–5. The
president saw this figure as an underestimate; because he wanted to
speed up the development of the new capital, additional funds would
be required. And President Shagari was committed to moving to
Abuja prior to the next presidential elections in 1983. In the 1981

estimates out of the federal share of the Federation account, ₦259 million was allocated. The revenue allocation formula which had been arrived at called for 2.5 per cent of total revenues to be allocated to the development of the federal capital. Naira 350 million was to be made available according to this formula. Thus the federal capital was allocated a not insignificant amount out of the estimated revenue for 1981 of ₦14.745 billion.

Once Abuja's construction began, the flow of funds could not be turned off easily. There are many costs associated with Abuja, including the construction of a main access road from Kaduna. There are many problems in co-ordinating construction. When Nigerian revenues were diminished by the downturn in oil prices in 1981, government determined to press ahead with Abuja nonetheless. It first assumed it would have enough cash to meet commitments. When Nigerian oil production fell after a refusal to lower prices until late 1981, there were some delays in paying contractors. (However, Abuja contractors, both internal and external, did better on receiving payments than many others who were owed money by state governments.) The Nigerian government by late 1981 came to the view that credits would have to be sought to finance new contracts at Abuja. But the strong political commitments of a regime with a political base in the north and among various minority groups led to the continued determination to fund the construction of a capital which would be near the northern center of Kaduna yet would be on neutral ethnic territory, which was a plus for so called minorities people who were neither Hausa, Yoruba nor Ibo.

The 1979 price rises for oil enabled the civilian government to push ahead on large steel projects as it did on Abuja. In order to speed up construction, President Shagari located the Steel Development Office in the Office of the President. In the 1981 budget estimates, the steel complex received about 13 per cent of capital spending or about ₦1.16 billion. This was about the same as that funding proposed for agriculture.

The steel complex includes the Aladja and Ajaokuta steel mills and mills at Katsina, Jos and Oshogbo. The development of a steel industry in Nigeria has been a controversial matter. The complex has been criticized for being too costly and for trying to do too much at once. The Aladja complex is a direct reduction plant being built by a German–Austrian consortium. It is near natural gas deposits at Warri but it requires imported iron. The large complex at Ajaokuta is being built by the Soviets and by western private companies. Most observers believe that it will turn out very expensive steel.

Nigeria can consume the steel to be produced by its new plants but it will have to encourage intermediate industries which can use the local steel. The decisions to build the steel complexes undoubtedly have to be understood in terms of Nigeria's conception, or at least its leaders' conception, of the country as the Giant of Africa. To be modern has been understood as to be industrialized and self-reliant. Steel, it is said, is required for defense needs and for the country to project itself as a major force in African and international affairs. Also, the hope has been to shift the economy to an industrial base while the revenues from the wasting asset can be utilized. But it is hard to escape the conclusion that the construction all at once of direct reduction and blast furnace systems rested on political and prestige concerns as much as on an estimate of economic needs.

Yet Nigeria has not yet pushed ahead with the development of a large natural gas industry. Nigeria is currently flaring gas which represents about 400,000 barrels of oil a day. Apparently, the economics of the development of a gas industry are favorable but the capital costs are very large since exports would have to be almost completely through LNG. The Bonny LNG plant costs have been estimated at $14 billion although it may be possible to have a feasible gas industry at lower cost. The Nigerian government itself has not pushed ahead to build a gas industry as it has on Abuja and the steel complexes at Aladja and Ajaoukuta. Almost no attention is paid to the gas industry in the *Guidelines to the Fourth National Development Plan*. In a later statement of March 1981, the Fourth Plan funding was put off until 1984.

No doubt, the Nigerian government was worried about making major new funding commitments at a time of falling oil revenue when it was both capital short, and the markets for its energy exports looked weak. Seeing its revenues and economy tied to seesawing oil prices may make the government wary of massive development for a gas industry. However, since present known gas reserves would almost double Nigeria's known oil reserves in oil equivalents, and since Nigeria's gas provides Europe with an alternative to Soviet and North African gas, the government's gas policy bears more analysis in the future.

The 1978 lesson that oil prices can fall was learned, to some extent even before the 1980/4. The 1980 and 1981 budgets were cautious ones and the 1981 budget provided a reserve of 25 per cent of capital expenditures. But the steel projects and new capital city could not be abandoned in mid-stream. One of the major lessons of the post-military period is the difficulty of reversing expenditure commitments made in times of abundant resources. Moreover, aside from large new capital commitments, Nigeria's decision makers faced three other persistent pressures on expenditure: the determination to finally begin to fund agriculture; continued demands for defense spending; and revenue allocation problems with the states and local governments.

The civilian budget presented in March 1980 called for agriculture to receive high priority. Military administrations had claimed that agriculture was a high priority also but, as we have seen, agriculture had received small shares of the military budgets and the allocations had not been spent fully. President Shagari's budget for 1981 increased the capital allocated to agriculture from 11 per cent to 13 per cent, but it is difficult to know how much was actually spent on agriculture and what were the specific breakdowns beyond the increases of 25 per cent to the Nigerian Agricultural and Cooperative Bank which received ₦40 million.

The increases in agriculture were supposed to reflect the commitment to a new Green Revolution strategy which was written by a team of Nigerian and World Bank specialists, and which became the model for Nigeria's Fourth Development Plan agricultural approach. This strategy recognized the limited success of past government-operated large firms and encouraged joint private–public concerns. Towards this end, agricultural production and processing has been transferred from schedule II to schedule III of the Nigerian Enterprises Promotion Act, allowing foreigners to own up to 60 per cent of the equity in an agricultural enterprise. The Green Revolution strategy suggests that the smallholder is the centerpiece of food production. The Green Revolution program calls for the expenditure of ₦4.36 billion over a five-year plan period. There will be strong economic pressures to invest in agriculture and, once funds get into the pipelines in larger numbers, there may emerge for the first time in Nigeria a strong bureaucratic pressure group interested in agricultural expenditures. This has been missing in Nigeria as compared to Kenya or Senegal where built up agricultural extension, training services and marketing structures have pushed for more funds to agriculture.

CONCLUSION

An unusally great share of Nigeria's oil windfall after 1973 was expended on expanding public services, particularly education and physical infrastructure, notably roads. Service expansion was greatest in urban areas. Agriculture received little attention despite its large role in the economy. With stagnant technology, and labor drawn into public construction and schools, agricultural output fell rapidly relative to the size of the non-oil economy. Inadequate infrastructure and distribution and a stop–go import policy resulted in the multiplier effects of spending out of sharply increased public programs being dissipated in inflation and exchange overvaluation rather than large increases in real consumption, since the supply of a key consumption good was inelastic.

This 'serviced-based' expansion was not unpredictable. Neither was it undertaken in opposition to popular demands. Regional inequalities had long been more politically controversial than those among income groups, and class-based political movements were weak. There was no landed class target for redistributive pressure and the federal and state bureaucracies were themselves powerful interest groups. there was, thus, little demand for directly redistributive measures and productive factors specific to a sector (such as agricultural labor) had no political basis for exerting pressure.

Pressures from the rural economy were blunted, too, by the strength of the desire to 'exit' and recognition of the crucial importance of education in determining the ability to compete in modern-sector labor markets. Growth, the extension of highly visible public services, indigenization (to the extent that it did not endanger growth) and the unification of the nation-state were more important goals than improving rural productivity and redistributing income directly.

At the same time, institutional constraints and the extreme political pressures to spend rent quickly contributed to shape the pattern of expenditure. Intervention in the rural economy was difficult and had previously been minor. In the absence of a tradition of successful measures, it was perceived, probably correctly, as impossible on a large scale in the short-run. Expanding roads and education – traditional functions of the Nigerian state – was far easier. The primary enrollment ratio shot up from only 37 per cent in 1970 to 79 per cent in 1978, while secondary enrollment rose from 4 per cent to 10 per cent. These are notable achievements, despite the inevitable caveats on education quality. Priorities began to shift somewhat back to agriculture and towards heavy industry after the election of the civilian government.

Other oil exporters have chosen different options for disposing of the windfall after 1974. Some, such as Algeria, invested particularly heavily in capital-intensive heavy industry, a trend which only became apparent in Nigeria after 1979. Indonesia devoted a substantial share of its resources to agriculture. How successful the Nigerian strategy of transforming oil wealth into human infrastructure capital (hence into non-traded assets with a wide development impact) has been, will only become apparent after a number of years, required for effects on productivity to be demonstrated.

It is clear that Nigeria's use of oil revenues for expanding services and its commitments to investing in infrastructure and latterly heavy capital intensive projects could not be sustained as oil revenues fell. Nigeria did not get enough immediate production payoffs and went heavily in debt as the 1980s progressed. It continued to use scarce foreign exchange to import foodstuffs. As the international debt crises intensified, Nigeria became one of the large problem cases, a developing country deeply in debt, which could not repay on time and was involved in debt reschedulings. Its own economic problems now revolved around debt issues as well as those of revenue allocation.

NOTES

1. For Nigerian and other capital importing oil exporters' revenue figures see Alan H. Gelb, 'Capital Importing Oil Exporters: Adjustment Issues and Policy Choices', Development Research Center, The World Bank, Washington DC, February 1981.
2. The history of this period and accounts of various elections can be found in James Coleman, *Nigeria: Background to Nationalism*, Berkeley, University of California Press, 1964; Richard Sklar, *Nigerian Political Parties*, Princeton, Princeton University Press, 1966; and Oyeleye Oyediran, 'Background to Military Rule', in Oyeleye Oyediran (ed.), *Nigerian Government and Politics Under Military Rule, 1966–79*, New York, St Martins Press, 1979, pp. 1–24; S. K. Panter-Brick (ed.), *Nigerian Politics and Military Rule: Prelude to Civil War*, London, The Athlone Press, 1970; B. J. Dudley, *Instability and Political Order: Politics and Crises in Nigeria*, Ibadan; University of Ibadan Press, 1973; John Mackintosh, *Nigerian Governmental Politics*, Evanston, Northwestern University Press, 1966.
3. For discussions of revenue sharing in Nigeria see Lawrence A. Rupley, 'Revenue Sharing in the Nigerian Federation', *The Journal of Modern African Studies*, vol. 19, no. 2, June 1981, pp. 257–78; Douglas Rimmer, 'Development in Nigeria: An Overview', in Henry Bienen and V. P. Diejomaoh (eds.), *The Political Economy*

of Income Distribution in Nigeria, New York, Holmes and Meier, 1981, pp. 29–88.

4. See Sayre Schatz, *Nigerian Capitalism*, Berkeley, University of California Press, 1977, F. A. Olaloku, *Structures of the Nigerian Economy*, London, MacMillan, 1979; O. Teriba and M. O. Kayode (eds), *Industrial Development in Nigeria*, Ibadan, University of Ibadan Press, 1977. The plan documents include: *The Guideposts for Second National Development Plan* Lagos, Ministry of Economic Development, 1966; the *Second National Development Plan 1970–4*, Lagos, Federal Ministry of Information, 1970 and the 'First' and 'Second Progress Reports' on this plan published by the Central Planning Office of the Federal Ministry of Economic Development and Reconstruction at Lagos in 1972 and 1974 respectively; the *Guidelines for the Third National Development Plan 1975–80*, Lagos, Central Planning Office, 1973; the *Third National Development Plan 1975–80*, two vols, 1975, the 'Revised Vol. II', 1976, and the 'First', 1977, and 'Second', 1979, 'Progress Reports' on this plan, all published at Lagos by the Central Planning Unit; and the *Guidelines for the Fourth National Development Plan 1981–85*, Lagos, Federal Ministry of National Planning, 1979.

5. *Nigeria: Optimal Long-Term Development*, World Bank Country Economic Report, Baltimore, The Johns Hopkins University Press, 1974; *Nigeria: Basic Economic Report*, World Bank, August 1981; Gelb, *op. cit.*

6. For figures on oil production, see Rimmer, *op. cit.*, pp. 50–2. Rimmer has used the Central Bank of Nigeria's Annual Reports.

7. For discussion of Nigeria's indigenization policy, see Thomas B. Biersteker, *Distortion or Development: Contending Perspectives on the Multinational Corporation*, Cambridge, MIT University Press, 1978 and Biersteker's, *Indigenization and the Nigerian Bourgeoisie: Dependent Development in an African Context*, Yale University, November 1980, unpublished paper; Adeoye A. Akinsanya, 'State Strategies Towards Nigerian and Foreign Business', University of South Carolina, paper presented to the Conference on Nigeria, Johns Hopkins, SAIS, 1981; Akinsanya, 'Economic Independence and the Indigenization of Private Foreign Investments: The Experiences of Ghana and Nigeria', unpublished paper; *Nigeria's Indigenization Policy, op. cit.*

8. For the early years of the Nigerian oil industry see Scott R. Pearson, *Petroleum and the Nigerian Economy*, Stanford, Stanford University Press, 1970; L. H. Schatzl, *Petroleum in Nigeria*, Ibadan, Oxford University Press, 1969. For accounts of the early 1970s see Ronald K. Meyer and Scott R. Pearson, 'Contribution of Petroleum to Nigerian Economic Development', in Scott R. Pearson and John Cownie (eds), *Commodity Exports and African Economic Development*, Lexington MA, Lexington Books, 1974, pp. 155–78; Aprad von Lazar and Althea Duerstein, 'Energy Policy and Patterns of National Development and Social Change: Lessons from Venezuela, Nigeria and Trinidad-Tobago', paper delivered in Edinburgh at the International Political Science Association Congress of 16–21 August 1976.

9. von Lazar and Duerstein, *op. cit.* p. 11. It was not Nigeria's imposition of OPEC terms on foreign companies which affected their willingness to invest in Nigeria's oil potential in the late 1970s and early 1980s, but the fact that Nigeria was consistently a price hawk within OPEC. However, indigenization may well have affected capital flows, especially after 1977. And there may have been indirect costs associated with restrictions on foreign managers and technical personnel. Some companies, especially textiles whose shares were bought by states, probably were poor purchases and costly to public purses.

10. Biersteker, 'Indigenization and the Nigerian Bourgeoisie', p. 11. Also, Angie Hoogvelt, 'Indigenization and Foreign Capital: Industrialization in Nigeria', *Review of African Political Economy*, no. 14, 1979.

11. Biersteker, 1980, p. 18. New foreign capital has continued to enter Nigeria at an overall annual amount of $331 million in the 1970s, rising after the 1972 decree but falling to around $200 million per year after the 1977 decree.

12. For the debate see *Nigeria's Indigenization Policy, Proceedings of the 1974 Symposium*, Nigerian Economic Society, Ibadan, Department of Economics, especially pp. 77–8.

13. Omafume F. Onage, 'The Indigenization Decree and Economic Independence: Another Case of Bourgeois Utopianism', in *Ibid.*, p. 61.

14. *Third National Development Plan*, vol. 1, p. 29, Lagos, Central Planning Office, Federal Ministry of Economic Development, 1975.

15. See chapter five.

16. From interviews with Nigerians and with expatriate participants in the *Third Plan* formulation.

17. Rimmer, *op. cit.*, p. 57.

18. *Ibid.*

19. A committee was appointed by notice on 9 August 1975 to study the question of a new federal capital. It recommended a new capital in the report *Location of the Federal Capital of Nigeria*, Lagos, December 1975. The government's own view on the report was published in 1976 as *Government's Views on the Report of the Panel on the Location of the Federal Capital*, Federal Ministry of Information, Lagos, 1976.

20. This plan was presented by the International Planning Associates to the Executive Secretary of the Federal Capital Development Authority. It is published by that authority as *Master Plan for Abuja: The New Federal Capital of Nigeria* (no date).

21. From *Technical Report No. 1 of the Capital Development Program Report*. These capital costs did not include furniture, moving of agencies, etc. Another report estimated a 20-year cost, measured in 1978 naira, of about 9 billion naira, with the public sector to absorb about 6 billion naira. Average annual rates of investment were estimated at ₦214 million between 1976–86, and growing thereafter. In the Special Report, 'Preliminary Analysis of Costs and Financing in the New Federal Capital', Lagos, nd, the Draft Plan's estimates worked out to a total of around 9 billion naira cost by the year 2000 but with an average annual cost between 1980–6 of about ₦452 million of which ₦51 million were to be born by private interests.

22. Schatz, *op. cit.*, p. 31.

23. *West Africa*, 3 March 1975, p. 244, cited by Sayre P. Schatz, 'The Nigerian Petro-Political Fluctuation', unpublished paper, Temple University, 1981.

24. O. Oyediran and W. A. Ajibola, 'Nigerian Public Service in 1975', *Survey of Nigerian Affairs, 1975*, London, 1978; Richard A. Joseph, 'Affluence and Under-development: The Nigerian Experience', *Journal of Modern African Studies*, vol. 16, no. 2, June 1978, pp. 221–40.

25. Schatz, 1981, p. 5.

26. Kesiah Awosika, 'Nigeria's Anti-Inflationary Policies in the 1970's', in *The Nigerian Economy Under the Military*, Proceedings of the 1980 Annual Conference of the Nigerian Economic Society, Zaria, Gaskiya, 1981, p. 285.

27. Alan Gelb, The World Bank, forthcoming.

28. M. I. Obadan and I. I. Ihmodu, 'Balance of Payments Policies Under the Military Regime in Nigeria', in *The Nigerian Economy Under the Military*, Proceedings of the Nigerian Economic Society, Zaria, Gaskiya Publishing, 1981, p. 250.

29. Subsequently, although oil prices shot up again from April 1979 to February 1980, from an average of $19 per barrel to $34 per barrel, the new civilian government of Shehu Shagari was cautious about the possibilities of maintaining this rate of increase in oil prices. The civilian government knew it faced wage pressures; it

had escalating domestic prices; and it was worried about future oil revenues. Nigeria's external reserves had fallen to ₦3 billion by the time the Shagari government came to power in late 1979. Even with the large increase in oil revenues for a ten-month period from April 1979, reserves were still only at ₦5.5 billion. Thus, the second Shagari budget, presented in November 1980, was still a cautious one. This caution was well placed because Nigeria's anticipated revenues of ₦14.745 billion for the 1981 budget year were not achieved. The 1981 oil slump affected Nigeria greatly.

30. This argument is from V. P. Diejomaoh and E. C. Anusionwu, 'The Structure of Income Inequality in Nigeria: A Macro Analysis', in Bienen and Diejomaoh, *op. cit.*, p. 48.
31. *Ibid.*
32. *Ibid.*, p. 101.
33. *Ibid.*
34. *Ibid.*, p. 115. Also see Peter Matlon, 'The Structure of Production and Rural Income in Northern Nigeria: Results of Three Village Case Studies', in Bienen and Diejomaoh, *op. cit.*, pp. 323–72.
35. Rimmer, *op. cit.*, p. 38.
36. See Shahrzad Gohari, 'Military Expenditures in Capital Importing Oil Exporters: Some Indications', unpublished World Bank Paper, February 1982, p. 22.

CHAPTER THREE

The Politics of Income Distribution: Institutions, Class and Ethnicity

AIMS AND ORGANIZATION OF THIS CHAPTER

The aim of this chapter is to try to understand how political actors have defined distributional issues in Nigerian politics. Politics is the competition for wealth, status and power. While these are goods that can be created, they also must be distributed in any society. Societies are distinguished not by the fact of struggle over valued goods, but by the amounts and resources available for competition and by the forms and intensities of the struggles which take place. The aim here is to try to understand the various ways that Nigerian politics have affected the formulation of economic policies. For, just as an economy sets the contexts in which political groups are formed and demands are raised and played out, so do political groups and institutions affect the elaboration of economic policies as well as the growth and structure of an economy.

Needless to say, these are huge themes of political economy. And Nigeria, while one of the most interesting countries in which to examine them, also poses many difficulties by virtue of data problems and by its very size and its economic and ethnic diversity. The material described and analyzed here can at best be a partial account of the politics of distribution in Nigeria.

This chapter focuses first on party leaders in the civilian period and then moves on to discuss the concerns of the military and civil service elite in regard to distributional issues. Formal plans are discussed along with political commitments. The second half of the chapter continues to look at the politics of income distribution in Nigeria by examining social groups and wider political cultures rather than the beliefs and concerns of the ruling elite. It also asks: What kinds of political space exist in Nigeria for the formulation of distributional policies? In what ways do class and ethnic groups define issues and constrain policy formulation and implementation?

Nigeria shares the same features of many smaller and poorer black African states. It still has low *per capita* income; the World Bank's Development Report ranks it forty-third or forty-fourth out of 110 countries.[1] While this puts Nigeria in the middle-income category, it is toward the low end of that category. Then, too, Nigeria, like a number of African countries, has done very badly in *per capita* food production. Its growth rate for public consumption was high in the 1970s, but low for private consumption. Population growth and especially urban growth are very high. Life expectancy remains low although it has improved over the decade.

While Nigeria shares these features with many African countries, it is atypical in important respects. Nigeria's economy, once dependent on its export of agricultural commodities, has been drastically altered as the country became a major oil exporter in the 1970s.[2] The world boom in oil prices after 1973 gave the Nigerian government immense new revenues; removed, for a time, foreign exchange constraints; and fueled a massive inflation in the late 1970s. During the period in which Nigeria became an important oil producer, fundamental transformations were wrought in the political structure. Civilian rule gave way to military rule. Multiple coups brought about new military leaders. One of the largest and costliest civil wars in the twentieth century was fought. A four-region Federation was turned into a 12- and then a 19-state system by military edict. A new constitution was created, and in 1979 elections were held for legislative and executive positions. The military handed power over to civilians and a new executive president took power in October 1979. Substantial plans for a new federal capital have begun to be implemented.

I do not review all these events here,[3] nor do I analyze the important political changes of 1979. It can be noted, however, that during the election campaigns, demands were made for a more equitable distribution of the economic pie.[4] The new political arrangements were vulnerable to pressures at a time when major social and economic changes, planned and unplanned, were underway. Nigeria's oil revenues, not unlike Iran's, Indonesia's, and Mexico's, have produced large plans for social and industrial transformation; but the government has not been able to put the cap on inflationary pressures since 1975. Plans predicated on continuously growing foreign reserves had to be carried out in the context of falling exchange reserves in 1978, although Nigeria received a reprieve with high oil prices in 1979. Before the 1979 price increases, Nigeria had to borrow in the international money markets in 1978. High recurrent costs have been generated by large startup costs of transportation projects, a construction boom and the proposed new capital. And all this in the face of declining *per capita* food production.[5]

Nigeria would appear to have the ingredients for a difficult, if not explosive, situation in the future. In order to try to understand the form and content of the politics of distribution in Nigeria, we must sort out the ways in which the ruling institutions have come to grips with distributional problems in Nigeria. This is a view from the top. We must also try to understand the nature of the demands, and the class and ethnic content of these demands from below.

DEFINITION OF THE ISSUE

It is a large generalization but perhaps not too inaccurate to say that the ruling civilian elite − i.e., former party politicians, civil servants and military officers who have ruled Nigeria since 1966 − was committed to economic strategies which focused on overcoming under-development and increasing Nigerian control of the economy. Distributional issues were raised during the civilian rule prior to 1966, but in terms of revenue allocations between regions and then states. Until recently, however, less attention was paid to income distribution as a matter of rural−urban cleavage or as between groups defined in income, occupational, or class terms. Although Nigeria had periods in its history when welfare politics were salient, the primary meaning of *distribution and welfare* was in terms of the division of public resources among territorial units. The factors that led to the ascendance of ethnic-territorial criteria for distribution were: general poverty; the introduction of electoral politics; the attempt to mobilize support by appeals to communal blocs; the weakness of class groups, given the relative lack of differentiation within the Nigerian economy of the 1950s and 1960s; and ideas of welfare which stressed raising absolute levels rather than interstrata comparisons.[6]

Arguments have also been made that elite commitment to communal politics − to competition structured in communal/ethnic terms − has been a mask for the maintenance of class privilege in Nigeria.[7] That is, the elite has deliberately fostered ethnic competition to obscure exploitation of one class by another. We would still have to account for the reasons why the elite was successful in so doing even if we accept that explanation. Indeed, we can start with the proposition that the Nigerian elite was based in its separate regional entities. Even those who operated in national arenas had regional party bases for their national power. The ability of the elite to operate at the center of power in Nigeria depended on maintaining regional power and building regional constituencies. One major shift that took place when the military took power in 1966 was that the armed forces, although split by ethnic origin and having ties to ethnic groups, had a national institutional base of power. That segment of the armed forces which tried to create a regional base failed when Biafra collapsed.

Putting aside for a moment the reasons why economic strategies and political competition have not been defined primarily in income strata, class, or functional terms, there probably would not be much dispute that the overt political struggles for distribution in Nigeria were largely defined in regional and ethnic terms for the first decade or so of independent rule in Nigeria, and well before. The matter becomes somewhat less clearcut from the mid-1970s on. During the earlier period, territorial entities and ethnic groups tried to influence central government policy on revenue allocation.[8] Relatively little attention was paid to shares of income within groups. Even competition between regions was more over disparities in services and facilities than over disparities in regional *per capita* income.

During the period of civilian rule, political parties did not organize around class issues, nor did strong opposition movements emerge within trade unions or splinter parties that articulated income distribution concerns programmatically in class or occupational terms.

I am not suggesting that class issues were never raised in Nigerian politics. Important strikes took place, particularly the general strike of 1964, and political leaders did from time to time articulate class grievances and appealed to class consciousness, especially in a general or populist way. The first *Nigerian National Development Plan 1962–1968* lists a more equitable distribution of income both among people and among regions in its statement of goals. But it is difficult to see from this plan any direct attack on distributional problems, even rhetorically speaking. The plan aimed at providing more services to business people, more export of agricultural crops, the introduction of more modern agricultural methods, expansion of electricity and more job creation to modernize and achieve more equitable distributions. In order to expand opportunities, the plan called for the training of more doctors and the expansion of primary school education and hospital services.[9] There was criticism at the time of publication that the plan lacked an explicit discussion of income distribution targets,[10] and it is hard to find an incomes policy in the plan.

An examination of the literature on the organization, operation and functioning of ruling political parties, their manifestos, and the ideologies of party leaders fails to demonstrate any translation from general statements to policies that deal with inequality in programmatic terms. This is striking even when one examines populist leaders like Aminu Kano, Adegoke Adelabu and Chief Awolowo or when we look at 'populist' parties which were operating in situations of structured inequality.

It may be useful to try to generalize crudely from the literature on Nigerian political parties and leaders as we look back to the period before military rule. The analyses of parties tell us much about the composition of Nigerian political life as it pertained to inequality, the kinds of resources that were available for competition and the kinds of leaders who were able to mobilize political resources. This brief retrospective examination will be followed by a discussion of the military period and then by a discussion of class and ethnicity in Nigerian political life.

PARTY POLITICS, PARTY LEADERSHIPS AND DISTRIBUTIONAL CONCERNS

None of the major Nigerian political parties that controlled national or regional governments in the 1950s and up to 1966 could be called socialist parties or parties strongly committed to equity issues. This statement covers the Action Group (AG), the Nigerian National Democratic party, the National Council of Nigeria and the Cameroons (later called the National Convention of Nigerian Citizens (NCNC) and the Northern People's Congress (NPC). Even major opposition parties, some of which had distinctive social compositions were not organized on a class basis and did not structure their opposition primarily on a platform of redistribution. An example of such a party was the Northern Elements' Progressive Union (NEPU), which was officered by petty tradespeople, shopkeepers and craftspeople. NEPU can be considered a populist party. Although it used the language of class struggle,[11] its appeals were very heterogeneous and were made to leaders of the tribal unions in the Middle Belt (Moslem northerners of the Ma'aikata class) such as teachers, native administration workers and ex-servicemen.[12] The conservative NPC had a larger following among wage laborers than NEPU.[13] The image of NEPU party leadership was that of politicians living off politics, and that hurt NEPU with its would-be followers.[14]

One of Nigeria's major political figures during its struggle for independence and during civilian and military rule has been Chief Obafemi Awolowo. Chief Awolowo has been leader of the Action Group, premier of the Western Region, and minister of finance in the military government of General Gowon. He was a contender for, and lost, the presidency in 1979 and 1983. In his book, *The People's Republic*, Chief Awolowo critiques capitalism and states his conception of a necessary socialist government. This includes abolition of rents, profits, dividends, private property and limitations on consumption.[15]

However, the AG, which Chief Awolowo led, did not function as a party of redistribuion either in or out of power. As Richard Sklar has noted, the AG, more than any Nigerian political party, tried to organize the peasantry, but its backbone was composed of men of the 'new class' − i.e., the rising professionals, business people and traders.[16] There were Marxist intellectuals within the AG (Awolowo distinguished himself from Marxists over means more than ends), and the party espoused some populist causes − especially, free primary education in the 1950s. In power, the AG was not a party which redistributed wealth, except to party leaders, nor was it split fundamentally by ideological concerns.[17]

Along with Chief Awolowo, two other major leaders of parties defined themselves in populist and socialist terms:[18] Aminu Kano and Adegoke Adelabu. Aminu Kano was the leader of the aforementioned NEPU and a vice president of the NCNC. Under the military government he, like Awolowo, became a member of the Federal Executive Council. The north's most famous radical politician, Aminu Kano, came from a prominent Moslem family. At one time his father was Acting Chief Alkali of Kano. Aminu Kano was able to articulate traditional political ideas, and his own egalitarianism was bound up with Islamic teachings. Like Awolowo, Aminu Kano referred to himself and has been understood as a pragmatist. He stressed equality of opportunity, extension of education and

elimination of privilege. But it is hard to find in Aminu Kano a translation from general goals and ideals to specific policies.[19] Both
Aminu Kano and Chief Awolowo have been criticized for failing to
make an impact on the military government in which they served as
commissioners for health and finance, respectively.[20]

Adegoke Adelabu was another leader who failed to translate
general socialist ideas and relate them to specific Nigerian conditions.
Adelabu was the leader of both a major Ibadan party (the Mabolaje
Grand Alliance) and the NCNC. He frequently discussed socialist
ideas, or what he called radical socialism, with reference to education
and agriculture, but without reference to Nigeria.[21] Perhaps he,
more than other Nigerian politician in the 1950s, focused on the need
to redistribute wealth. Yet his biographers state:

> ... it is somewhat difficult to see Adelabu, who had spent so
> much time and effort attempting to make his way in the world
> of private enterprise, as a Revolutionary Socialist. There is no
> reason to doubt the genuine nature of his sympathy for the
> masses ... On the other hand, his ideas on Socialism were
> unsystematic, and tended to suggest a compromise with capital
> rather than revolution.[22]

Adelabu's Ibadan party hardly functioned as a radical party.

What to make of all this? Populist leaders defined themselves as
socialists, but they rarely translated their general ideas into Nigerian
specifics. Nor did they lead parties that were socialist in composition
or organization. One clue to this civilian period of 'socialist' leaders
without socialist parties can be found in the following passage from
Richard Sklar's *Nigerian Political Parties*:

> ... a paradox in Adelabu's career may be remarked. In principle,
> Adelabu was progressive ...; in national politics he was a radical.
> But in local politics he was too astute and ambitious not to
> appear as a conservative and traditionalist.[23]

This passage suggests that the pursuit of personal advantage was not
irrelevant to Nigerian politicians. It also suggests that the conditions
were absent for a party whose politics were based on class struggle
and redistribution of income. These two facts linked together have
led many observers of Nigerian politics to suggest that during the
civilian period, an elite was in the saddle which simple tried to mask
its class interests. It has been said that the prospect and subsequent

reality of power precipitated a fusion of elite groups into a single dominant class in each region of Nigeria.[24] 'This class,' comments Sklar, 'is an actual social aggregate, engaged in class action and characterized by a growing sense of class consciousness. It may be termed the political class ...'[25]

I would prefer to understand this period of civilian rule as a time when class issues did not dominate organized party politics because of the complexity of those politics, which in turn reflected the complexity of Nigerian society in ethnic/communal terms as well as in occupational/class terms. Populist parties could be conservative, for example, when they upheld the importance of chieftaincy. Communal appeals were made as regionally-based parties contended with each other; they were also made to offset the potential appeal of radicalism to lower class elements. The fact is that conservative and communal appeals were frequently successful.

We will have to return to these themes later as we try to understand the social basis for organized politics in Nigeria. Now, however, it is necessary to turn to the period of military and civil service rule.

MILITARY AND CIVIL SERVICE RULE

There has come to be a general consensus in the literature on military rule in developing countries that 'the military' is a label pasted over many different governments. We know that military regimes differ in terms of the mixture of civilian–military authority, the size of their armed forces, policy outlooks and the degree of centralization of authority, among other factors. As case studies have been carried out[26] and as cross-national aggregate data analyses have been undertaken,[27] the view has become widespread that military regimes in Africa faced the same types of economic constraint, as well as the same social and ethnic cleavages as the civilian regimes. The argument then has become that the civilian-military distinction is irrelevant for the important outcomes of economic development, urbanization, and political stability that may take place. The argument has been that these outcomes would not be determined in Africa either by specific institutional format or by specific political constellations.[28]

It is not surprising that empirical work should conclude that (1) in aggregate, military regimes do not form a distinctive regime type in terms of performance and (2) the degree of diversity found within military regimes is not dissimilar to that found within civilian regimes. But this does not decide the issue as to whether there are or are no important differences between civilian and military regimes within a country. I have argued with respect to Nigeria that while lines between civilian and military authority became blurred, especially from 1967 onward, and that while there were various patterns of inter-penetration and coalition between military and civilian actors, there are distinctive patterns of politics under military regimes as compared to civilian ones.

These patterns had more to do with political processes, with a failure to represent constituencies, and with a form of decision making than they had to do with outcomes for economic and social policy. There were important differences in economic policies and patterns between the military and civilian regimes in Nigeria, but these were more a function of a changing Nigeria and new resources that became available than they were of military rule *per se*.

Observers can argue about the effects of military rule on Nigeria in terms of what specific policy outcomes can be traced to the military itself or to the military in conjunction with civil servants. But there is widespread agreement that the period of military rule has been one of centralizing authority in Nigeria and that the military and civil service elite has been an active agent in the process of centralization. It was not just that centralization went on coterminously with the period of military rule or that the Civil War and the breakup of the regions into many states increased the power of the center. It was also that the attitudes and interests of both military and civil servants fostered the development of stronger central institutions of the national state. This pattern was consequential for the politics of income distribution.

I am not suggesting that there were no factional or communal tendencies within the military or civil service. Rather I am saying that, on balance, both were strongly in favor of more effective central institutions and of extending the scope of national authority outward. Neither civil servants nor the military were especially interested in penetrating downward into Nigerian society; they did not easily carry out representative functions or operate at the grass roots. But they did want to extend the scope of the central government's authority. Buoyant oil revenues made this possible.

The military government embarked on a massive universal primary education program; pushed forward measures to indigenize the economy; moved toward a uniform tax law in 1975; and expanded the parastatal sector of the economy. One can view these measures as stemming from a desire to create socialism or to expand state capitalism, but their effect was to give, in the short-run at least, an expanded role to state officials. This expansion can be seen in vastly increased federal expenditures and federal control by decree and practice over many activities formerly carried out by regions and states − e.g., control of commodity prices set by the marketing boards.

The army and federal civil services expanded from 1966 to 1978. The pre-Civil War Nigerian army was about 10,000. By the mid-1970s, prior to any contraction of the armed forces in 1978−9 the Nigerian forces were close to 240,000. Now the armed forces number around 160,000. The Civil War gave the army enhanced technical capabilities. The Nigerian Civil War, like other civil wars before it in the United States, the Soviet Union and France, produced a much stronger central government with enhanced power and status.

Nigeria's ethnic politics also pushed the system toward increasing centralization. The well-being of people in Nigeria who belong to smaller ethnic groups has been widely perceived to rest on a strong central government. Support for breaking up the four regions into 12 states was generated in the smaller ethnic communities, or 'minorities areas', in 1967. The states that were carved out of the old regions gave administrative form to non-Yoruba, non-Hausa and non-Ibo communities. Moreover, the centralizing institutions in Nigeria − i.e., the federal civil service and the military − have had a disproportionate number of minorities in key roles. In the federal civil service, significant positions among permanent secretaries or principal assistant secretaries and members of parastatal organizations have been held by people who are natives of the state of Bendel.[29] Among the military, officers holding critical commands were from the north, but often from the Middle Belt areas (Tiv, Angas, Idoma, Birom and others); enlisted men and noncommissioned officers from these areas have been especially prevalent. Although there has been a large influx of Yoruba into the Nigerian armed forces since 1967, it is striking that many Yoruba officers have come from what is now the state of Kwara rather than from the Yoruba core areas.

What of the officials themselves? There are numbers of ways to look for evidence concerning the military and civil service elite's understanding of the structure of inequality in Nigeria and its various commitments to alter that structure. One way is to look at statements of concern as expressed in major policy announcements such as budget speeches, five-year plans, short-run economic surveys and analyses. Of course, an analysis of the actual translation of general statements into specific policies is crucial for an assessment of commitment. But it could be argued that short-run pressures, administrative bottlenecks and lack of information and know-how can intrude on commitments which are strongly held. Therefore, we should try to look directly at the attitudes of civil servants and military personnel toward the distribution of income. This can be done by interviews and by analyses of statements of self-definition of roles and interests. While there has been some interviewing with military personnel and civil servants, especially in the old western state of Nigeria, we do not have good attitudinal data to evaluate. However, military officers and civil servants have stated their positions and what they have seen as their major priorities in Nigerian economic and political life.

Military personnel and civil servants have been partners in military rule. Civil servants had expanded roles under the military and played major and overt roles in policy formulation. For example, they filled political vacuums in the states and at local levels, served as chairpersons of important public corporations and sat on executive bodies (although not continuously). They have been vulnerable during periods of intense military factionalism and turnovers of military personnel. Widespread purges of civil service ranks have also taken place. While we cannot assume that high-level military and civil servants always saw political economy issues in the same way since 1966, there seems to have been widespread agreement on the contours of economic policy, as well as on major economic issues.

Civil servants and military personnel were interested in control of the Nigerian economy. They were concerned about settling the matter of the number of states in the Nigerian Federation, creating a formula for allocating revenues between states, and establishing order and a stable process of development. These leaders were also desirous of rapid economic growth and of asserting Nigeria's place in Africa and in the international economic and political order. A frontal assault on low-end poverty or on relative shares of the economic pie was not high on their agenda.

Nigerian military regimes can be demarcated roughly as follows. General Ironsi ruled from January 1966 until July of that year when he was killed. General Gowon ruled from mid-1966 until 1975 when he was replaced by General Mohammed in a peaceful coup. General Gowon's rule can be broken around midpoint in 1970 when he was near his highest level of support. General Mohammed was killed in an aborted coup in February 1976. General Obasanjo was Head of State until the transfer of power to civilians in October 1979. General Ironsi formed the first military regime in January 1966 but was not the instigator of the coup which replaced civilians in Nigeria.[30] The young officers who actually carried out the coup thought of themselves in the Nigerian political context as radicals and populists. Major Nzeogwu, one of the coup leaders, attacked civilians for the corruption, disorder, and despotic rule. Lieutenant Colonel Ojukwu attacked civilians for their incompetence, inefficiency, abuse of office and disregard of the common man. But this was as close as these officers came to a statement about the inequalities of Nigerian life;[31] they were more concerned about the disorder and corruption of that life.

The first two military regimes – the Ironsi government from January–July 1966 and the Gowon government from mid-1966 until 1970 – were concerned, above all, with the form of the Nigerian polity, the Civil War and national reconstruction. Establishment of national authority and resumed growth were the key issues during this period.

By October 1970, the Gowon government was well established. It had won the Civil War and enjoyed wide respect and authority in Nigeria. Indeed, it was better accepted than any independent Nigerian government had ever been. In October 1970, General Gowon announced a Nine-Point Program that had to be fulfilled before a civilian regime could be reintroduced in Nigeria. This was the Gowon military government's manifesto. General Gowon stipulated that it was necessary to have reorganization of the armed forces, implementation of the national development plan and repair of war damage, eradication of corruption from national life, settlement of the question of more states, preparation and adoption of a new constitution, introduction of a new formula for revenue allocation among states, a new population census, organization of 'genuinely national' political parties and organization of elections of popularly elected governments in the states and the center. Again, the issue of equity among income groups was not salient.

It would be largely accurate to say that the Gowon military regime perceived government in an administrative rather than in a bargaining and coalition context.[32] Above all, this government wanted national unity. Politicians whom I interviewed in 1972–3 – i.e., participants in military cabinets and former elected officials – agreed that the military officers focused on narrow and parochial interests which pertained to military interests *per se*. The politicians believed that military officers operating in broader policy realms were averse to representational politics and unsuccessful at it. Nor did the politicians believe that the military had been especially successful in developing health or educational services or in promoting economic development. The military people were given high marks for their creation of more states and for their accomplishments on the national unity question.[33]

The Nigerian military government under General Gowon, while continuing to ban political parties, might have tried to create redistribution through administrative edicts, consistent with its vision of the political process. Or, it might have tried to create organizations for mobilizing and controlling reformist tendencies, as the Peruvian military tried to do.[34] (Most students of Peru's and other reformist military regimes emphasize the constraints, both external and self-imposed, on the militaries' undertaking income distribution reforms.) The Nigerian military in the Gowon period, however, hardly seemed interested in probing the administrative and political constraints – although, there were policy innovations, especially in education – and tax reform and wage policies were implemented.

However, the Second Five-Year Plan (1970–4) stated an increased emphasis on income distribution and the welfare of the common man.[35] As Sayre Schatz has pointed out, the Second Plan spoke of the need to reduce areas of unearned income, broaden the social base of capital ownership in the economy, reduce the high degree of concentration of stock shareholding and enable Nigerians to share in the increasing profits being generated.[36] The means to achieve these goals were said to be a new national leadership that would be honest and dedicated, and an investment policy that would be consistent with national goals.[37] Indigenization and Nigerianization were seen as a means to these ends, as well as good things in and of themselves. Schatz has called the Second Plan period one of 'guided internationalist nurture-capitalism with a welfare tendency.'[38]

In practice, whatever welfare to be brought about was to come from the government or from private economic initiatives but not through structural change. That is, the government was supposed to guide investment and to some extent increase the services it was delivering. There was no intended direct assault on equity problems. Indeed, given the formula the government had for economic development and the conditions of Nigerian political and economic life, such an assault would have been difficult to mount because the government did not face a landed aristocracy whose land it could expropriate throughout the country.

Traditionally elite groups usually were not bothered by the military government. As for private accumulations of industrial wealth, the government wanted growth through partnership with private investors; it also wanted to increase the scope of Nigerian private enterprise. The government was not about to attack private Nigerian accumulators either by helping to create new institutions designed to bring about redistribution through popular participation, or by implementing policies from above for rapid alteration of income distribution. Nor was the government's indigenization policy designed to cope primarily with distributional problems. Professor Aboyade has argued that indigenization from 1972 to 1974 worsened inequality.[39]

No doubt there were differences of opinion within the government on both the nationalization and indigenization programs. Not all transfers went to private owners. State governments and parastatals bought up large quantities of the shares offered. There is dispute as to whether the government's major aim was to support orderly indigenization through public purchases or whether the idea was to lessen private investment and to be able to socialize wealth in order to deal with equity problems later on.[40] My own view is that the public control of corporations and resources is consistent with economic nationalism and with public officials' own sense of identity with the state. Their sense of corporate and professional well-being is tied up with the expansion of state power, and their first order of motivation in Nigeria stemmed from the identity of public officials' interests and expansion of the state. This view receives support when we look at what outspoken civil servants themselves said during the period of formulation and implementation phrase of the Second Plan.[41]

Over and over, civil servants emphasized growth objectives and a concern for an 'independent' economy. They addressed themselves to welfare objectives, and increasingly so as the 1970s progressed. The civil servants were still concerned with regional shares of income and with interstate disparities. Rural–urban income distinctions received more rhetorical attention than before, and the theme of concern with

employment became heard more and more. Civil servants have had
a bias for dealing with inequality by trying to deliver more services
and to reform the government's ability to deliver the services well.
Discussions of confiscatory policies or direct reallocations through
tax policies were not heard, although, as we shall see, wage and price
policies become more salient after the Second Plan period.

So far, I have been referring to high level civil servants. At the
highest levels of the state and federal services, civil servants were often
aggressive in moving to fill political vacuums from 1966 to 1974. At
local levels, though, Nigerian civil servants found it difficult to both
represent and administer. And, there seemed to be a disposition at
all levels of the civil service to question whether the military had a
mandate for radical reform.[42]

In public documents, at least, civil servants did not seem consumed
by a concern for dealing head-on with income inequalities. Of course,
if we did a close analysis of civil service attitudes and behaviors,[43] we
would have to distinguish within the civil service by rank and background, and by whether the administrators were technocrats or
generalists.

Civil servants pushed very hard for large increases in their salaries,
and these were granted after a two-year inquiry of the Public Service
Review Commission (the Udoji Commission), which submitted its
report in September 1974. Many salaries were doubled retroactive to
April 1974. The civil service salary increases mightily fueled Nigerian
inflation. The Udoji Commission had provided recommendations for
administrative class civil servants. Professionals and public sector
workers in general clamored to keep up, but the great majority of
the population had little protection against the inflationary consequences of Udoji.[44] One commentator has seen the Udoji wage
increases as the Gowon regime's attempt 'to encourage acquiescence
to its retention of power by giving a pivotal section of the population
a sizable share of oil wealth.'[45]

During the period of military rule, military officers served as
governors of the states and at various times headed economic ministries
in the states and at the federal level. I have not carried out any
systematic scanning of officers' statements over a ten-year period to
try to gauge their commitments on distribution and equity issues.
However, I did interview military officers in the western state of
Nigeria in 1972–3 and discussed with them the large-scale unrest and
violence that had taken place in 1968–9 in the west and which came

to be known as the 'Agbekoya.'[46] Agbekoya was an agrarian populist movement and a revolt against high taxes and poor services which centered in areas where cocoa production had been on the decline. Military officers tended to see Agbekoya as a plot hatched by former politicians, and were insensitive to the farmers' plight. General Adebayo, who then was governor of the western state, refused to see the protest as directed against levels of taxation. He argued that tax agitation was most rampant in better-off areas where people had basic services such as water and electricity, although he reproached traditional and local leaders for not showing more concern about their areas.[47] Military officers in the western state were more concerned with re-establishing law and order than with coming to grips with the economic and social problems.

The Third National Development Plan was formally promulgated by General Gowon in March 1975 and was meant to cover the period 1975–80. The plan was embraced by General Mohammed, Gowon's successor.[48] The Third National Development Plan lists a more even distribution of income as its second goal after an increase in *per capita* income; reduction of unemployment is listed next and then an increase in the supply of high-level manpower, diversification of the economy, balanced development and indigenization of economic activity.[49] The plan also noted that the development policy must be directed at economic growth and development, price stability and social equity, and that the emphasis given to each goal would vary depending on prevailing economic situations and political philosophies. The main concern of the Third Plan's policy was said to be the need to effect a more equitable distribution of income and to control inflation.[50]

The strategy to be adopted in this period with respect to income distribution was for the public sector to provide subsidized facilities for the poorer sections of the population; these were to include electrification, water supplies, health services, cooperatives, and community development programs in the rural areas, and housing in the urban areas. The government felt that these programs would directly raise the level of living of the poorer classes and constitute a more practical means of income redistribution than other more direct measures.[51] The government stated its intention to continue to use fiscal measures of progressive income taxation to reduce existing inequalities in the distribution of income. Universal free primary education was a major policy to bring about equal opportunities.[52]

I am not going to try to assess the military government's performance or the indirect effects on income distribution of the military's own practices and defense spending.[53] It can be pointed out that when the Central Planning Office published the First Progress Report on the Third National Development Plan to cover 1975–6, neither the general survey of the economy nor the review of specific sectors looked at the income distribution effects of various programs. Indeed, income distribution was not mentioned in this report.

The Third Plan called for the establishment of an Income Analysis Unit in the Federal Ministry of Economic Development and Reconstruction; earlier, a national accounts study team was to provide information on an incomes profile of Nigeria. But data on incomes remained very weak, and assessments of the impact of policies on distribution were not forthcoming. Sayre Schatz, who predicted that there would be a marked discrepancy between stated commitment to reducing income disparities and achieved goals, noted that 'in the face of the powerful income-differentiating tendencies in Nigeria's early-capitalist society, little direct income policy was even proposed.'[54]

It is apparent that military personnel from 1966 to 1975 did not really focus on income distribution issues. Thereafter, the story is more complicated. Murtala Mohammed's government has been called 'corrective' and 'populist,'[55] but if these designations have merit it is largely because General Mohammed started demobilization of the army and put life back into the process of the transition to civilian rule. He moved to create a new constitution. These were all important measures.

General Mohammed increased the salience of concern with equity issues. He also increased producer prices for agricultural commodities, although this move was a continuation of earlier measures. In early 1973, under General Gowon, the power to fix producers' prices was transferred from state marketing boards to the Federal government. Export duties and the states' produce sales tax on crops that the boards dealt with were replaced by a single federal tax of ten per cent *ad valorem*. In 1974 this tax was removed. The idea was to give producers higher prices. Between 1974 and 1976, agricultural producer prices doubled for many commodities and tripled for palm oil. As noted, in 1977 the state marketing boards were replaced by a national board for each commodity. These reforms then continued after General Mohammed's assassination.

Agricultural reform, then, did not begin or end with General Mohammed, nor was it strikingly successful. Since the cost of living was going up rapidly from 1967 on, the increase in producer prices for commodities no more than offset other price increases. Schatz, among others, has pointed out that there was a decrease in aggregate agricultural output from 1970 to 1971 through 1974–5, and an even greater reduction in output per farmer. He states that the rural–urban income disparity was aggravated by indigenization and Udoji wage increases.[56] Military regimes had not closed urban–rural gaps in income, nor had they redressed intrasectoral inequalities.

It has been argued that the massive purges that General Mohammed conducted of the army, police, civil service and universities can be thought of as a radical move on the equity front. 'The Government was to acquire a favorable reputation as a 'poor man's government' but this was because the abuse of office is, in a rural society with reasonably free and equal access to land, the chief source of inequality.'[57] There is some truth to this point of view, and certainly General Mohammed's historical image is now that of a populist because of his attack on corrupt practices, his confiscation of urban land and some farms gathered by public officials, and his crackdown on business run by high-level civil servants.[58]

It is also true that General Mohammed and his successor, General Obasanjo, pursued a policy of compressing wage differentials. They also restricted government loans for the purchase of expensive automobiles, and automobiles were taxed more heavily. The Land Use Decree of 1978 promulgated under General Obasanjo was designed to reduce the cost of urban land and to increase access to farmland. These measures and revisions of priorities in the Third Five-Year Plan to emphasize basic needs have led some observers to want to distinguish between the programs of General Gowon and those of Generals Mohammed and Obasanjo.

There is no doubt that equity issues had a greater salience once General Mohammed came to power. But reforms cut many ways at once and often had unanticipated consequences. There were great difficulties in implementing tax and educational reforms, nor do spending priorities appear to have been radically altered. Nigeria entered a reformist period with the ascendance of General Mohammed. But the country did not witness a period of either radical reform or major change toward more equitable income distributions.

It is not possible here to analyze fully the political campaigns of late 1978 and 1979, nor the programs and appeals of the new parties. Once again, all parties declared for the provision of more services

– especially health, education and housing. The emphasis was more on service delivery than on direct redistribution of personal incomes.

The two parties that most consistently took populist stands were the Unity Party of Nigeria (UPN), led by Chief Awolowo, and the Peoples Redemption Party (PRP), led by Aminu Kano. Spokespeople for the UPN accused the ruling party, the National Party of Nigeria (NPN) of being led by capitalists. Indeed the NPN, led by Shehu Shagari, was clearly more conservative in tone than the UPN. The UPN called its ideology 'socialist' and argued that free education, free medical care, rural integrated development and full employment could come about only in a socialist system.[59] The UPN also called for a lifting of the ban on import controls and removal of government restrictions on trade and commerical activities. It thus tried to appeal to business people, too. Indeed, at the very time that the UPN renewed its pledge to introduce a minimum income of ₦2,500 per annum for workers and farmers within its first term, four-year government if elected, it also announced its intention to let Nigerians invest and establish new businesses. The UPN seemed to show a suspicion of state controls.[60]

The major parties continued to have a large ethnic group as their constituency base, and their candidates were selected with a view toward appealing to other ethnic groups. Chief Awolowo and Shehu Shagari chose Ibos as their vice-presidential candidates whereas Dr Nnamdi Azikiwe, leader of the Nigerian Peoples Party and himself an Ibo, did not.[61] While there were programmatic distinctions between the parties, and while they campaigned all over Nigeria, their strengths were less that of a programmatic appeal to economic strata than an appeal to personality and ethnic coalition-building. There was a strong correlation between the electoral success of a presidential candidate and ethnic constituency. Thus, Chief Awolowo carried the Yoruba states of Lagos, Ondo, Oyo and Ogun. Indeed, the presidential election marked the first time that Chief Awolowo carried Ibadan constituencies, and the Yoruba rallied around him.

Similarly, Dr Nnamdi Azikiwe was extremely successful in the Ibo states of Imo and Anambra; he also did well in the state of Plateau. Alhaji Ibrahim was able to get a majority of votes only in Borno among his own Kanuri people, although he competed well in the neighboring state of Gongola.

Alhaji Shehu Shagari's strength was the most widespread of the candidates. He was able to win in non-Hausa areas where he made electoral coalitions, and ran well in the state of Bendel. However, his support came predominantly from the north, although another northern candidate, Alhaji Aminu Kano, was able to carry his own home state of Kano.[62]

Gubernatorial and presidential elections were closely correlated. In only two states did a governor win who came from a party different than the presidential candidate. In Gongola, one percentage point or so separated the presidential candidates of the NPN and the Great Nigerian People's party; the same figures held in the gubernational elections, although the results were reversed. Similarly, the legislative elections correlated with the executive ones. Only in the state of Kaduna did a governor come from a party that did not have plurality of seats in the legislative elections. Kaduna was the other state in which a governor was not from the same party as the leading presidential candidate. The candidate of the PRP – i.e., Aminu Kano's party – won in Kaduna. It was this state, perhaps more than any other, in which we can see some clear differentiation between class and ethnic appeals in the elections. The PRP gubernatorial candidate, Alhaji Abdulkadiri Balarabe Musa, explicitly appealed to *talakawa*, or commoner, interests. In his maiden postelection speech, he promised to 'free the masses from the bondage of all forms of oppression by the powerful and rich class.'[63] And, on taking power at the state level, the PRP abolished the community or poll tax (*harji*) and cattle tax (*jangali*) in Kano and Kaduna. These taxes were viewed by the governor as taxes on the rural areas in favor of urban ones. He saw them as pillars of feudal oppression.

The UPN also moved to implement some of its campaign platforms in states where it had won. In the state of Lagos, fees in schools were ended and private schools were abolished. At the national level, the UPN made it a condition for entering the Shagari government that:

> free and compulsory secondary school education be adopted;
> a guarantee of a national minimum wage or income of not less than ₦200 per month for workers and certain defined categories of self-employed persons be instituted from April 1, 1980;
> free curative and preventive health services be made available to all Nigerians

These conditions were restatements of the UPN's campaign programs, and the NPN did not agree to them.

Programmatic politics, then, was more in evidence in the 1979 elections than it had been in earlier elections. Nonetheless, on the basis of the campaigns and elections of 1979, it would be hard to argue that party politics in Nigeria had altered radically from the 1960s.

This leads us back to exploring the kinds of political space that regimes have had in Nigeria for formulating policy. It is necessary to try to find out what kinds of pressures policy makers have faced. How have equity issues been defined, and by whom? What has been the basis for organizing dissent from below? We now turn to these questions in order to try to understand why there has been such little direct focus on income distribution as an issue of Nigerian political life.

A SHIFT FROM THE COMMUNAL BASE OF COMPETITION?

Most discussions of political competition in Nigeria have focused on ethnic or communal conflict. Examinations of equity issues for the most part have been in terms of formulas for interregional of interstate allocations of federal funds, and on the siting of industries and infrastructure. Territory and community rather than class and occupation seem to have been the organizing concepts used in the analyses of political competition and economic distributions in Nigeria.

However, the process of centralization of authority (described above) and the creation of more states, in conjunction with the central control of oil revenues, have shifted the focus of the debates on distribution away from interregional and interstate conflict to some extent. True, it is still posisble to measure the flows from the Federal government to the states.[64] It is not really harder to do the calculations with more rather than fewer units. However, the political visibility and impact have been greatest when regions − not states − feel they get the short end of the stick.

The former regions were dominated by the large ethnic groups. Now, some states are controlled by smaller ethnic communities while larger ethnic groups inhabit more than one state. The creation of states dilutes regional competition.

Territorial competition was still intense when a specific formula existed for revenue allocation to the states, albeit a formula in which the values in the equation were heatedly debated. I refer, of course, to the alterations over time in shares based on derivation going from the distributable pool to the states and what came, after the Raisman

Commission, to be stipulated as criteria of size of population, basic responsibilities of each government, need for continuity in regional and public services and need for balanced development of the Federation as a whole.[65] Except for the size of population, the very meanings of these criteria were open to a good deal of interpretation. And, as students of Nigerian censuses are aware, size of population was not a fact easily agreed upon in Nigeria.

When the number of units grew from 4 to 12 and then 19, it could not be argued that whole regions benefited in a consistent way. Thus, Rimlinger cites *per capita* allocations as a percentage of the national average to Ibo-speaking states in the former Eastern Region, with Imo having 103.4 per cent but Anambra, 90.4 per cent in 1976–7. For Yoruba-speaking states in the old Western Region, Ogun has 128.6 per cent whereas Ondo has 91.8 per cent and Oyo 69.6 per cent. Similarly, some of the northern states are above national average while others are below (although the states of the 'dry north' are all below average).[66] Direct federal spending in the states has become increasingly important as compared to revenue allocations, but it is hard to measure the impact of such spending.

While I cannot speculate on how much commitment there is on the part of inhabitants to their states, it would appear that regional groupings of states no longer provides a sufficient base of national power for elites.

The complicated constitutional provisions for winning the election for president of the Nigerian Federal Republic insisted that a candidate receive a plurality plus at least a quarter of the votes in two-thirds of the states.[67] A runoff required members of the national and state legislatures to choose between the two top candidates.[68] Thus, getting allocations for one's own state remained important, but contending electorally for national power did not rest on the success of such an effort.

The proliferation of states, and the facts that the center is ever more the source for funds in Nigeria and that derivation is less taken into account for distributions to the states may work to diminish the intensity of competition between states in Nigeria.[69] Does this mean that as politics becomes more national we might expect a shift to seeing distribution and equity issues more in terms of income categories, economic sectors and occupations? Income differences can be expected to remain intertwined with communal and state identifications because communal identities remain strong in Nigeria; the average income of wage earners and the self-employed show significant differences by states within the upper-, lower- and middle-income categories; and the number of people within each category differs by states.

Still, we can predict a relative increase in the salience of equity issues defined in class and sectoral terms, while ethnic and communal definitions remain strong and relevant. The rapid growth of the Nigerian economy from oil revenues, rising inflation, the trend toward urbanization and stagnation in the agricultural sector all portend this occurrence.

The growth in importance of class and sectoral terms of reference will not take place in any simple manner in Nigeria, nor will it come at the expense of communal ties. Some of the difficult subjects that must yet be explored include the following: the degree and manner in which equity issues are raised; whether low-end poverty will be featured in debate; the values that equity issues speak to; and the political structures and interests that must be taken up and articulated in Nigerian society.

CLASS, ETHNICITY AND INEQUALITY: GENERAL COMMENTS

There has been a long-standing debate and a growing literature on the matter of classes in Africa. Many studies argue the pros and cons of the existence of classes, class consciousness, and the meaning of 'class' in the African context. African leaders past and present have been prominent in this debate, too. The early articulation of African socialism by leaders like Touré, Nkrumah and Nyerere revolved around the issue of the relevance of class analysis in African political life and the inevitability of class formation in Africa.[70] Contemporary debates deal with the relationship of class to ethnicity;[71] the relationship of domestic classes to international capitalism (i.e., dependency[72]); and the relationship of classes to categorical and situational elites (e.g., the debate on whether the military and bureaucratic elite should be considered as classes themselves, or as spokespersons or surrogates for classes;[73] and whether trade-unionized workers are a labor aristocracy or not).[74]

No one doubts that groups organize for competition and cooperation on the basis of economic interests and motives; nor does anyone doubt that occupational distinctions and income differentiations have political consequences. The issue at stake in the debate is whether the term 'class politics' means that people have to be conscious of their position in relation to the means of production and the social and political consequences that flow from those relations, or whether it means that classes can exist objectively, regardless of whether or not people are conscious of their situation.[75] Also, does any hierarchy of inequality constitute a class system? Should conflict over access to public resources be defined as *class* conflict? That is, are all distinctions between rulers and the ruled to be defined as dichotomous and zero-sum, and as distinctions between classes?

Before taking up these issues in the Nigerian context I want to declare myself on a number of definitional and analytical points. When I say that a group is an 'ethnic' one, I am making an analytical distinction or a simplification for analytical purposes. In the real world, people have bundles of feelings, attachments and motives – all at one time. Individual identities – that is, the way a person describes him/herself – are a function of many things: the 'name' given at birth by one's parents, ties to relatives and how one is perceived by out-groups. An individual can either accept or reject these identifications. The way a person works, lives and moves about affects his/her self-identification over time.

In some cases, groups give identities which are sometimes difficult to reject. Migrants to Abidjan or Kinshasa may be referred to by an ethnic term which is not their own in their place of origin. New groups arise based on the use of lingua francas such as Swahili or Lingala. People may deliberately alter their identities or 'pass' in order to get jobs or social acceptance. This has happened to people with caste identities in India, religious affiliations in the United States and even racial identifications in some societies. Elsewhere, the state may insist on an ethnic identity for an individual.

Ethnic affiliations may be hard or fluid from societal context to context and can change over time. They are not always 'givens' or primordial. The distinctions between ascriptive and nonascriptive variables is not always very helpful. These are subjective, not objective phenomena. Identifications may be derived from language, skin color, or place of origin in some societies (but not in others). Political factors like economic ones, are usually important in the process of identification. Thus, people who defined themselves as Arabs before independence in Kenya may now define themselves as Coastal Kenyans. Depending on where he is and who asks the question, 'What are you?,' a Lebanese Christian might reply. 'Lebanese,' 'Christian,' 'Maronite,' or some subgroup of Maronites.

It is not easy to isolate analytically the ways in which 'communal' and 'ethnic' (I use the words interchangeably here) relationships are different from class relationships. It is said that communal groups encompass the full range of sex and age divisions within society, but this is also true for class groups. Communal ties are said to provide a network of groups and institutions extending throughout a life cycle. This can be true also for occupational and class groups who form sports, burial and health societies. Within what we normally refer to as 'class' and 'communal' groups, internal differentiation of status, power and lifestyles usually takes place. True, if by class we mean 'income group', then differentiation by income group can take place only within communal groups by definition while it must take place between class groups by definition.

Common cultural identification may occur for class as well as communal groups. Most communal groups, certainly large ethnic-language ones, do not share cultural symbols across the whole group. Language communication may be hard for an ethnic group, when there are many dialects within a group that traces its origins to a common ancestor. There are also societies in which class groups who supposedly speak the same language cannot be easily understood by other class groups who are also nominally members of the same language group.

We may get the idea that a communal group is simply one in which people claim to share a commonality of identity across many relationships. With this understanding of the term, some class groups would then be 'communal.' Indeed the term 'cockney' implies not only the use of a language dialect but also shared food tastes, lifestyles, income, and status.

The concept of 'class' as distinct from 'communal group' is not so clear either. Normally we refer to class affiliations as stemming from people's social and economic relations, which are derived from their place in the processes of production. More broadly, we refer to economically-based ties as achievement- rather than ascriptively-oriented memberships. Class is thought of by many anthropologists as nonbirth-ascribed status. However, while it is true that class status is identified by such features as income, education and occupation, it is also true that our idea of class has birth and holistic lifestyle characteristics.[77] We make distinctions by referring to 'upstart people,' 'classes,' 'parvenues,' and '*nouveau riche.*'

How people spend their income – that is, their consumption styles – seems related to broader, non-income characteristics. These associations with class may be more applicable to a society that has many occupational and income differentiations within it as compared to a society where most people are rural and very poor. But we should not think that highly industrialized societies are the only ones in which the notion of class is slippery in application.

UNDERSTANDINGS OF CLASS, WEALTH AND POVERTY IN NIGERIA

Because Nigeria is a large heterogeneous society with many culturally distinct groups and subgroups, we cannot expect that culturally associated understandings of wealth and poverty and the way people are to be grouped will necessarily be the same throughout the country. For some areas, we have extremely detailed empirical work on the relationship of social values to social structural variables such as patterns of landholding and stratification,[78] the relationship between fertility and attitudes[79] and perceptions of inequality as related to occupational data.[80]

I want to present some vignettes culled on a selective basis from various authors who have done detailed studies in Nigeria. My aim is to show the variety of terms and their usages in people's thinking about wealth, poverty and equality in different parts of Nigeria. My aim also is to root understandings of inequality in the population's own contexts and vocabularies so that we avoid facile generalizations about class consciousness and class politics. We should not deduce values from certain structural conditions, much less deduce political behavior from those conditions.[81]

P. C. Lloyd argues that 'tribally structured societies ... tend to have a variety of terms with which to designate men of prestige, emphasizing variously their wealth, their moral standing, or their generosity. And these terms are applied to individuals and not groups.'[82]

Wealth itself is not an unambiguous concept. Students of fertility have been very conscious of the need to explore the ideas about wealth. A. O. Okore tells us that, 'Wealth, to an Ibo man, still consists of land, crops and livestock, children, money and other forms of material goods.'[83] Ukaegbu notes that 'numerous children are regarded as 'true wealth' and there is a tendency to regard couples who have large families as being rich or potentially so.'[84] Caldwell says that four-fifths of all Yoruba hold that children are either better than wealth or are wealth.[85]

Studies of fertility in Nigeria and elsewhere indicate a sense of the variety of ideas about wealth in different societies. Ideas concerning children and wealth have to do with what we call 'this worldly income' – that children provide security, labor and income. There are also considerations that have to do with maintenance of a family after the death of a couple and the ability of children to provide for the demands of the community at burial ceremonies. In rural Yoruba society it is still taken as one of the immutable facts of existence that size of family, political strength and affluence are not only interrelated but one and the same thing.[86]

Polly Hill insists that the Hausa informants of the Dorayi people near Kano City relate the concept of wealth specifically to economic well-being. They distinguish the *economic* from other factors. 'The use of the word "wealth" is meant to convey the importance of economic security.' Wealth is separated out from political power.[87] Hill goes on to argue that the concept of wealth, *arziki*, is a mysterious personal attribute necessary for success in this world. It is a gift which cannot be explained rationally in terms of inheritance, hard work, many sons, intelligence, or religious piety.[88]

It is important to know whether ideas of wealth are the same when applied to both individuals and groups. Analysis of legitimacy will depend on the answers. In a work devoted to Yoruba perceptions of social inequality, Lloyd argues that distinctions should be made between how the Yoruba see themselves in society and how they view society. For example, equals of the same age are considered to be 'class mates' rather than people of equal status or income.[89] According to Lloyd, answers to questions of social rank depend on differences in ethnic terms between 'indigens' and 'strangers,' or between, for example, the Oyo or the Ekiti Yoruba. Lloyd says that his respondents made distinctions of wealth but to do this descriptively was not to raise questions of legitimacy or to attribute causal factors. People made distinctions between the poor and rich but did not use class terms.[90] Lloyd also tells us that the Oyo and Ibadan Yoruba complained of not getting enough resources compared to other Yoruba; but these disparities between the ethnic subgroups did not lead to distinctions in class terms. Distinctions between the ethnic groups were made in terms of diet and speech.[91]

There are, of course, many places in Africa where differences between ethnic groups have come to be defined in terms of economic inequality. But the relationships between ethnic and class definitions are usually complex and sometimes the reverse of what might be expected. In some West African societies all herdsmen are called *fulani*, an ethnic term. Occupations are given an ethnic identification. Lloyd, however, says that perhaps the Hausa language allows for the terminology of caste to be adapted to the terminology of class — for example, the terms *talakawa* (commoner) and *sarakuna* (officeholders and their kin) form categories into which the population may be divided. But while the stratified societies of the savanna have this terminology, Lloyd says that the concepts of class are largely absent from the West African vernacular languages.[92]

All diversity cannot be comprehended exclusively in ethnic or class terms. Territorial/neighborhood interests have been evident in many African cities, and the nature and salience of issues determine the contours of conflict. People move in and out of associations and give weight first to one group then another. Demands are pressed forward by shifting groups. The sets of interests which operate must be shown, not deduced, from a presumed class structure. Furthermore, it is a mistake to deduce lifestyles, social status and political stance from income differentiation, land and other asset holdings. Undoubtedly, there are relationships between these things which are not random, but the nature of the relationships varies within and between societies. Not only must we avoid facile generalizations for Nigeria as a whole, but social and political patterns and historical experiences are varied even within language groups.[93]

We would like to be able to relate social structural variables to attitudes and political behaviors. We would like to be able to see the impact that change, say in land price or the pace of migration, has on attitudes, political organizations and behaviors. This would enable us to say something about the ways in which patterns that develop in subsistence settings persist, are strengthened, give way, or are adapted in new contexts. We could then assess both the political implications of change and the possibilities for different strategies of distribution and development.

In the pages that follow we rely on secondary sources to get at some of these questions, albeit very imperfectly. There are huge gaps in information which are only partially remedied by micro-surveys or the few national surveys and censuses that exist for Nigeria.

CLASS POLITICS IN NIGERIA

There are a number of facts about which most observers of Nigerian politics agree: communal politics has become less overt and the states are less significant bases of power than were the old regions. The social composition and occupational structure of society have changed since 1960. Occupational differentiation has proceeded; the industrial working class is growing in size, although it is still a small part of the urban-employed. The commercial and business sectors have expanded along with the strengthening of parastatal and public sector organizations. That is, the growth of the private business sector and the middle class in private employment have gone on along with the growth of the state sector. This growth has not been mutually exclusive, although recently, employment in the public sector has grown at about twice the rate of the private sector. The public sector, including the teaching service, now accounts for about 65 per cent of total modern sector employment, which is placed at about 1,500,000. Yet Nigeria is an atypical African country in that high-level manpower has been moving from the public into private sector employment.

Different observers seeing the same 'facts' have come to these diverse conclusions: that state capitalism is proceeding in Nigeria; that Nigeria is becoming a private capitalist-dominated state. No one has concluded that Nigeria is becoming a socialist state. Perhaps more significant than the debate over what label to put on Nigeria, has been disagreement as to the kinds and intensities of pressures that are building from below for egalitarian change.

As yet, it is difficult to see the development of a strong set of industrial working class organizations. Nigeria has a history of strike action, including a large general strike in 1964. As in many African countries, the government has moved to control the trade union movement by co-ordinating trade union affairs through a central labor organization. The banning of individual trade unions, arrest of leaders, creation of state frameworks for settlement of industrial disputes and the making of strikes illegal have occurred in Nigeria. But, strikes have occurred despite the fact that Decree Number 7 of 1976, a trade disputes decree, continued restrictions on the right to strike and established a complex hierarchy of bargaining institutions.

As Waterman has noted, Nigeria has moved toward a corporate structure for industrial labor relations.[94] The Nigerian Labour Congress was established in 1975 and incorporated a statutory regulation for the federation of unions. However, as Waterman also notes, despite the increased regulation since the Civil War, industrial relations remain anarchic. After both the Udoji report in 1975 and the earlier Adebo Wage Commission in 1970–1, large-scale strikes took place. Procedures for the settlement of disputes have been extremely various, which reflects the heterogeneity of the Nigerian economy with its state sectors, private foreign firms, private local capitalists and extreme regional variations.

Studies of Nigeria give us a very complicated picture of the relationship of class to communal interests as expressed in behaviors during strikes, trade union organizing, demands for better work conditions, employment, security of job and wages. Micro-studies of workers in Nigeria indicate that there is a great deal of variation in the relationship of ethnicity to class and in the development of class consciousness. The variables that appear explanatory include the specific issue of protest, the structures available through which people compete, the homogeneity or heterogeneity in ethnic terms of the labor force and the place of residence. That is, significant factors include the kind of city, pattern of migration and place where the industrial work force is recruited from and its relationship both to rural areas and to the informal sector.

We cannot ignore the wider urban environment in which workers live. The content of traditional customs also matters. In addition, the source of capital and technology, degree of product differentiation within the corporate structure, nature of the industry as domestic or foreign controlled, relationship of wages to total costs, all shape the kinds of demands workers make, the responses to demands and the organizations which evolve.

It is possible for one to accept the proposition that industrial workers in Nigeria respond to limited choices with rational action toward situations of structured inequality, and still not accept the idea that workers have class interests only and that their other concerns are simply manipulated by the elite in order to obscure class interests. In order to see and explain the weakness of class action by workers, one does not need to have recourse to explanations that rely on ignorance, intransigent traditional values and apathy on the part of first-generation factory workers. Job insecurity, limited alternatives of income, gaps between union leaders and the rank and file and repression may all be important factors.[95] Desired patterns of social mobility, the structuring of political conflict and economic competition as affected by ethnic factors also may be important.

Ethnicity has affected recruitment to industrial jobs in Nigeria. For example, in Kano, the withdrawal of Ibos affected the ethnic composition of the working force after 1966. Labor in Kano's factories has become increasingly Hausa-Fulani. Studies of factory employment show that in cases where the labor pools are ethnically heterogeneous, ethnic sponsors intervene with management to hire clients put forward by ethnic associations. Such is the pattern described by Dorothy Remy in Zaria.[96] This is by no means an unusual pattern in Africa. Remy goes a step further to show the importance of the urban environment on workers' behavior. 'The size and concentration of the industrial proletariat and the relative importance of formal and informal economic activities in the city shape the external parameters of industrial action.'[97]

In some Nigerian cities, in Lagos and Kano especially, factories are concentrated on large industrial estates built by the government. Workers frequently live on the estates in dormitories. Yoruba workers tend to migrate to Lagos while Hausa tend to migrate to Kano. Workers are more mixed in Zaria, and Yoruba dominate Ibadan, but in both cities there are fewer industries than in Lagos or Kano and they are individually sited. Workers live in occupationally heterogeneous neighborhoods scattered throughout these cities.

The high concentration of workers in the estate areas of Lagos and Kano has created a need for large informal sector opportunities to service the workers. 'Strangers' to these cities are frequently involved in this sector in entrepreneurial roles. (In Lagos, 'strangers' comprise Yoruba people who have migrated recently and are non-indigenous to the city.) Strangers find it harder to establish large networks of customers in Zaria and Ibadan.

The relationship between formal and informal sectors is affected by the relationships between the ethnic groups occupying them. In Ibadan and Zaria a number of factors work to maintain close ties between industrial workers and their ethnic communities. One is the tie between informal sector ethnic affines. Another is the relative scarcity of alternative sources of income, which places pressure on the people who have industrial jobs to keep them and to maintain links with the ethnic associations that have been influential in getting them such jobs. This situation reduces workers' class consciousness and hampers the effectiveness of sustained collective action.[98] Ethnicity does not necessarily dilute class consciousness. For example, in Ibadan and Zaria the tenuous links between industrial workers and

the informal economy reduce the economic interest of local entrepreneurs in industrial disputes. Therefore, workers are thrown back
on their ethnic ties for job security and support.

Nigerian workers frequently see upward mobility in terms of
leaving industrial factory work and accumulating enough capital to
take up a trade, artisan job, or small business activity. Whether or
not this leads to a diminished demand for wages and a weakening of
class consciousness is a matter for debate. Adrien Peace argues that,
in Lagos, the workers' desires to leave industrial employment and
enter the informal sector, as well as their willingness to enter collective
action in Lagos in order to obtain funds to set up small businesses,
increase the pressures for higher wages.[99]

The visible success of local economic entrepreneurs also provides
an alternative pattern of mobility, and demonstrates that an individual
can rise in the system. Wage labor is seen as a means to a different
kind of life, not as a means of achieving redistribution through
collective action.[100] Nigerian workers place a premium on personal
independence. The suggestion here is that class action is weakened
because social mobility and welfare are perceived as arising outside
of the industrial sector.

On the other hand, formal and informal sector workers may
contrast their salaries and benefits to managers and owners, and the
income difference between formal and informal sector workers may
be insignificant in light of the larger contrasts. Paul Lubeck makes
this argument for workers in Kano:

> ... because the urban workers in Kano emerge from the common
> inequality status of being a *talakawa* before they became urban
> laborers and because marriage patterns, mutual aid, Islamic
> institutions, household and community relationships integrate
> the formal and informal sector workers, there is no objective or
> subjective cleavage between them ...[M]embers of the informal
> sector, by servicing the formal sector workers, participate in a
> redistribution of high income such that informal sector workers
> regard the formal sector workers as a political elite pursuing the
> class interests of the laboring population as a whole.[101]

Undoubtedly, what we call formal and informal working-class
sectors are highly differentiated internally. Lifestyles as well as income
vary within these categories, and cultural and ethnic patterns affect
the development of class ties. Furthermore, we have to take account

of the situational distinctions among groups in Nigeria. John C. Caldwell, referring to African societies in general, argues: 'The obsession with *per capita* analysis has obscured situational gain, which is of particular importance to patriarchial males.'[102]

Here, Caldwell is referring to the unequal division of wealth or consumption within the family, but the point can be generalized. There are inequalities by sex, age and family status. *Per capita* income may remain static but the person at the top of the pyramid controls more resources, has access to more services and enjoys more power if the families grow in size. This phenomenon accounts in part for certain resistances to change in highly structured pyramidal societies. People at the top of the heap may resist changes that will clearly benefit them materially in the short-run but that, in the not-so-long-run, will alter their status within the group or shift the bases of authority to a very different status system.

Individual political action is based on an assessment of situational gain. It is true that such action may be structured by the channels available for activity, group and communal pressures and the demands of the state, but we can start with the assumption that individual actors make a judgment about their prospects for gains in different contexts – those of family; community; locality; and, for some actors, state and nation.[103] Action taken to improve one's own family situation rather than class action may be highly likely[104] if the following circumstances take place:

> Individual head of household benefits are seen to increase by having more children;
>
> The system is understood to be one in which social mobility and increased economic well-being are possible and even likely;
>
> It is true that 'perhaps the single most important consumption good for the successful family is meeting all family obligations in a more generous way ...'[105]

There are, of course, obstacles and costs to political action by the urban poor and the organized working class.[106] The urban poor have unstable residences, low membership rates in voluntary associations, little trust in their leaders (often for excellent reasons), lack of funds, few meeting places and are frequently divided by ethnic origin. If the connection is made between collective acts and individual interests, the collective acts are perceived, and accurately so, to be of a very high cost in the short run. Political organizations that might help people make these connections have been the exception rather than the rule in Nigeria, as the government bans individual trade unions and radical parties.

For all their weaknesses, the industrial workers in Nigeria have a greater capacity for collective action than peasants and individuals in the informal urban sector. Should we describe trade-unionized workers in Nigeria as a 'labor aristocracy'? The labor aristocracy thesis has been in vogue in Africa with Marxists, Fanonists and conservative analysts. They have all pointed to the fact that cities have expanded much more rapidly than employment opportunities, and that employed workers have appeared as a relatively privileged group when compared to peasants and other people in the urban informal sector. It is true that industrial workers have usually wanted higher wages more often than they have demanded expanded opportunities for new entrants into the working class. The ratios of skilled workers' salaries are three times higher than salaries of those unskilled workers.[107] Yet when we try to come to grips with applying labor aristocracy theories to Nigeria, we are struck by the heterogeneity of the working force and the complexity of inter- and intrasectional, rural–urban and public–private relationships.

I have already noted that there are some difficulties in accepting a neat dichotomy between formal and informal workers, both politically and economically. In Nigeria, a buoyant informal sector may be as important for social mobility as increasing the size of the industrial working force. The reduction of jobs in the informal sector through growth of imports or new capital intensive techniques may close off important mobility and income opportunities. Moreover, wage earners often form the focal point of the urban networks of their less fortunate kinsmen.[108] Still, even after we take into account that urban wages have not kept pace with cost-of-living increases, especially in Lagos, industrial jobs are preferable for urban migrants while casual labor is at the bottom of the informal sector. This is evidenced by the long lines in front of factories that are hiring.

For most rural Nigerians, industrial employment is preferable to farming. People in rural areas seem to be voting with their feet. Whatever the colonial and postcolonial intentions for equalizing rural and urban incomes, the phenomenal rates of growth of the state of Lagos and of cities like Ogbomosho, Oshogbo, Port Harcourt, Kaduna and Ilorin, as well as smaller towns like Akure and Oyo,[109] tells us that millions of Nigerians perceive that they will be better off in urban areas rather than remaining in rural ones.

This should not lead us necessarily to describe formal sector labor as an aristocracy, however. The terminology is unfortunate because it implies a status elite, which the urban proletariat does not appear to be. Workers in the formal sector do appear relatively privileged economically compared to rural dwellers and most dwellers in the informal urban sector, but they do not enjoy the independence or wealth of managers, civil servants and military officers.

The crux of the matter is political. Labor aristocracy theorists suggest that the urban proletariat is in alliance with the elite to divide peasant-produced surpluses and to keep wages high by restricting entrance into the organized working class. One observer, rejecting these ideas, argues instead that the Lagos proletariat, which he calls 'populist militants,' is best viewed as the locally-based elite of the urban masses, or the vanguard of those who see a highly inegalitarian society.[110] Terminology aside, most observers see the proletariat in Nigeria as having, compared to peasants and urban marginals, a capacity for collective action and a relative awareness that collective rather than individual action produces results.[111]

It is debatable whether urban workers, by their class demands for furthering their economic situation, display strong antagonism to the existing order.[112] Nor does one have to assume that trade-unionized workers' economic demands are antithetical to the interests of those worse off; they may or may not be, depending on how resources are collected to meet those demands and what are the spin-off effects of higher wages. A critical question is whether the economic demands for 'more' can be accommodated incrementally or whether they require a radical restructuring of society in order to produce more egalitarian outcomes.

In order to come to grips with this issue, we need to inquire into the nature of the demands made, the channels for demands, the responsiveness of government to demands, and the alliances that are formed. Adrian Peace suggests that workers' specific grievances in Lagos are set in a general framework of perception of social injustice: 'Perceptions of gross inequality are continually reinforced by day-to-day experience of exceptional conspicuous consumption in an urban arena overwhelmingly characterized by the poverty of the majority.'[113] But he gives no survey data to support this. Surveys of industrial workers suggest that although workers feel exploited, they do not view those who get ahead as having done so through unjust means.[114] Furthermore, one can feel that a situation is unjust and yet think that there are no good alternatives − or, that the system remains full of mobility alternatives.

John Saul, in reconsidering his labor aristocracy thesis as applied to Nigeria, cites the absence of revolutionary ideology and revolutionary intellectuals in Nigeria.[115] He also notes that the wider political economy context must be analyzed. Agreed. As I suggested earlier, government is not a passive actor. Its programs for reform, its willingness to repress and co-opt, and its ability to do so are critical factors in the development of reformist or radical politics.

The growth rates of the economy and its structural changes are critical factors, too. The creation of a workable variant of machine politics or patron−client relations depends on a continually growing pie so that the elite and non-elite do not perceive politics as a zero-sum game. 'The conservatism of the workers, like the poor in general, is itself ambiguous. It represents a claim on the rich and powerful that they should protect their poor brethren, a demand on the economy that it should permit everyone to become a successful trader.'[116] In order to work, some of these claims and demands must be met for incremental reform strategies. The congruence of demands and political structures also must be considered.

It is hard, for example, to make the politics of economic redistribution work through the channels of decentralized political and bureaucratic structures. Demands for redistribution and equity are not likely to be satisfied by providing a cleaner water system. So far, the demands in urban Nigeria and in developing countries generally have not been for redistribution, but for better living standards. Demands for 'more' in absolute terms can be destabilizing, although a political system has an easier time handling them than demands for redistribution − i.e., unless the targets of redistribution are defined as marginal ethnic groups (e.g., Asians in Uganda) or foreign nationals. A politics of redistribution is much more difficult when embedded class groups must be attacked.

ETHNICITY AND CLASS AND REDISTRIBUTION IN NIGERIA

Ethnicity and distributional issues can be grouped under two major headings in Nigeria: (1) foreign ownership and indigenization;

(2) communal–class relationships. I shall say no more here about foreign ownership and indigenization except to note that worker/owner relationships must be differentiated in Nigeria according to whether industries are basically controlled by multinational corporations, or whether they are foreign-owned single product industries or Nigerian-owned processing industries.

In Nigeria, private national ownership of sizeable industrial companies tends to be regionalized. This does not mean, however, that ethnicity has no relevance. Nigerian-owned processing industries are the ones in which wages constitute a large proportion of total costs. Wages tend to be below government minimum wage standards. Nigerian owners resisted strongly in 1970 and 1971 the Adebo awards to workers. The economic environment is more competitive for such owners. But there is an ethnic link here, too. For example, workers in Kano see themselves as Hausa, like the owners of the processing industries or the managing directors they may have contact with. When economically squeezed, they see a violation of Islamic norms and a repudiation of ethnic brotherhood. This intensifies ill feelings. In January 1971, when owners did not pay the Adebo awards and as the Moslem festival of Idl Fitr approached – when gifts are to be given and celebrations made – traditional Islamic customs 'interacted with industrial conflict so as to buttress the class solidarity of workers ...'[117]

It is not easy to sort out the impact of ethnic values on class in these situations. Dorothy Remy tells us that the workers she interviewed in Zaria had both a clear perception of the status hierarchy within the factory and the realization that schooling was a prerequisite for higher paying jobs. No one she interviewed thought it unfair that those in management (supervisory positions) should receive an annual income as much as four times as great as their own.[118] The status conferred by education justified income differentials to workers. The idea that education justified status and income inequalities derived from an 'ethnic' set of values. Do the Hausa owners who pay their workers low wages justify this in traditional terms? Kano workers are illiterate, rural-born migrants. Few of Kano's urban-born work in factories 'because both the local entrepreneurial ethic and relatively higher urban status orient the urban-born to trading and commerce of all varieties.'[119] Do owners justify their actions because they are dealing with non-locals who are not really of their community?

Observers tell us that in Kano and in northern Nigeria more generally, class-based deprivation and criteria for leadership are likely to be mediated through an Islamic ideology 'less because of deep religiousity, but more because, for uneducated workers, it is the only known and accepted standard of legitimacy.'[120] Thus religion cuts different ways. Islam provides a vehicle for demanding greater equity by stressing fairness and dignity, but it also justifies status hierarchies.

When looking at any complicated set of values in a belief system, one can almost always pull out strands which would justify action or inaction in coping with situations of inequality. While traditional values have to be examined for their content, ethnicity must be expressed through some channels; and, ethnicity and class must be understood situationally – that is, in specific social, political, economic and spatial contexts.

An analysis of protest by the Port Harcourt proletariat illustrates that in the mid-1960s political and economic groupings which centered on occupational and income differences proved transient. They were 'once again subordinated to the communal identities of region and nationality.'[121] Indeed, it has been argued – correctly, I believe – that while support for strikes in Port Harcourt cut across communal lines, 'this meant not the erosion of communal identities but, rather, their temporary displacement.'[122] Yet it has been maintained that in Nigeria communalism is not an independent political force in its own right, 'but rather a channel through which other interests are directed and made manifest.'[123] And, the assertion is made that in Nigeria ethnic movements have been created and instigated by new men of power who try to further their own special interests 'which are, time and time again, the constitutive interest of emerging social classes. Tribalism then becomes a mask for class privilege.'[124]

It is true that in Nigeria – and elsewhere – men who strive for political power have used communal feelings and have built on old antagonisms for their own ends. These ends may well be the further-ance of their own status, power and economic well-being. Rural as well as urban areas provide contexts for politicians' or state officials' use of communal cleavage. It seems odd though to conclude that communalism is not a force in its own right and always a phenomenon dependent on other forces. Observers do make such conclusions, perhaps, because they see virtually all communal conflict as rooted in competition between individuals for the scarce resources of wealth, status and power. Modernization, it is said, exacerbates cleavage both because it has 'the effect of reorienting formerly separate peoples to a communal system of rewards' and because it makes men more alike in that they have the same wants.[125]

It is not evident to me that the wants of people in Nigerian urban areas are more alike than those of peoples in rural areas. It is true that access to resources has changed for different groups at different times in Nigeria and that new resources became available to new men – resources such as education, organization, oil and new occupations. But competition is always over wealth, status and power. 'Class' and 'non-class' societies do not differ in this regard, nor do rural and urban societies.

What differs in urban contexts are the amount and kinds of resources available for competition, as well as the structures through which people compete. The form of the struggle and the relative weight of the factors lead us to describe 'conflict' as either class or communal. Naked opposition of cultures – that is, the dislikes of some people for the habits, smells, foods, or hairstyles of others – may be quite rare as a dominant motive for conflict. Such conflict is more likely to occur in urban than in rural societies, if for no other reason than the proximity of different groups in urban contexts.[126]

I conclude that Port Harcourt and other Nigerian cities retained communal cleavages at their base because it was easier for the elite to organize around communal – that is language and ethnic-geographic – ties. Where it is easier to organize groups on the bases of language, geography and ethnicity – no matter who is doing the organizing and why – we might well talk of communcal societies. Urban life may provide new frustrations and insecurities based on class; but old ties, or new ones formed on non-income and non-occupational bases, may be easy to maintain. Language, a sense of belonging, blood relationships, or the very desire to belong to a communal group (even to an invented group) are all resources for would-be leaders and are building blocks of organization as effective as union dues or shared job experiences.

We must ask, why are those people who use communal feelings around which to organize so often successful in accomplishing their short-run goals? For some, these geo-ethnic conflicts have a class base. But in Port Harcourt, the poor Onitsha Ibos threw in their lot with the rich Onitsha Ibos rather than with poor Owerri Ibos. It was difficult for those Ibo leaders to function who wanted a political base beyond their own groups. And it was hard for non-Ibo leaders to emerge as city-wide powerful figures since their support rested on neither a large voting bloc nor a commercially strong base.[127] Although ethnic conflict was interwoven with inequality, ethnic or communal conflict was not synonymous with inequality of resources.

We must further ask, why did the new men of power in Nigeria so frequently contend with each other in ethnic terms? Why didn't they see their class interests? Why didn't they form a cohesive elite against the have-nots? Stratification exists within as well as between communal groups.

Again, Port Harcourt provides some interesting examples. A class of men, who were apart from the communal rank and file, emerged within each of Port Harcourt's geo-ethnic communities. Yet these men led communal groups against each other, thinking that it would be to their own advantage to organize mass support on a communal basis. Moreover, these men remained tied to communal groups – not only by political needs but also because they sought prestige, succor and belonging in communal groups. Elites remained self-conscious about their roots. Indeed, new elites have been created by modernization in many industrial and non-industrial countries, frequently from minority groups but also from majority groups. Members of the new elite are often carriers of ethnicity.

In answer to the question: Why do leaders organize around communal identities? Wolpe states that communalism in Port Harcourt 'impinged only upon political recruitment and patronage – issues upon which the prestige and recognition of immigrant groups depended – and did not affect routine council/municipal deliberations such as finance, road and market maintenance, school construction and the like.'[128] Perhaps patronage and recruitment seemed the key issues in Port Harcourt and then became infused with communalism. Because residences in Port Harcourt were communally heterogeneous, school construction and access to roads were not communally defined issues. Elsewhere in Africa, where residences in cities are communally segregated, fierce communal struggles have arisen over market sites, occupation of market stalls, roads and schools. The political behavior in urban areas cannot be understood unless neighborhood settings are examined and the relationships between power holders and groups that organize demands are put in the spatial context of the urban environment.

For example, Pauline Baker has given us a political history of Lagos from 1917 to 1967 which analyzes group demands in the changing Lagos contexts by gathering both historical information and survey data on local leaders.[129] Lagos has retained traditional characteristics of ethnic homogeneity and communal land tenure; at the same time it is a booming industrial port and a commercial and administrative center. Spatial distributions are very important in Lagos. The indigenous core of the city is made up of a landed lower class consisting mostly of Yoruba Moslems. The city is built around a permanent traditional community, but the majority of urban residents are more recent migrants.[130] Because of the severe shortage of land, there is no complete ethnic segregation anywhere in Lagos, but lower-class people tend to live in much more homogeneous ethnic communities than wealthy people.

Lagos abounds in contradictions. As in Port Harcourt, political changes among the elite there did not constitute a simple transformation from traditional to modern attributes. The sequence went from modern characteristics of wealth and education possessed by a small number of Africans (often non-Nigerians), to wealth separated from education in an ethnically mixed group of Nigerian nationalists, to a new middle-class group of Yoruba immigrants, to dominant indigenous Lagos Moslems whose ethnicity – and Lagos origin – was their strategic resource. The ruling political strata in Lagos changed from aristocracy to nationalist oligarchy, to ethnically homogeneous middle class, to communally-based leaders.[131] Each group utilized different resources. Economics was never irrelevant, but a movement from communal to class politics did not occur. The process of urbanization in Lagos led to class differentiation expressed in different styles of housing, distributions of wealth, and occupations and wages. Spatial distributions and ethnicity always interacted with changing economic and demographic patterns to produce complicated political alignments. Except for one period – 1917–38 – of all the major groups in Lagos, the ones based on class or economic cohesion proved to be the weakest; and, during that exceptional period, the African elite based on education and wealth was also a highly distinct cultural group, united by origin as much as by socioeconomic background.[132]

The lack of class solidarity in the urban community can be attributed to the social composition of the working class and the structure of the labor movement: 'The majority of the urban working class is a heterogeneous collection of wage earning immigrants whose economic concerns are limited to personal and immediate material gains.'[133] Urban workers seek no alliance with the rural peasants or the urban unemployed. Trade unions protect the privileges of those who have jobs, and ethnic unions provide more gratifications for their members than trade unions. Only the 'old' indigenous Lagos Moslems who live in central city areas are united by blood, locality, land, origin, class and ethnicity. For other groups, the plurality of identities conflicts with rather than reinforces interests.[134]

In Lagos, power and status do not rest only – or even principally – on economic resources: 'Vertical class divisions are crosscut horizontally by ethnic, clan, kindship and communal stratification.'[135] Leadership is fragmented, and Lagos is a city that is socially unintegrated and in which the boundary between local and national politics is not clear.

All studies of the politics in major cities must come to grips with the relationship between national and city politics. Local differentiations are played out in the context of the centralization of national resources. More generally speaking, political behaviors are affected by authoritative institutions through which community influence is channeled. That is, the outputs of government affect patterns of competition and participation. The government's performance is an independent factor that affects support for or disaffection from the regime. Thus, in the future, as in the past, government's own policies and performance – which are at the same time a response to pressures from below and an expression of elite preferences – will themselves be consequential for the development of politics in class or communal directions.[136]

SUMMARY AND CONCLUSIONS

I have generally tried to describe important institutional and authority changes and to examine their effect on distributional issues. I have also tried to make an argument about the social and economic context in which policymakers operate.

Nigeria is undergoing rapid social and economic change: the composition of exports has altered vastly in the last decade; urbanization is extremely rapid; indigenization of the economy has been undertaken in the industrial and banking sectors; and authority has been centralized within a new multistate system and through a civil-service-military coalition which has seen its own interests furthered by centralization.

Income distribution issues were not salient in the first civilian period of Nigeria's independence. During the military rule, various plans and pronouncements mentioned equity concerns with increasing frequency, especially toward the end of the period of military rule, but income distribution has not been the main concern of public policy in the economic and political realms. Nor has there been strong pressure from below to move the system to deal frontally with equity issues — either conceived as rural–urban distributions or in class terms. Insofar as Nigeria has seen its politics governed by distributional issues, these have been communally defined for the most part and have centered on allocations from the center to regions and states in the Nigerian federation.

There has been no clear development of a class-based politics in Nigeria. Neither peasant organizations nor trade unions in the industrial sector have been strong organizations pushing for redistribution of income. Nor have people in the urban informal sector constituted a force for effective radical change. The relationships between formal sector and informal sector workers are complicated and variable by city, region and ethnic community.

The elites themselves have been highly fragmented in Nigeria, which may provide a wedge for reformist politics and strategies since Nigeria does not have strong countrywide landed aristocracies or large-scale national capitalists. Thus, while there still seems to be much political space in Nigeria for rulers to avoid a politics of reform since demands from below are not well organized, there are policies which will be undertaken in the name of strengthening the state or increasing national authority, which can be more egalitarian in their thrust.

The rural sector is still being relatively ignored, which is a consequence of its political weakness. However, Nigeria is not a country where an entrenched national elite is holding on for dear life against reform for more egalitarian distributions. Rather, it is more accurate to say that the country's policies have aimed more at growth and control of the economy than at income redistribution.

There does not appear to be sufficiently effective pressure from below to alter these directions fundamentally in the short-run. They might, however, be altered by reform-minded elite members for their own purposes and goals because, in places and at times, pressures will build especially on state governments and the local elite. The people who control Nigeria at its center, whether civilian or military, will respond selectively and contend with each other for support.

Thus, equity concerns will and do get a hearing in Nigeria, and will be present in the calculations made by political competitors.

NOTES

1. *The World Bank Development Report*, Washington, DC, World Bank, 1979, pp. 128–9.
2. Many features of the old Nigerian economy remain. Not only does agricultural productivity remain low but, while there has been a large shift in the structure of GDP from agriculture to industry between 1960–76, a majority of the labor force remains employed in agriculture. However, that sector accounts for less than one-quarter of GDP. Manufacturing remains small as a share of GDP.
3. For a discussion of the political economy in Nigeria in the late 1960s and mid-1970s and the impact of oil, see Keith Panter-Brick (ed.), *Soldiers and Oil: The Transformation of Nigerian Politics*, London, Frank Cass, 1978. For a discussion of oil wealth and Nigerian poverty, see Richard A. Joseph, 'Affluence and underdevelopment: the Nigerian experience.' *Journal of Modern African Studies*, vol. 16, no. 2, June 1978, pp. 221–40. For current political events, see various issues of *West Africa*.
4. See chapter 5 on the 1979 election.
5. For a cogent statement of these problems, see Joseph, *op. cit.*
6. For discussions of electoral strategies, see B J. Dudley, *Instability and Political Order. Politics and Crisis in Nigeria*, Ibadan, University of Ibadan Press, 1973, Richard Sklar, *Nigerian Political Parties*, Princeton, NJ, Princeton University Press, 1963. For communalism in Nigeria, among others, see Robert Melson and Howard Wolpe (eds), *Modernization and the Politics of Communalism*, East Lansing, Mich., Michigan State University Press, 1971.
7. Howard Wolpe, *Urban Politics in Nigeria: A Study of Port Harcourt*, Berkeley, Calif., University of California Press, 1975; Richard Sklar, 'Political science and national integration: a radical approach', *Journal of Modern African Studies*, vol. 5, May 1967, pp. 1–12.
8. Much of the academic study of Nigeria has been devoted to the problems of revenue allocation and the various revenue commissions. For major studies of revenue allocation in Nigeria, see, among others, A. Adediji, *Nigerian Federal Finance*, London, Hutchinson, 1969; O. Teriba, 'Nigerian revenue allocation experience, 1952–1965', *Nigerian Journal of Economics and Social Studies*, vol. 8, November 1966; P. N. C. Okigbo, *Nigerian Public Finance,* Evanston, Ill., Northwestern University Press, 1965. For recent reviews, see Ali D. Yahaya, 'The creation of states', in Keith Panter-Brick (ed.), *Soldiers and Oil: The Transformation of Nigerian Politics*, London, Frank Cass, 1978, pp. 201–23; S. Egite Oyovbaire, 'The politics of revenue allocation', *ibid*, pp. 224–52. Major commission reports include the following: Hicks-Phillipson in 1950, the Chick report in 1954, the Raisman Commission report in 1958 and the Binns Commission report in 1965. These reports were reviewed in Teriba, *op. cit.*, and Chief I. O. Dina, 'Fiscal measures', in A. A. Ayida and H. M. A. Onitiri (eds), *Reconstruction and Development in Nigeria*, Ibadan, Oxford University Press, 1971, pp. 374–414.
9. Ayida and Onitiri, *op. cit.*, p. 12.
10. Jerome C. Wells, *Agricultural Policy and Economic Growth in Nigeria, 1962–1968,*

Ibadan, Oxford University Press, 1974; Reginald H. Green, 'Four African development plans: Ghana, Kenya, Tanzania, and Nigeria', *Journal of Modern African Studies*, vol. 3, no. 2, August 1965, pp. 249–79.

11. NEPU saw a dichotomous class struggle between members of the native administrations and the ordinary *talakawa*, or commoners. See Billy Dudley, *Parties and Politics in Northern Nigeria*, London, Frank Cass, 1968, p. 169. Dudley says this dichotomy can be translated into one between Fulanis and Habes — that is, into an ethnic one.

12. James S. Coleman, *Nigeria: Background to Nationalism*, Berkeley, Calif., University of California Press, 1963, p. 365.

13. Sklar, *Political Parties, op. cit.*, pp. 335–7.

14. Dudley, *op. cit.*, pp. 179–80. For another important discussion of NEPU, see C. S. Whitaker, *The Politics of Tradition: Continuity and Change in Northern Nigeria*, Princeton, NJ, Princeton University Press, 1970, passim.

15. This book was published in 1968, Ibadan, Oxford University Press.

16. Sklar, *op. cit.*, p. 256.

17. Richard Sklar has argued that the 1962 split of the AG into the Awolowo and Akintola wings can be seen as a split between radicals, or left-socialists, and liberal capitalists, Sklar, *op. cit.*, p. 281. I conducted interviews with former members of the Western House of Assembly in 1972–3. Out of 54 respondents, only one thought that the different social and economic bases of the AG were consequential for the split; 32 people mentioned personal struggles between the two leaders; 18 mentioned ethnic factors; 16 mentioned different views about an alliance with the North. (More than one cause could be listed by a single individual.)

18. Whitaker, *op. cit.*, pp. 329–30 and 394. There were othere 'left' leaders, of course, like Samuel Ikoku of the Eastern Region of the AG who was elected federal secretary of the AG.

19. For a biography of Aminu Kano, see Alan Feinstein, *African Revolutionary: The Life and Times of Nigeria's Aminu Kano*, New York, Quadrangle, 1973.

20. Chief Awolowo resigned after two years as commissioner. Aminu Kano held the commissionership for close to a decade.

21. Ken Post and George Jenkins, *The Price of Liberty: Personality and Politics in Colonial Nigeria*, Cambridge, Cambridge University Press, 1973, p. 134.

22. *Ibid.*, pp. 134–35. Adelabu's major work is *Africa in Ebullition*, Ibadan, 1952.

23. Sklar, *op. cit.*, p. 294.

24. Sayre O. Schatz, *Nigerian Capitalism*, Berkeley, Calif., University of California Press, 1977, p. 156.

25. Richard Sklar, 'Contradictions in the Nigerian political system', *Journal of Modern African Studies*, vol. 3, no. 2, 1965, p. 204. Edwin Dean, in *Plan Implementation in Nigeria, 1962–66*, Ibadan, Oxford University Press, 1972, pp. 52–3, also points to the influence of local politics on national decision makers. He has added that Nigerian politicians were shaped by foreign influences and that they did not focus on national development. Dean argues that there was an attachment to specific examples rather than to abstractions and a tendency to engage in paternal exhortation. All of these phenomena may have been derived from the difficulties of moving from the general to the specific and formulating strategies for growth and distribution.

26. See, for example, Thomas S. Cox, *Civil–Military Relations in Sierra Leone*, Cambridge, Mass., Harvard University Press, 1976; Samuel Decalo, *Coups and Army Rule in Africa*, New Haven, Conn., Yale University Press, 1976; Anton Bebler, *Military Rule in Africa: Dahomey, Ghana, Sierra Leone and Mali*, New York, Praeger, 1973.

27. See Robert W. Jackman, 'Politicians in uniform: military governments and social

change in the third world', *American Political Science Review*, vol. 70, December 1976; R. D. McKinlay and A. S. Cohan, 'A comparative analysis of political and economic performance of military and civilian regimes', *Comparative Politics*, vol. 8, no. 1, October 1975; McKinlay and Cohan, 'The economic performance of military regimes: a cross-national aggregate data study', *The British Journal of Politics*, vol. 6, no. 3, July 1976.

28. Henry Bienen, *Armies and Parties in Africa*, New York and London, Holmes & Meier, 1978, pp. 194–5.

29. *Ibid.* The Federal government's revenues are overwhelmingly derived from oil that exists either offshore or in the states of Bendel and River, which have 4.3 and 3.2 per cent of the population, respectively. This makes Bendel and Rivers twelfth and sixteenth in size, respectively, out of the 19 states. The ethnic groups which inhabit these states are so-called minorities peoples. That is, they are not Hausa, Yoruba, or Ibo speaking although there are Yorubas in Bendel. Bendel (which was the old Midwest Region) was carved out of the Western Region in 1962–3, specifically to remove non-Yorubas from the control of the Yoruba Western Region.

30. See Robin Luckham, *The Nigerian Military*, Cambridge, Cambridge University Press, 1971.

31. Leo Dare, 'Nigerian Military Government and the Quest for Legitimacy', *Nigerian Journal of Economic and Social Studies*, vol. 17, no. 2, July 1977, pp. 95–118.

32. Valerie P. Bennett and A. H. M. Kirk-Greene, 'Back to the barracks: a decade of marking time', in Keith Panter-Brick, *op. cit.*, p. 23.

33. A discussion of the interviews and the results can be found in Bienen, *op. cit.*, pp. 192–260.

34. For a discussion of the Peruvian experiment, see Ellen Kay Trimberger, *Revolution from above: Military Bureaucrats and Development in Japan, Turkey, Egypt, and Peru*, New Brunswick, Transaction Books, 1978; Alfred Stepan, *The State and Society: Peru in Comparative Perspective*, Princeton, NJ, Princeton University Press, 1978; Abraham Lowenthal (ed.), *The Peruvian Experiment*, Princeton, NJ, Princeton University Press, 1975; and the papers presented to the workshop on the 'Peruvian Experiment Reconsidered', The Wilson Center, Smithsonian Institution, Washington, DC, November 1978.

35. Schatz, *op. cit.*, p. 22.

36. *Ibid.*

37. *Ibid.*, p. 23.

38. *Ibid.*, p. 24.

39. See O. Aboyade, 'Closing remarks', in *Nigeria's Indigenization Policy, Proceedings of the 1974 Symposium,* organized by the Nigerian Economic Society, Ibadan, Department of Economics, pp. 77–8.

40. For this dispute, see Aboyade, *Nigeria's Indigenization Policy, op. cit.*, especially pp. 60–72.

41. The following publications contain accounts of high-level Nigerian civil servants who have spoken their minds: *The Quarterly Journal of Administration; The Nigerian Journal of Economic and Social Studies;* Ayida and Onitiri, *op. cit.*; Mahmud Tukur (ed.), *Administrative and Political Development: Prospects for Nigeria*, Kaduna, Baraka Press Limited, 1971; A. A. Ayida, 'The Nigerian revolution, 1966–1976' (address to the Nigerian Economic Society Annual Meeting, Enugu, 1973). In 1972 a conference was held at Ahmadu Bello University in Zaria at which permanent secretaries addressed themselves to the questions of institutional and administrative perspectives for national development. A number of papers were subsequently published in the *New Nigerian*, Kaduna, especially in the 25 November 1972, issue.

42. This point was made in interviews with civil servants in Lagos and Ibadan in 1972–3.

43. Terisa Turner, 'Commercial capitalism and the 1975 coup', in Keith Panter-Brick (ed), *op. cit.*, pp. 166–97, looks at the tensions between generalists and technicians in the nationalized oil industry, and their relationships with private foreign and Nigerian business people.

44. See, among others, Ian Campbell, 'Army reorganization and military withdrawal', in Keith Panter-Brick (ed), *op. cit.*, p. 74.

45. Joseph, *op. cit.*; also O. Oyediran and W. A. Ajibola, 'Nigerian public service in 1975', *Survey of Nigerian Affairs*, 1975, London, 1978.

46. *Agbekoya* means in Yoruba 'farmers who reject injustice.' The most important accounts of *Agbekoya* are in Christopher Beer, *The Politics of Peasant Groups in Western Nigeria*, Ibadan, University of Ibadan Press, 1976; Christopher Beer and Gavin Williams, 'The politics of the Ibadan peasantry', in Gavin Williams (ed.), *Nigeria: Economy and Society*, London, Rex Collins, 1976, pp. 135–58; *Report of the Commission of Inquiry into the Civil Disturbances Which Occurred in Certain Parts of the Western State of Nigeria in the Month of December, 1968*, Ibadan, Government Printer, 1968, known as the Ayoola report.

47. Robert Adeyinka Adebayo, 'The Truth About Tax Riots: Governor Adebayo speaks', Ibadan, Government Printer, 1969.

48. *Daily Times*, Lagos, 14 August 1975, p. 5.

49. *Ibid.*, p. 33.

50. *Third National Development Plan*, vol. 1, p. 29, Lagos, Central Planning Office, Federal Ministry of Economic Development, 1975.

51. *Ibid.*, p. 31.

52. *Ibid.*

53. Victor Olorunsola, in *Soldiers and Power. The Development Performance of the Nigerian Military Regime*, Standford, Calif., Hoover Institution Press, 1977, makes such assessments, but the analysis is not systematic. Also see Nelson Kasfir, 'Soldiers or policy makers: the comparative performance of Nigerian military regime', unpublished paper, Hanover, New Hampshire, 1978.

54. Schatz, *op. cit.*, p. 54.

55. Martin Dent, 'Corrective government: military rule in perspective', in Keith Panter-Brick (ed.), *op. cit.*, pp. 101–40.

56. Schatz, *op. cit.*, p. 31.

57. Dent, *op. cit.*, p. 118. Dent notes that in Hausa the word for 'oppression' and 'official abuse of office' is almost the same and would both be translated as *zalunci*. The word in Hausa for 'poor man', or 'commoner', is the same for 'man without office,':*talakawa*.

58. It is difficult to know the impact of these purges on corrupt practices. Although individuals left universities and the civil service to pursue business full time, this may simply have been a reaction to changing circumstances for getting ahead.

59. See the statement by Chief Bola Ige, gubernatorial candidate of the UPN for Oyo State, in the *Daily Times* (Lagos), 6 February 1979.

60. See *Agence-France Press*, Paris, no. 2587, 25 May 1979.

61. The other major party was the Great Nigerian People's Party, headed by Waziri Ibrahim, a wealthy businessman who founded the Nigerian Peoples Party but broke with it. Aminu Kano of the PRP was disqualified for standing as president toward the end of the campaign and was then reinstated.

62. For an analysis of electoral results, see chapter 5. Here, only aspects of the election relevant to the discussion on class and ethnicity are presented.

63. *The Punch*, Lagos, 22 October 1979, p. 5.

64. Yahaya does so, *op. cit.*, p. 217; so does Oyovbaire, *op. cit.*, pp. 237 and 242. Also see Gaston V. Rimlinger, 'Communalism and gains from development', Rice University Program of Development Studies, Houston, Texas, paper no. 74, 1976.

65. Rimlinger, *op. cit.*, p. 25.
66. *Ibid.*
67. Shehu Shagari did not win 25 per cent of the votes in 13 states. He had over 25 per cent in 12 states and just under 20 per cent in the thirteenth state (Kano). Shagari was declared elected by the Federal Election Commission on the grounds that the ordinary meaning of 'one quarter of the votes cast at the election in each of at least two-thirds of all the states ...' is one-quarter of the votes in 12 states and one-quarter of two-thirds, or one-sixth of the votes cast in the thirteenth state in a 19-state system. Although this interpretation was contested in the courts by Chief Awolowo, it was sustained.
68. The constitution called for the two top candidates to run against each other in an electoral college consisting of state and national legislatures. This was not necessary, however, and the military government amended the constitution by decree before leaving power, to allow for a subsequent runoff to be handled through a second national election.
69. The distributable pool to states has increased. Half of it goes on the basis of population, the other half is divided equally among states. The Federal government received large revenues from its petroleum profits tax and ran surpluses which allowed it to abolish export data or compensation grants to states, increase the size of the distributable pool and introduce uniform rates and allowances for income tax. Rimlinger, *op. cit.*, p. 31, concludes from all this that the new allocation formula and state structure have established a higher degree of distributional equity among communal groups than had existed under any previous arrangements. It would be more accurate to say that there is now a distributional formula for equity between the territorial–administrative expression of communal entities.
70. Several of the many statements by African leaders are included in the following: Julius Nyerere, *Freedom and Socialism*, Dar es Salaam, Oxford University Press, 1968; Kwame Nkrumah, *Consciencism*, London, Heinemann, 1964; Leopold Senghor, *African Socialism*, New York, 1959; Sekou Touré, *Experience guineenne et unite africaine*, Paris Presence Africaine, 1961; Sessional Paper No. 10 'African socialism and its application to planning in Kenya', Nairobi, Government Printer, 1965. See also William Friedland and Carl Rosberg, Jr. (eds), *African Socialism*, Stanford, Calif.: Hoover Institution Publications, 1964.
71. To cite only a few studies: Melson and Wolpe, *op. cit.*, in Howard Wolpe, *Urban Politic in Nigeria*, Berkeley, Calif., University of California Press, 1974, Henry Bienen, *Kenya: The Politics of Participation and Control*, Princeton, NJ, Princeton University Press, 1974; Victor Olorunsola (ed.), *The Politics of Cultural Sub-Nationalism in Africa*, New York, Anchor Books, 1972; Crawford Young, *The Politics of Cultural Pluralism*, Madison, Wis., University of Wisconsin Press, 1976; Pauline Baker, *Urbanization and Political Change: The Politics of Lagos, 1917–1967*, Berkeley, Calif., University of California Press, 1974.
72. Again, to cite only a few studies: Colin Leys, *Underdevelopment in Kenya*, Berkeley, Calif., University of California Press, 1974; Giovanni Arrighi and John S. Saul, *Essays on the Political Economy of Africa*, New York, Monthly Review Press, 1973; Richard Harris (ed.), *The Political Economy of Africa*, New York, Halsted Press, 1975.
73. Irving Markovitz, *Power and Class in Africa*, Englewood Cliffs, NJ, Prentice Hall, 1977; Amilcar Cabral, *Revolution in Guinea*, London, Stage 1, 1969; Henry Bienen, 'State and revolution in Africa: the work of Amilcar Cabral', *Journal of Modern African Studies*, vol. 15, no. 4, 1977, pp. 555–68; Miles D. Wolpin, 'Marx and radical militarism in developing nations', *Armed Forces and Society*, vol. 4, no. 2, Winter 1978, pp. 245–65; Michael Cohen, *Urban*

Policy and Political Conflict: A Study of the Ivory Coast, Chicago: University of Chicago Press, 1974.

74. R. Sandbrook and R. Cohen (eds), *The Development of an African Working Class*, Toronto, University of Toronto Press, 1976; Issa G. Shivji, *Class Struggles in Tanzania*, London, Heinemann, 1976; Robert Bates, *Unions, Parties and Political Development: A Study of Mineworkers in Zambia*, New Haven, Conn., Yale University Press, 1971; E. de Kadt and G. P. Williams, *Sociology and Development*, London, Tavistock, 1974. Many issues of the *Review of African Political Economy; Development and Change;* and *Manpower and Unemployment* are relevant to this debate.

75. Markovitz, *op. cit.*, p. 9.

76. Cohen does this in his study of the Ivory Coast because he concluded that public authority is so important; that access to government is so critical in the accumulation of private property and power, and that 'political conflict in Africa, when it concerns public policy and resources, is in fact class conflict,' Cohen *op. cit.*, p. 195.

77. Ronald Cohen illustrates this idea in his discussion, 'Social stratification in Bornu', in Arthur Tuden and Leonard Plotnicov (eds), *Social Stratification in Africa*, New York, The Free Press, 1970, esp. pp. 253−63. Cohen discusses class distinctions between the Kanuri in terms of styles of dress, dialect distinctions in speech and differences of power and authority − and also in terms of numbers of clients and dependents. '... [W]e must also view class differences as another status distinction in and of itself, since it is such a broadly inclusive feature and is, therefore, in a number of senses a multifaceted variable instead of a dichotomous category when it is actually utilized by people themselves to judge and generalize about someone else's or one's own high or low status in the society', pp. 255−6.

78. See Polly Hill, *Population, Prosperity, and Poverty: Rural Kano 1900 and 1970*, Cambridge, Cambridge University Press, 1977.

79. A. A. Okore, 'The Ibos of Arochukwu in Imo state, Nigeria', in John C. Caldwell (ed.), *The Persistence of High Fertility, Part I*, Canberra, Australian National University, 1976.

80. See Oshoma Imoagne, *Social Mobility in Emergent Society: A Study of the New Elite in Western Nigeria*, Canberra, Australian National University, 1976; P. C. Lloyd, *Power and Independence: Urban African Perceptions of Social Inequality*, London: Routledge and Kegan Paul, 1974.

81. As J. D. Y. Peel says when he examines the Yoruba concepts of development: 'the linguistic vehicles of central concepts enable particular experiences, solitary or shared, to be linked into something of a unified interpretation of a collective historical experience.' See J. D. Y. Peel, 'Olaju: A Yoruba concept of development', *Journal of Development Studies*, vol. 14, no. 2, January 1976.

82. P. C. Lloyd, *Africa in Social Change*, Baltimore, Penguin Books, 1967.

83. Okore, *op. cit.*, p. 316.

84. Alfred Ukaegbu, 'The practice of traditional birth control and attitudes toward family planning in rural eastern Nigeria', in press, cited in *ibid*.

85. John C. Caldwell, 'Towards a restatement of demographic transition theory', in Caldwell, *The Persistence of High Fertility, op. cit.*, p. 75.

86. *Ibid.*

87. Hill, *op. cit.*, pp. 110−13.

88. *Ibid.*, p. 155.

89. Lloyd, *Power and Independence, op. cit.*, p. 140.

90. *Ibid.*, p. 168.

91. *Ibid.*, p. 177.

92. Lloyd, *Africa in Social Change, op. cit.* p. 314.

93. Imoagene, *op. cit.*, calls attention to the degrees of egalitarianism within Yoruba political systems and the extents of social mobility which have obtained within Yoruba subgroups.

94. Peter Waterman, 'Industrial relations and the control of labour protest in Nigeria.' This is an unpublished and shortened form of the forthcoming paper, 'The Nigerian state and the control of labour: the case of the Lagos cargo-handling industry', in Paul Collins (ed.), *Administration for Development in Nigeria*, Ibadan, Ibadan University Press. Also see *Report of the Tribunal of Inquiry into the Activities of Trade Unions*, Lagos, Federal Ministry of Information, 1977 and *Federal Military Government's Views on the Report of the Tribunal of Inquiry into the Activities of Trade Unions*, Lagos, Federal Ministry of Information, 1977.

95. For detailed discussions about the workers in Nigeria, see the following publications among others: Paul Lubeck, 'Unions, workers, and consciousness in Kano, Nigeria: a view from below', in Sandbrook and Cohen, *op. cit.*, Paul Lubeck, 'Contrast and continuity in a dependent city; Kano, Nigeria', in Janet Abu-Lughod and Richard Hay, Jr. (eds), *Third World Urbanization*, Chicago, Maaroufa Press, 1971, pp. 281–89. (I am in Professor Lubeck's debt for making available unpublished material.) Howard Wolpe, *Urban Politics in Nigeria, op. cit.* Dorothy Remy, 'Economic security and industrial unionism: a Nigerian case study', in Sandbrook and Cohen, *op. cit.*, pp. 161–78. Dorothy Remy and J. Weeks, 'Income, occupation and inequality in a non-industrial town', in K. Wohlmuth (ed.), *Employment in Emerging Societies*, New York, Praeger, 1973. Adrian Peace, 'Industrial protest in Nigeria', in Emanuel de Kadt and G. P. Williams (eds), *Sociology and Development*, London, Tavistock Publication, 1974. Adrian Peace, 'The Lagos proletariat: labour aristocrats or populist militant', in Sandbrook and Cohen, *op. cit.* Robert Melson, 'Ideology and inconsistency: the cross pressured Nigerian worker', in Melson and Wolpe, *op. cit.*, pp. 581–605. Robert Melson, 'Nigerian politics and the general strike of 1964', in Robert Rotberg and Ali Mazrui (eds), *Protest and Power in Black Africa*, New York, Oxford University Press, 1970, pp. 171–87. T. Yesufu, *An Introduction to Industrial Relations in Nigeria*, London, Oxford University Press, 1962. Waterman, *op. cit.*

96. Remy, 'Economic Security ...', *op. cit.*, pp. 163–4.

97. *Ibid.*

98. *Ibid.*, p. 164.

99. Peace, 'Industrial Protest ...', *op. cit.*

100. Lloyd, *Power and Independence, op. cit*, p. 226. Lubeck says that four-fifths of Hausa workers look to the entrepreneurial sector for mobility. 'Contrasts ...', *op. cit.*, p. 288.

101. Lubeck, *op. cit.*, p. 289.

102. Caldwell, *op. cit.*, p. 80.

103. This assertion puts me within the camp of 'rational-actor models of politics'. However, rational-actor models refer not only to income maximization, but also to maximization of wealth, power, status, or security. The rational-actor models of most economists and political scientists have been individual-choice centered, but in some societies, and for many important purposes, the choosing unit is communal. Wealth and security also may be diffuse and communally based.

104. Caldwell, *op. cit.*, p. 91. For a detailed discussion, see Aderanti Adepoju, 'Rationality and fertility in traditional Yoruba society, South West Nigeria', in Caldwell, *op. cit.*, pp. 123–51, and 'High fertility and the rural economy: a study of the Yoruba society in Western Nigeria', in *Ibid.*, pp. 331–60.

105. Many surveys in Africa show that extended families remain intact and provide mutual aid for the unemployed. Relatives take on dependents who are unemployed,

and unemployed heads of households tend to have expenditures per unit of consumption which are not way below those of unskilled laborers — reaching four-fifths the expenditures of artisans and small shopkeepers. See among others, Helen Ware, 'Economic strategy and the number of children', in Caldwell, *op. cit.*, pp. 541–55. Among professionals, expenditures per household are almost four times greater than those of unskilled laborers (from a survey in Dakar), but expenditures per consumption unit are less than twice as great. Richer heads of households acquire more dependents because they are affluent. Imoagene's survey of the new elite in western Nigeria found the continuation of intimate family ties. Help to families was persistent and diffuse, and extended to a wide network of relatives — although civil servants were less involved with seeing and helping relatives than politicians and business people. (See Imoagene, *op. cit.*, pp. 117–40.) One study of Liberia found that kin networks were most effective among those ethnic groups with the longest tradition of urbanization. See M. Fraenkel, *Tribe and Class in Monrovia*, London, Oxford University Press, 1964.

106. The work of Joan Nelson is especially wide-ranging because she uses data on Latin America, India, and Africa. See Joan Nelson, 'The urban poor: disruption or political integration in third world cities', *World Politics*, vol. 22, April 1978, pp. 393–414. Also, Joan Nelson, *Political Access to Power: Politics and the Urban Poor in Developing Nations*, Princeton, NJ, Princeton University Press, 1979.

107. Giovanni Arrighi and John Saul, 'Socialism and economic development in tropical Africa', *Journal of Modern African Studies*, vol. 6, no. 2, 1968, pp. 141–69. Arrighi calls special attention to the need for multinational corporations to stabilize labor. He and others also call attention to the role of multinational corporations in fostering labor aristocracies in Africa. See Arrighi, 'International corporations, labor aristocracies and economic development in tropical Africa', in Robert I. Rhodes, *Imperialism and Underdevelopment: A Reader*, New York, Monthly Review Press, 1970, pp. 220–67.

108. Peace, *op. cit.*, p. 288.

109. See, among others, H. I. Ajaegbu, *Urban and Rural Development in Nigeria*, London, Heinemann, 1976, pp. 33–4.

110. Peace, *op. cit.*, p. 289.

111. Peter Waterman, 'Conservatism amongst Nigerian workers', in Williams, *op. cit.*, p. 171, raises some questions as to the workers' commitment to collective action. A majority of the respondents viewed workers as furthering themselves through self-help and government aid. A minority of his respondents listed trade union demands as being most important for bettering conditions.

112. As suggested by Peace, *op. cit.*, p. 289.

113. *Ibid.*, p. 296.

114. Waterman, *op. cit.*, p. 168, says that only a small minority of responses from interviews with workers suggest that one gets to the top by unfair means in Nigeria, although over half the respondents felt that top salary earners were privileged and exploiting.

115. John S. Saul, 'The Labour Aristocracy' Thesis Reconsidered', in Sandbrook and Cohen, *op. cit.*, pp. 303–10. Saul cites Waterman's 'Communist theory in the Nigerian trade union movement,' *Politics and Society*, vol. 3, no. 2, spring 1973.

116. Waterman, 'Conservatism ...', *op. cit.*, p. 181.

117. Lubeck, 'Unions, Workers ...', *op. cit.*, p. 152.

118. Remy, *op. cit.*, p. 169.

119. Lubeck, *op. cit.*, p. 144.

120. *Ibid.*, p. 158.

121. Wolpe, *op. cit.*, p. 194.

122. *Ibid.*, p. 178.

123. *Ibid.*, p. 233.
124. Richard Sklar, 'Political science and national integration − a radical approach', *op. cit.*, p. 6.
125. Wolpe, *op. cit.*, p. 7 and 233.
126. See Henry Bienen and Michael Danielson, 'Urban political development', *World Politics*, vol. XXV, no. 2, January 1978, pp. 264−95.
127. See Wolpe, *op. cit.*, pp. 155−6.
128. *Ibid.*
129. Baker, *op. cit.*
130. *Ibid.*, p. 45.
131. *Ibid.*
132. *Ibid.*, p. 73.
133. *Ibid.*, p. 113.
134. *Ibid.*
135. *Ibid.*, p. 114.
136. *Ibid.*, p. 8.

CHAPTER FOUR

Religion and Economic Change
in Nigeria

When we explore the relationships between religion and economic structures and change in Nigeria, we are engaged in an extremely complex analytical and empirical undertaking. If we try to seek the impact of behavioral consequences of religion, we must be careful to distinguish the doctrinal aspects of religion, the practical religion (interaction between original doctrine and social, political and economic conditions of the time), and the impact of religious organizations and structures acting as political and economic units themselves. The behavioral consequences have to do with individuals, groups, and very large categories called societies in which political culture can be examined.

The analytical problems we confront have been examined by Weber and the many commentators on his work.[1] Sociologists have long been concerned with elaborating complex models to try to understand the impact of religion, and these models include accounting for the growth of new religions in specific contexts. Religion can be understood as an outcome of social, political and economic conditions as well as a cause of change. Where religious changes are produced or affected by political integration or economic growth, religious changes in turn have their influence. In Africa there have been many attempts to examine what Balandier has called the colonial condition,[2] to see the growth of new religions as a product of political relations, and anthropologists have studied 'praying religions' and millennial cults with the aim of exploring industrialization and alterations in status as components of social change.[3]

The central theme of Weber and those who reacted to his work can be stated: To what extent does religion stabilize, change, or reformulate non-religious beliefs and actions?[4] Posing the question in this way implies that religious beliefs can be empirically isolated from wider attitudes associated with ethnic or national communities. In some ways Nigeria provides a good testing ground because Islam, Catholicism, and various Protestant denominations, including African churches, exist along with so-called traditional religions. However, it is not always possible to separate ethnicity from religion. Most Catholics in Nigeria are Ibo; most Hausa and Fulani are Moslem (although not all Moslems by any means are Hausa or Fulani or even from northern Nigeria). The Yoruba have been seen as an extremely interesting group because they continue to have traditional believers and also divide roughly between Moslems and Christians. David Laitin, intending to examine the differential impact of Christianity and Islam (see table 20 for breakdown of population by religion) on Nigeria and wanting to control for nationality (or ethnicity), economy, numbers of generations in the presence of a world religion, motivations for conversion, and ecology – all of which are different in many Moslem and Christian areas in Nigeria – concentrates on a part of Yorubaland and is carrying out micro-analysis on the historical process of conversion as well as on contemporary attitudes and behavior.[5] This is a sophisticated and sensible strategy.

My task is somewhat different. I want to try to relate economic changes in Nigeria to underlying values on which they may be based. The task is not easy. Few studies examine the import of religious

Table 20
Religious Affiliation by Region, 1952 and 1963

Region	Per cent Moslem		Per cent Christian		Per cent Other	
	1952	1963	1952	1963	1952	1963
North	73.0	71.7	2.7	9.7	24.3	18.6
West	32.8	43.4	36.9	48.7	30.3	7.9
East	.6	.3	46.2	77.2	50.2	22.5
Lagos	41.0	44.3	53.0	54.6	2.0*	1.1
Mid-West	–	4.2	–	54.9	–	40.9
TOTAL	44.4	49	22.0	34	33.6	17

* Plus four per cent other.

Source: *Nigerian Census*, 1952, *Nigeria Yearbook*, 1969, Lagos, Times Press, 1970, p. 193. As found in J. N. Paden, *Religion and Political Culture in Kano*, Berkeley, University of California Press, 1973, p. 44, table 4.

values on economic change and ask whether religious values are consistent with or contradictory to economic change in Nigeria. Even the micro-studies of entrepreneurship do not usually focus on religion. At a general level, there is more concern in the literature on Nigeria with religion and political integration than with religion and economic development. But religion's impact on economic policy may be a second-order effect which works through political variables. For example, one might conclude that Islamic values and institutions have not had direct impact on central economic policy, leaving aside for the moment their impact on individual behavior of investors and workers. But even so, Islam and Islamic institutions have had a major impact on politics and governmental structures in northern Nigeria. The heated debate over a Sharia federal court of appeals during deliberations on the Constituent Assembly which was considering Nigeria's new constitution made evident how important Sharia law remains to many Nigerian representatives from the north. Centralized institutions based on Sharia law, administrative modes tied to emirate structures and a concern for central control, have limited opportunities for private entrepreneurship in the north. Islam has worked through political institutions to affect economic behavior and policies.[6]

Another example of indirect effects would be the conscious separation of church and state which motivated British colonial rulers in southern Nigeria. This had the consequence of the British refusing to allow Christian education to be pushed in the north, as well as leading to a separation of church activity from direct governance in the south. One could go further and argue that the idea of a secular state is itself a religious value of sorts and that this idea had an impact in Nigeria. The British idea of a Protestant colonial state was consequential for the evolution of the Nigerian economy in the south. Christianity was introduced in Nigeria by economic liberals and thus the idea of an open economy was to some extent tied up with Christianity.[7]

The impact of world religions in Nigeria has to be seen historically, and often mediated through political administrations and values. Even so, it is not easy to describe what has occurred in the Nigerian economy over the last decades and to account for it in terms of religion and social change. Our conclusions depend on whether we focus on the decisions of policy makers at the center of the economy and on macro-economic changes, or on the behavior of individuals and economic units. Moreover, religious institutions in Nigeria have themselves played economic roles. Churches and mosques, religious brotherhoods and orders are sometimes direct and sometimes indirect producers, consumers and controllers of assets.[8]

Looking at the evolution of the Nigerian economy, some observers would put more emphasis on external variables of colonialism, trade and the expansion of a world capitalist system, than on any factors indigenous to Nigeria. There are also peculiarly difficult problems in coming to grips with values in Nigeria. We have very few surveys of national or group attitudes. The society is extremely heterogenous by communal association, language, religion, ecology. Large-scale macro-economic changes cannot easily be related to growth of world religions (which are relative latecomers to Nigeria) or national values. In the end, the complexity of factors, the uncertainty of data on attitudes and gaps in our knowledge of behavior (how many people give according to *Zakat?* Are there biases towards size and capital intensity that can be traced to religious values?) force us back to some classic questions. We must again ask, for example, about entre-preneurship and about attitudes toward equality and organization, which must be understood in terms of individual as well as group behavior and about which we have some information. These matters have large consequences for the Nigerian economy and they can be translated into questions about the sociology of religion.

RELIGION AND ECONOMICS

We have seen that civil servants and military personnel were com-mitted to indigenization, as were the businessmen who benefited from buying shares from foreign corporations. These were from many ethnic groups but were overwhelmingly Moslems or Christians. There is little reason to suspect that religion distinguished these actors with respect to their economic nationalism. It is true that the northern part of Nigeria was less penetrated by foreign trade and investment than the south. It is also true that on most indices of modernization, the Moslem north lags behind the south, whether we measure education, income, or infrastructural development. The wealthy in Nigeria are concentrated in the southwest and the oil-producing areas. The poorest are in remote areas of the country: Ibibio in the southeast, Idoma, Tiv and others in the Middle Belt, particularly those who are neither Moslem nor Christians. Among Moslems, Fulani and Kanuri in the north are poorer than Hausas.[9]

Modernization lags in Nigeria have been frequently attributed to the impact of Islam. Admittedly, agreements between British colonial authorities under Lord Lugard and the traditional Islamic rulers kept out Christian missionaries and their attendant schools, roads and skills. Peter Kilby and others have asserted that the north and south differ in the intensity of their desire for modern consumer goods and that these differences can be accounted for by the conservative influence of religion and the sociopolitical system of northern Nigeria. 'Islam, the semi-feudal emirates, and the exclusion of western [missionary] education on religious grounds combined with a later and less intensive contact with the western world, have meant that in the north the whole process of modernization – changes in the way of living, values and skills, as well as directly material terms – has lagged behind that of the east and west.'[10]

I am much more comfortable with the supply side of this argument than with the demand side of it. Relative lack of contact with external skills and technology did put the north at a disadvantage. And the political system of the north did hinder social mobility as compared to the west and east. Ecology was also less favorable for much of the north. The non-Islamic north did not fare well.

How much of northern conservatism should be attributed to Islam, rather than to the vested interests of ruling elites and the stuctures they built to maintain their political and economic control? It is quite possible that religion has been an important component of political control and the idea of state intervention in economic life in the north. The problem with focusing on Islam simply as a conservative religion has been much discussed. Many have pointed to the variety of entrepreneurial activities in Iran, Turkey, Pakistan and Islamic black Africa.[11] Hausas in Nigeria frequently say that *they* are the Jews of Africa in that they spread over much of West Africa and they stress their trade and merchant activities. If many Hausas went into trade rather than invested in business, so many Christian Ibos and Yorubas went into professions and gravitated to the civil service in the mid-twentieth century. It was characteristic of much of Africa for relatively educated people to work to obtain professional degrees or a place in the state hierarchy. But there were many reasons for the commitment to civil service, profession, and trade rather than to industrial enterprise. The structural bottlenecks to entrepreneurial activities have been widely discussed.[12] Outsiders with capital and access to broader markets had certain advantages over African businessmen starting small, although African traders had advantages of lower information costs. Still, by 1960 officials estimated that there were already more than one and a quarter million enterprises in Nigeria. As restraints were put on foreigners and as markets grew and Africans acquired skills and capital, large-scale entrepreneurial activity quickened.

It is thus hard to accept the view that either Islam or traditional religions were barriers to entrepreneurship in Nigeria, although Islamic political structures and educational developments may well have inhibited the growth of the private sector. It has been argued that traditional religions and culture caused Africans to be averse to risk because they attributed misfortune to malevolent personal interventions. Whether we should treat this belief, if it was widely held, as religious or cultural is a question. If it was held across religions, as most have argued, we must understand it in broad cultural terms. But how then can we account for rising entrepreneurial activities when structural conditions altered? Did the cultural beliefs change so rapidly too?

By the 1970s Nigerians were leaving the public sector to enter private business. Civil servants were using their contacts to form lucrative partnerships and smooth the way for foreigners in Nigeria. The civil service as a career had also become riskier after General Murtala Mohammed in 1976 purged civil servants appointed during and before the Gowon regime. Also, the private sector was booming, and for people with high education wages were higher there than in the public sector. Nigeria proved to be an unusual African country in that the private sector became a magnet for highly educated people. Public positions no longer dominated the aspirations of university graduates. Private and public sectors should not be seen as two ends of a scale in Nigeria in the 1970s, one going up as the other goes down. Rather, the public sector became a more vigorous actor as centralization proceeded and oil revenues grew. But private opportunities also increased and with greater national integration in the 1970s, private actors had a wider field on which to play.

Government policies and economic opportunities plus the growth of management skills appear to have been much more important in enhancing private activities than changes in religion and/or culture. But even scholars who have dealt with cultural variables as important elements in entrepreneurial activities have stressed the patterns of extended family and social mobility more than religious values. Kilby has argued that the roots of Nigerian entrepreneurial deficiencies may run deeper than lack of experience or training, and lie in the under-lying disposition and attitudes of entrepreneurs. These attitudes in turn affect business ethics and the delegation of managerial authority. But Kilby does not single out religion as an independent variable nor does he isolate religious components of Nigerian culture. He empha-sizes traditional sociocultural phenomena common to all Nigeria's ethnic groups[13] (and thus common to all religions). He argues that while Ibo and Yoruba patterns of status mobility based on achieved wealth provide a strong incentive to establish a business enterprise as a means of obtaining high social status, once established there are no antecedent roles conferring respect for efficient managerial performance.[14] Others have argued that the desire to get rich quick, willingness to channel resources to family, or engage in corrupt acts stem from traditional sociocultural patterns. But again, few have isolated the part of religious variables in these patterns.

It is not that analysts have been unaware of religion as a factor. But they have found that ethnicity, not religion, is critical in social and economic networks through which business is carried out. Cohen reports that Yoruba Moslems objected to Hausa Moslems' religious and economic separatism in Ibadan.[15] When analysts have tried to treat religion as an independent variable, they have had difficulties parceling religion out from ethnic subcultures. LeVine and others have speculated that individualism, childrearing and individual achievement norms would be related to individualistic concepts of man's relation to God.[16] Ibos, however, are known as perhaps the most individualistic of Nigeria's ethnic groups and they are largely Catholic, whereas Catholicism stresses the individual's direct relation to God less than does Protestantism. Commentators have emphasized elements in Ibo culture more than religion in accounting for Ibo desire for upward mobility. Individual initiative, not inherited position, establish an Ibo's place in the system. Willingness to innovate and a fluid world view structured as a marketplace characterize Ibo views. Religious views have not been seen as critical to commercial success.[17] Nor has traditional religion much affected agricultural practices, although certain ceremonies are performed by those who practice traditional religion in connection with their farming activities. The Smocks write that:

> the extent to which economic factors override religious tra-ditions and sentiments can be seen in the gradual displacement of yams by cassava as the principal crop ... the traditionally

unchallenged significance of yams in the diet and the economy meant that yams were elevated to sacred status, and they continue to play a central role in religious ceremonies ... [that] Cassava gives higher per acre yields, requires less work, and presents fewer storage problems is considered more significant than the religious status of the yam.[18]

Islam is often described as a religion of obedience and respect for authority and thus understood to discourage individualism and presumably to discourage achievement orientation. Yet Islam like Christianity involves individual, not group adherence to beliefs which are held as valid. In his study of Nigerian schoolboys, LeVine found among Hausas in his sample indications of lower frequency of a need for achievement – of what, following McClelland, is defined as a latent disposition to compete with a standard of excellence.[19] He found a strong positive association between Christianity and the percentage of his achievement imagery-dreamers for the sample as a whole. Religion was almost completely confounded with ethnicity, since the ethnic groups with the highest percentages were Ibos and southern Yoruba. The only ethnic group in his sample which had both Christians and Moslems was northern Yoruba and here he found no significant association between Christianity and the frequency of achievement imagery.[20]

It is true that studies of Yoruba social mobility have shown a high percentage of Christians as compared to Moslems who attained political prominence during the colonial period. For example town councilors in Lagos were overwhelmingly Yoruba and Christian between 1920 and 1947. During 1950–5 Christians still dominated, although many more Moslems appeared. From 1959 on, some Lagos wards elected Moslems overwhelmingly and these individuals came from a wide variety of occupations. A shift had occurred from political power resting on elite educational background to political power resting on communal ties and economic associations.[21] This shift occurred in Lagos in the mid- to late 1950s but not in all the Yoruba-speaking Western Region. In 1958 the Federal Executive Committee of the Action Group, the Yoruba-based ruling party in the Western Region in the 1950s and early 1960s, had 45 Christians, 5 Moslems, and 12 unknown in an area which by this time was about half Christian and half Moslem.[22] While some prominent Moslem Action Group politicians were educators, the Moslem Yoruba political

elite tended to have backgrounds in business and trade rather than
in education and law. Yoruba Christians used their education to
become socially mobile and politically involved, but it is not clear that
Yoruba Christians as compared to Moslems were more entrepreneurial
or business-oriented in general. They were able to rise in bureaucratic
organizations, both public and private, in which western education
was a key qualification.

In his examination of Moslem and Christian converts in Ile-Ife,
Laitin notes that both religions took root there in the early years of
this century. 'Both won converts because their virtuosos had reputed
healing powers, and because they were associated with progress and
civilization (formal education and advanced technology for the
Christians; associations with Lagos business life for the Moslems),
and because neither religion presented itself initially as an exclusive
alternative to the traditional religions.' Laitin could find no discernible
difference in occupation of the original converts to Islam or Christianity
in Ile-Ife.[23]

To raise questions about entrepreneurship is to ask about the
motivations for individual and family behavior and to operate at the
micro-level. Coming back to macro-levels, one of the most interesting
and difficult questions is that of the impact of religion on matters
of equity in Nigeria. But is very hard to sort out the impact of ethnicity
and religion on class consciousness, organizations and on demands
for equality.

EQUALITY AND RELIGION

Having a sense of the ethnic and language complexities involved in
understanding inequality should make us very careful as we approach
the subject of inequality and religion. One can find highly egalitarian
strands in Christianity and Islam, and depending on the social and
historical milieus in which we look at the propagation and organization of these religions, we can find them acting as vehicles for
egalitarian demands or as justifications for the *status quo*.

Laitin argues that Moslems have a rigid sense of social equality
and that this is not just a doctrinal matter but observable in behavior.
All members of the mosque have a moral responsibility to enforce
community standards; modes of prayer are simple and dress is austere
at the mosque; all prostrate themselves while praying and the floor
is an equalizer. Laitin notes that Yoruba culture requires that young

men prostrate, or at least lean, to elders or social superiors. While prostration does not go on in church, leaning does, but in the mosque norms require an equal bowing from the knees for all greeters.[24] The women of the mosque which Laitin visited, however, were consigned to dank rooms away from the men. There is no equality of sexes at the mosque, nor is there much at the churches in Yorubaland either.

So far, we have been talking about equality and the life of the mosque. But what about life outside the mosque? As many have pointed out, Islam demands of the rich that they give *zakat* or alms to the poor. It also requires that inheritance be spread among heirs. But there are varieties of land tenure and inheritance patterns among Moslems in Nigeria.

In his work on Ile-Ife, Laitin suggests that differences between mosque and church mean very little outside of them. The norms of Yoruba culture dominate.[25] Yorubas, Christian and Moslem, are hardly bent on income redistribution or on abolishing status and the hierarchy of traditional authorities. (The Yoruba-based Unity Party of Nigeria campaigned in the 1979 elections on a populist platform which stressed the delivery of services. It did not campaign for redistribution of income, and the party platform stated a commitment to freeing the private sector from regulations, although some UPN governors took over some private enterprises.) It may be that if one controls for wealth, Christians have fewer wives than Moslems (this appears to have been true in Ife), but polygamy is widespread among Christians, and Moslems have justified their own need to accumulate in terms of supporting large households and more wives.

In the north, Islam cuts different ways with regard to equality. Islamic northern Nigeria is the most hierarchial part of the country. This is expressed in terms of relations between the sexes. Fewer women attend school in the Islamic north than in the south. Girls do not attend Koranic schools despite Nigeria's commitment to universal primary education. Women are channeled into a narrower range of occupations. Religion provides a rationale for the existing social order while providing an institutional framework through which women fulfill the economic and social roles assigned to them.[26] The wives of the Hausa ruling class experience seclusion in the husband's compound. Remy points out that better-off workers have begun to adopt the status symbols of the Moslem Hausa aristocracy, including the seclusion of women, which is justified in religious terms and which has important consequences for the development of a modern labor force in rural and urban areas.[27] The gulf between commoners and royalty seems large in the northern emirates. And Islam is used to justify status inequalities in both the political and economic realms.

However, we must be careful not to see Islam simply as a component of an ideology which justifies inequality. For Islam in the north has acted powerfully as an integrative mechanism through which demands for equality are made. Islam has provided a language and values through which to express egalitarian demands.

From 1980 to 1983 the most radical demands and implementation of policies came from a splinter faction of the Peoples Redemption Party (PRP) which controlled the governorship of two states, Kano and Kaduna. The PRP was led by Aminu Kano, who had been the populist leader of the old Northern Element's Progressive Union based in the Middle Belt areas of the north and in Aminu Kano's home areas of Kano city and emirate. Amino Kano, the leader of NEPU and the PRP was a *mallam*, a Moslem teacher.[28] After Nigeria returned to party politics in the late 1970s, Aminu Kano was able to gather support of some major trade union leaders and, with traditional support plus workers's support, was able to carry Kano State in the presidential election.

The PRP's manifesto called for the state to take command of the economy and was more socialist in orientation than the other parties' platforms, although many PRP ideas remained highly general. When two PRP governors won (although in Kaduna State the legislature remained in the hands of the National Party of Nigeria), they embarked on a radical program. They abolished head and cattle taxes and pushed to democratize local government procedures and reform land tenure systems. They made common cause with governors from parties other than the NPN and were expelled from their own PRP. Eventually the governor of Kaduna state, Alhaji Balarabe Musa, was impeached by the state assembly in 1981.

The point of retelling these stories is that it has been in the Moslem north, especially in Kaduna and Kano city, the largest urban concentrations in northern Nigeria, that radical and conservative forces have faced each other directly. The expelled PRP governors and their supporters see both the NPN and the established PRP as oligarchic and reactionary. They are viewed in turn as dangerous radicals. Very different economic and social interests and programs are developed in a context of struggle between traditional emirate authority and secular leaders; different religious and traditional authorities with bases in Kano and Sokoto also contend with each other; and different Moslem movements and sects operate in the fluid political and religious milieu of Nigeria's north.

In December 1980 large-scale rioting in Kano city led to the death of between one and ten thousand people as a sect led by Muhammudu Marwa Maitatsine fought pitched battles with Nigerian police and army. Marwa appears to have been a leader of the Yan Izala sect whose stated aim is to strike against materialism and privilege and purify Islamic practice. The sect has been supported by refugees from Chad and Niger, as well as by recent rural migrants to Kano city. Police and army put down the rioting with great violence and it may have been that the perception of the sect as heretical led to the lack of restraint by army and police.

In July 1981 riots again broke out in Kano. The governor of Kano state, Alhaji Abubakar Rimi, sent to the traditional ruler, the Emir of Kano, a letter in which he charged the Emir with disrespect to the secular authority. The Emir's supporters in turn took the governor's letter to be disrespectful and unacceptable. State government offices were sacked and the governor's political advisor was killed. In 1983–84 Moslem sect violence broke out again in Maiduguri and Yola.

Thus parts of northern Nigeria continue to be roiled by the movements of Islamic sects calling for reform and purification and by conflict between secular and traditional-religious authorities. The north, like other areas of Nigeria, continues to have syncretistic mixtures of world religions and ethnic cultures. There is a complicated history of reforms as purification, modernization, westernization, and secularization in the north and in and around Kano particularly.[29] Islam in the north has developed through brotherhood communities that 'reflect' ethnic, geographic and generational factors, all of which intersect with underlying economic patterns (such as urbanization and division of labor). The brotherhoods also create transethnic loyalties in Nigeria. The brotherhoods in Nigeria, as in other parts of Africa and especially in Senegal, engage in direct economic activities.[30]

While the Islamic brotherhoods link political and economic actors and achievement-oriented bureaucrats, in Iboland ethnic unions facilitated accommodation between tradition and modernity and have harnessed elements in the traditional political culture that have been conducive to political development.[31] There were many values in Ibo traditional society that were compatible with rapid development. But the traditional Ibo villages were isolated and not integrated into a wider community. As Smock describes the process, the ethnic unions, not religious groups or religious values, emerge as the critical transforming factors. 'By transforming religious facets of traditional culture into expressions of communal loyalty, the unions prevented communities from fragmenting as they went through the process of Christianization.'[32] Interestingly, Smock does not describe the process of Christianization as itself an integrative one for Ibos. She stresses the limited role of the Catholic Church in the areas studied. The Church was predominant and filled a vital role in community life. But most priests were Irish, not Nigerian, well after Nigeria's independence, and the Nigerians did not come from Eastern Region, and were therefore not involved in local disputes. Smock also argues that conversion to Christianity effected limited change in the convert: 'Membership in the church did not preclude participation in other rites, since former pagan festivals were transformed to celebrate the secular unity of the community, rather than the beneficence of a deity.[33]

It may be that Catholicism in Iboland like Islam in northern Nigeria affected attitudes toward political authority more than attitudes toward economic activities. Perhaps Catholicism played a role as Ibos came more to accept centralization of political authority.[34] Similarly, as political modernization and integration proceeded in northern Nigeria, reformist movements in Islam were important. Paden suggests that strands in Islamic political thought of repairing and holism have been merged with an accent on the former.[35] If this is the case, it may suggest possibilities for reform rather than extreme change being necessary in the core values and structures of society with all the political implications this entails.

CONCLUSION

No one concerned with the economic and political history of Nigeria could ignore the impact of Islam and Christianity. No one concerned with Nigerian culture and values could ignore these religions and the continued impact of pre-colonial traditional religions. Having said this, it is still difficult to isolate the effects of religion and especially to distinguish the importance of religion from a wider set of ethnic and cultural attitudes, values, and structures when we look at entrepreneurship, attitudes toward equality, or commitments to indigenization of the economy.

This is not to say that religion has not been important in affecting economic changes. Sometimes religious values and institutions have affected more directly political values and institutions and these in turn have been consequential for the relationship between, for example, private and public sectors in northern Nigeria and perhaps for a concern with state control.

Religion, acting on social structures and the formation of groups, and itself often an outgrowth of fundamental social, economic and demographic changes, is a critical component for the analysis of economic and social change. There is a broad agenda for research on religion in Nigeria and a great deal of work needs to be done in the interrelationship of religion and economic change and development in Nigeria. For example, we need much more work on the economic activities of religious institutions such as has been done in Senegal.[36] This would entail work on Islamic brotherhoods in Nigeria and an examination of the economic activities of Christian churches. We also need more interviewing of public officials to try to understand how general attitudes about economic matters relate to religious beliefs and whether diffuse attitudes translate into specific policies.

We have a better understanding of the ways that politicians both mobilize constituents through appeals to religion and use communal institutions to further political ends and organizations than we have of the relationship between religion and economy. A wide research agenda looms before students of Nigerian society. Historical and contemporary work needs to be undertaken at the level of individuals, firms and government agencies. No one with even a passing acquaintance of Nigeria would deny the historical and present importance of religious movements and the interaction of world religions with African religious beliefs and institutions that existed before the spread of world religions and co-existed with them. The need now is to understand the impact of world religions. It is especially important to examine these in the context of a rapidly changing society, an economy that retains many old features while manifesting important new ones associated with an oil economy, foreign financial and industrial interventions, and growing connections in trade and investment with the rest of Africa and the world.

NOTES

1. For an interesting analysis of religion and political culture see David Laitin, 'Religion, Political Culture, and the Weberian Tradition', *World Politics* 30, July 1978, pp. 563–92.

2. George Balandier, *Sociologie actuelle de l'Afrique Noire*, Paris, Presses Universitaires de France, 1955.

3. For a major study of the adoption of Aladura Christianity and the development of the Christ Apostolic Church and the Cherubim and Seraphim in Yorubaland see, J. D. Y. Peel, *Aladura: A Religious Movement among the Yoruba*, London, Oxford University Press, 1968. Peel describes the members of the Aladura churches as 'the middling men,' the 'industrious sort of people and recent immigrants to the town,' p. 228, as Walzer and Hill have written of adherents to Puritanism. Michael Walzer, *The Revolution of the Saints*, London, 1966; C. Hill, *Religion and Puritanism in Pre-Revolutionary England*, London, 1964. Peel is concerned to explain the fundamental character of a religion of industrialization in the Yoruba context as a new morality of obeying rules, p. 299. The difficulty with picking out individuals who themselves seek out a religion like the Aladura churches and then arguing that the religion has a particular impact is that the religion may be sought precisely for its compatibility with values and attitudes the individual already has. Peel is aware of this and does not hold that economic behavior stems from religious beliefs. He argues that the doctrine held by Aladura believers was determined by a particular world view they held, p. 298. This world view, as a system of ideas, seems to give rise both to church membership and to economic traits.

4. Laitin, p. 591.

5. David Laitin, 'Conversion and Political Change: A Study of (Anglican) Christianity and Islam among the Yorubas of Ile-Ife.' Paper delivered at the Annual Meeting of the American Political Science Association, Washington, 28–31 August 1980.

6. I am indebted to Larry Frank of Saint Lawrence College for these insights.

7. I am indebted to Graham Irwin of Columbia University for these insights.

8. I am not going to deal with the direct economic roles of religious institutions.

9. See Donald Morrison, 'Inequalities of Social Rewards: Realities and Perceptions in Nigeria', in Henry Bienen and Vremdia P. Diejomaoh (eds), *The Political Economy of Income Distribution in Nigeria*, New York, Holmes and Meier, 1981, pp. 173–92.

10. Peter Kilby, *Industrialization in an open Economy: Nigeria, 1945–1977*, London, Cambridge University Press, 1969, p. 32.

11. For one study which insists that Moslems have been encouraged by their religion to make profits, see Maxime Rodinson, *Islam and Capitalism* (New York, Panther, 1974.

12. Among studies of entrepreneurship in Nigeria see John Harris, 'Industrial Entrepreneurship in Nigeria', Ph. D. thesis, Evanston, Ill., Northwestern University, 1967, E. Wayne Nafziger, 'Nigerian Entrepreneurship: A Study of Indigenous Businessmen in the Footwear Industry', Ph. D. thesis, Urbana, University of Illinois, 1967, Peter Kilby, *African Enterprise: The Nigerian Bread Industry*, Stanford, Hoover Institution, 1965, Peter Marris, 'Social Barriers to Entrepreneurship', *Journal of Development Studies*, October 1968; E. O. Akeredolu-Ake, 'Values, Motivations, and History in the Development of Private Indigenous Entrepreneurship: Lessons from Nigeria's Experience, 1946–1966', *Nigerian Journal of Economic and Social Studies* 13, July 1971, pp. 195–220; E. Wayne Nafziger, 'The Effect of the Nigerian Extended Family on Entrepreneurial Activity', *Economic Development and Cultural Change*, October 1969.

13. Kilby, *Industrialization in an Open Economy*, pp. 341–2.
14. Ibid.
15. Abner Cohen, 'The Politics of the Kola Trade.' In Edith Whetham and Jean Currie (eds), *Reading in the Applied Economics of Africa*, vol. 1, *Micro Economics*, London, Cambridge University Press, 1967.
16. Robert A. LeVine, *Dreams and Deeds: Achievement Motivation in Nigeria*, Chicago, University of Chicago Press, 1966.
17. Audrey C. Smock, *Ibo Politics: The Role of Ethnic Unions in Eastern Nigeria*, Cambridge, Harvard University Press, pp. 16, 30. For studies of Ibo culture see Victor Uchendu, *The Ibo of Southeast Nigeria*, New York, Holt, Rinehart & Winston, 1965; K. Onwuka Dike, *Trade and Politics in the Niger Delta, 1830–1885*, London, Oxford University Press, 1956.
18. David R. Smock and Audrey C. Smock, *Cultural and Political Aspects of Rural Transformation: A Case Study of Eastern Nigeria*, New York, Praeger, 1972, p. 95.
19. See David McClelland, *The Achieving Society*, Princeton, Van Nostrand, 1961.
20. LeVine, p. 58.
21. Pauline Baker, *Urbanization and Political Change: The Politics of Lagos, 1917–1967*, Berkeley, University of California Press, 1974; appendices on socio-economic and political profiles of Lagos town councilors, pp. 286–306.
22. Richard Sklar, *Nigerian Political Parties*, Princeton, Princeton University Press, 1963, p. 484.
23. Laitin, 'Conversion and Political Change', pp. 5–6.
24. *Ibid.*, p. 18.
25. Peel makes the same point when he says that 'Yoruba Moslems have been tolerant and Yoruba before they are Moslems, except for the most orthodox.' Peel, *Aladura*, p. 4. See also J. S. Trimingham, *Islam in West Africa*, London, 1959.
26. Dorothy Remy, 'Underdevelopment and the Experience of Women: A Nigerian Case Study', in Gavin Williams (ed.), *Nigeria: Economy and Society* London, Collings, 1976, p. 124.
27. *Ibid.*
28. For a biography of this interesting political figure see Alan Feinstin, *African Revolutionary: The Life and Times of Nigeria's Aminu Kano*, New York, Quadrangle, 1973.
29. For the most detailed treatment see John N. Paden, *Religion and Political Culture in Kano*, Berkeley, University of California Press, 1973. For a review see Laitin, 'Religion and Political Culture.'
30. Paden argues that the *mallam* or teacher class was a natural link between political and economic classes in Kano and that the reformed brotherhoods facilitated social mobility in Kano. Paden, p. 392. It would be interesting to know if Christian ministers filled similar functions. Laitin ('Conversion and Political Change', pp. 11–12) says that there was a clear functional specification of roles in the Christian missionary tradition as opposed to role diffusion among Moslems: 'While the Christian missionaries saw the clear linking of trade, military might and religious conversion, they almost universally refused to take a direct role in the first two functions.' The missionaries, as Laitin points out, supported the growth of cash crops, farming and trade. Subsequently, church figures did play roles in party politics and appear to have been figures linking economic and political actors. Since the emphasis in this chapter is on religious values and economics, I am not dealing directly with the economic undertakings of religious institutions.
31. Smock, p. 237.
32. Ibid., p. 238.
33. Ibid., p. 140.
34. Christianity led to division in Iboland as well as to integration, because it caused

splits between pagans and Christians and later, as different missionary societies competed for converts, new sectarian differences divided communities. See Smock and Smock, p. 56.

35. Paden, p. 386.
36. Lucy Behrman, 'Muslim Politics and Development in Senegal', *Journal of Modern African Studies* 15, June 1977, pp. 261–77. Donal B. O'Brien, *Saints and Politicans: Essays in the Organization of Senegalese Peasant Society*, London, Cambridge University Press, 1975; L. B. Venema, *The Wolof of Saloum: Social Structures and Rural Development in Senegal*, Wagenigen, Center for Agricultural Publishing and Documentation, 1978.

CHAPTER FIVE

The 1979 Nigerian Elections

INTRODUCTION

One of the most important events in contemporary African history was Nigeria's return to civilian rule through elections for national and state executives and legislatures in 1979. Although there were many difficulties in administering the elections, most observers felt that the elections were generally free of the administrative and political interventions that had characterized many earlier Nigerian elections. Nonetheless, the elections were not without controversy over their outcomes, legitimacy, and meaning. The presidential results were contested in the special electoral tribunals and in the courts, as were many state contests.

As the electoral returns were analyzed, observers still could not entirely agree on what they had seen: to what extent the Nigerian political system was still structured around ethnic ties, whether parties become truly national entities and whether Nigeria simply reproduced the leaderships of the pre-1966 civilian regimes.

Before we can look directly at these issues, we have to understand the background to and context of the 1979 elections.

BREAKDOWN OF MILITARY RULE AND RETURN TO CIVILIAN RULE

Nigeria has been an independent country for more than 20 years. Electoral politics preceded formal independence; elections were held for the Federal House of Representatives in 1954 even before internal self-government was granted to the Eastern and Western Regions in 1957 and to the Northern Region in 1959. Federal elections were also held in 1959. A number of regional elections had been held in the east, west and north in the 1950s and early 1960s.

After independence, federal elections were again held in 1964–5 despite great controversy over the 1963 census. The southern alliance, the United Peoples Grand Alliance (UPGA) made up of the Action Group (AG), the Northern Elements' Progressive Union (NEPU), National Convention of Nigerian Citizens (NCNC) and the United Middle Belt Congress (UMBC) called for a boycott. The Nigerian National Alliance, made up of the Northern Peoples Congress and the Nigerian National Democratic Party (NNDP) in the west, won a disputed election.

In March 1965, elections were held in areas where there had been total boycott. In the fall of 1965, elections were held for the Western Regional Government amidst extreme violence in the west and internecine fighting among the Yoruba. Electoral politics broke down over the 1963 census, ethnic-regional conflict, the intervention of northern power into the west and internal factionalism within Yorubaland.[1]

The crisis in the Western Region from 1962 to 1965 was a critical turning point in Nigerian history. Chief Awolowo, leader of the Action Group had been premier of the Western Region. He contested the national elections of 1959 and was defeated, becoming the leader of the opposition in the National Assembly. His deputy leader in the Western Region, Chief Samuel Akintola, then became Premier in the Western Region where the AG remained the ruling party. In the tenuous coalition politics of Nigeria in the early 1960s, Chief Akintola wanted to form a ruling coalition based on the control of the Northern region by the Northern Peoples Congress (NPC). Chief Awolowo felt that westerners, who were overwhelmingly Yoruba, were being squeezed out of the federal civil service and the awarding of contracts by the Federal government. He believed that a conservative, northern-based government would fail and that he could create a new majority coalition by holding on to his base in the Western Region and by achieving enough support in parts of the Northern Region. Awolowo lost control of the government, however, in the west. A chaotic session of the Western House of Assembly failed to confirm a successor, and the Federal government declared a state of emergency and ruled through emergency powers.

A profound step had been taken in Nigerian politics because the Federal government had intervened in the very heart of the regional political process. In the past, each of the three large parties, the AG in the west, the NPC in the north, and the NCNC in the east had been left to rule their own regions. The leaders of the west, however, split.

Akintola became Premier of the Western Region after a six-month period of emergency rule, but he could not control the AG nor rule by consent in the west. The Federal government first brought Chief Awolowo to trial for treason and then imprisoned him. The Federal government increasingly intervened in western politics through police powers. Regional authority was undermined. The constitutional bargain was broken. Violence was rife throughout the west as intra-Yoruba factionalism intensified.[2]

Electoral politics broke down in the mid-1960s because of communal and factional strife. The one-party systems in each of the large regions had depended on the Federal government staying out of regional politics. When northern power was brought to bear in the Western Region through the power of the Federal government, fair elections could not be guaranteed. Factional politics within Yoruba-land opened up the possibilities for extreme ethnic tensions to be expressed by maneuvering within the Western Region. The perception that corruption was growing in Nigeria and that the civilian elites had lost legitimacy was widespread.

A military coup occurred in January 1966. This first coup brought formal representative government to an end. Nigeria returned to electoral politics after 15 years of military rule, when elections were held for executive and legislative bodies at state and national levels in 1979. Thus Nigeria has had a military government for more than half its existence as an independent nation. Military rule can also be thought of, however, as an interruption of electoral politics which preceded independence in 1960 and was reinstated in 1979.

What is clear even now is that Nigerians have taken elections seriously as a way of determining who will rule. This could not be said of all African political systems. In Nigeria, however, from the inception of military government under General Ironsi in 1966, the military committed itself to withdrawal from power. While this commitment was honored in the breach in Nigeria, it remained a strong element of legitimacy for the military regime. General Ironsi's successor, General Gowon, who emerged from the second coup of July 1966, also committed himself to withdrawal. On 1 October 1970, he announced a Nine-Point Program for return to civilian rule by 1976. When General Gowon was perceived to have reneged on the commitment to move toward civilian rule, he was replaced by General Murtala Mohammed in yet a third coup in 1975.

An important factor leading to the Mohammed coup was the

failure of the military government to carry out an acceptable census which was seen as a prerequisite for new elections. Unlike Mali or Somalia or many other African states that came under military rule in the mid-1960s, Nigeria (and Ghana) faced constant pressures for a return to civilian rule. Indeed, the period of military rule from at least 1967 on can be thought of as a military–civilian dyarchy. Civilians were reintroduced as commissioners at both the state level and the national level in 1967, to provide links to civilian constituencies and to allow for some aspects of representative government which military officers neither wanted to provide directly nor were capable of providing.[3] As the Nigerian Civil War proceeded, it was necessary to harness support through civilian consultative committees, sometimes called 'Leaders of Thought.' Support was also sought through the civilian commissioners who served as executive officers in cabinets of military governors throughout the 12 states, which were created in 1967 from the former four regions of Nigeria. (Subsequently, in 1976, Nigeria created seven new states.) Although military officers also served as ministers at the national level, the idea of formal civilian participation in the military government existed almost from the inception of military rule.

The civilians who served under military governments frequently were well-known political figures. Chief Awolowo, former Leader of the Opposition at the national level and Premier of the Western Region, was made Minister of Finance in 1967. Mallam Aminu Kano, former leader of NEPU, also became a federal commissioner. At state levels, some technocrats were appointed as commissioners, but so were many party leaders. Civil servants expanded their roles and power as they have elsewhere in Africa under military regimes. Because the civilians in government included highlevel party figures, many political networks were maintained during military rule. As will be discussed later in this chapter, the parties that emerged to contest the 1979 elections, though not simply recreations of the pre-1966 political parties, had important continuities of leadership, ethnic constituencies and political alignments and networks.

One reason for the restoration of civilian rule was the idea that civilian rule was the norm for Nigeria. Although no systematic, large-scale public opinion surveys exist to establish overwhelmingly that in Nigeria's political culture civilian rule was legitimate and military rule was not, the military's own words and actions show that it felt it had to stress its intention to return to the barracks.[4]

In the early 1970s politicians did not, however, take for granted that civilian rule would return.[5] After General Mohammed took power, he and his successors did make clear their commitment to return power to civilians, but the Nigerian military's withdrawal from power was neither easy nor straightforward. Indeed, a crucial factor in Nigeria's return to civilian rule was the military's own fear of internal fragmentation through a process of coup and countercoup. The Nigerian army, for all the internal bloodletting of 1966 and the civil war that followed, remained, in comparative African perspective, a relatively professional army with strong corporate values.[6] The longer the military ruled, the more political a segment of the officers became. The more politically effective the officers became, the more they needed to establish their own political client groups enmeshed with civilians. Many officers in the Nigerian military did not want to take up the tasks of representative government that they knew were essential if Nigeria was to be ruled effectively and peacefully. To 'represent' meant that the military would have to respond to constituency demands, which were especially complicated. They involved communal representation, the role of traditional leaders and conflict over ascendance to traditional positions, revenue allocation among states and the issue of the creation of more states and the rising demands of new social groups, labor and a growing bourgeoisie.

The Supreme Military Council (SMC) promulgated a rule stating that officers who stayed in ministerial positions during the last months of the transition before elections would have to resign their commissions. The idea was to remove officers who had been in politics at the end in order to widen the distance between the military and the civilians, and to re-enforce the idea that the military was out of politics. Officers who had served in political positions in the transitional regime would be perceived as political and should not continue to serve under new civilian rulers. This was important because senior officers were not completely trusted to be non-partisan. Military governors of the states were thought to have inflated state census results in 1973.[7] Military men were eventually to enter into the formation of some of the parties, and there was from the start the fear that officers would be involved in electoral politics.[8] In the end, Chief Awolowo, the leader of the Unity Party of Nigeria, accused the last military Head of State, General Obasanjo, of being against him and argued that the military threw the election to his opponent. But this view, apparently, was not widely shared in Nigeria, or at least widely shared outside

Chief Awolowo's camp. This was in good part because the military in July 1978 did post back to the barracks officers who had served as state governors. Some military federal commissioners also went back to armed forces regular duties at that time.

THE TRANSITION PERIOD

As early as January 1966, General Ironsi had talked about the military government as 'interim.' In 1967, a phasing of stages for return to civilian rule was announced that included preparation for elections in early 1969. This phasing was not adhered to. The military government still insisted, however, that it wanted civilian rule, and on 1 October 1970, it announced a Nine-Point Program for return to civilian rule by 1976. In October 1974 in the aftermath of controversy over a new census – a controversy reminiscent of the one that raged in the 1960s over an earlier census – General Gowon announced the military government's intention to stay in power beyond 1976. General Gowon said that the nation's military leaders had decided it would be 'utterly irresponsible to leave the nation in the lurch by a precipitate withdrawal.' He stated that the military had not abandoned the idea of a return to civilian rule, but he maintained the ban on political parties that had been in effect since January 1966.

In 1972–3, a number of trial balloons were floated by the military government. Nigeria's first president, Nnamdi Azikiwe, proposed a formal dyarchy, a combined military and civilian government, to last for at least five years after formal military rule ended. He argued that the military should constitute a fourth arm of government along with executive, legislative and judicial bodies.[9] While the press condemned these proposals, some military officers supported them. After 1974, civilian pressures for military withdrawal mounted.

General Murtala Mohammed commited himself to military withdrawal by 1979; he initiated the creation of a new constitution that was drafted after his assassination in February 1970.[10] He proposed that a draft constitution be completed by September 1976, that new states be created in the Nigerian Federation, and that local government elections be held without party politics. A Constituent Assembly would consider the draft constitution. By October 1978 the ban on parties would be lifted, and elections would be held for state and federal offices by October 1979. Despite the assassination of General Mohammed, his successor, General Obasanjo, did indeed hold to the schedule.

The period from 1976 to the elections of 1979 was a critical one not only for laying the ground rules for the elections, but also for creating the constitutional framework in which competitive party politics would be carried out. The events of these years and the procedures and institutions that developed have been discussed at some length. I want only to abstract the most critical aspects from these accounts.[11]

The Constitutional Drafting Committee (CDC) was appointed by the head of state. Most of its members could be called technocrats. Of its 50 members, 19 were from the universities; 12 were lawyers; 11 were connected with present or past governments.[12] Almost one-third of its members, however, had been civil commissioners, so they had served in political/executive roles. Two individuals were chosen from each state for geographic representation. The federal military government did provide instructions for the CDC, though not all the instructions were heeded. For example, the Supreme Military Council felt that there was no consensus on an ideology in Nigeria, and thus the constitution should not proclaim any particular ideology. One of the seven subcommittees that were created, the one dealing with national objectives, did propose that the constitution state a commitment to socialism and to public ownership of the means of production, but the plenary CDC did not accept this recommendation.[13]

The subcommittee on political parties and elections opted for a multi-party system after receiving many memorandums concerning the costs and benefits of multi-party systems and one-party systems.[14] The subcommittee recommended that parties should be national. The members were all conscious of the sectional nature of the old Nigerian party system. National elections had been competitive, but within each of the regions a single party became dominant over time.[15] Murtala Mohammed had even suggested that the CDC should feel free to recommend a no-party system if it felt that a government could be formed without political parties.

The CDC wrestled to make compatible the military's desire for a limited number of truly national parties and its own determination to have a free, democratic and lawful system of government that would ensure maximum political participation and an orderly succession to political power. Given Nigeria's heterogeneous character, a fair system of representation had to take account of social and ethnic diversity. Provisos toward these ends stated that members of the executive committees of parties must be drawn from at least two-thirds of the 19 states; that the objectives and programs of parties must conform to fundamental national objectives, though these were left undefined; that membership had to be open to all citizens; that headquarters must be in the federal capital; and that ethnic and religious labels were disallowed. Parties also had to hold open elections and could not maintain paramilitary organizations, as they had done in the past. These organizations had caused open interparty warfare in 1965, which was one of the main triggers of the 1966 coups. In the end, these provisos were accepted in the constitution by the military government along with the stipulation that only parties could canvass for votes or contribute to candidates. Parties also had to reflect the 'federal character of Nigeria', which was said to combine a desire for national unity with the diversity of Nigeria's peoples.[16]

The CDC submitted its report to the federal military government in September 1976. In April 1976, that government had already expanded the number of states from 12 to 19, setting the stage for a political system with many state arenas for competition.[17] The CDC recommended that a Federal Election Commission be established by decree which had wide powers to certify and regulate party life and to establish candidates' ability to stand for office. It proved to be crucial in deciding how the 1979 elections would be contested, who could contest and in determining the final outcome. In October 1976, the military government appointed a 24-member Federal Electoral Commission (FEDECO) to draw up voters' registers, to organize state and federal elections and to delimit constituencies.[18]

In 1976, the federal military government imposed a set of reforms on Nigeria's local government structure that were designed to make local government more uniform throughout Nigeria and, above all, to make it more efficient, accountable and responsive. The CDC had itself included a section on local government, but the military government reorganized local government prior to a new constitution coming into being.[19] Elections were held for the newly established local government councils in December 1976 – the first elections in Nigeria since 1965. State governments could opt for direct or indirect elections. Nine states, seven in the north and Anambra and Cross River in the south, opted for indirect elections. No party activity was allowed even in states with direct elections.[20] Periods of registration for voters had to be extended in Lagos state because registration results were so disappointing. In other states, registration was more robust. Chiefs and persons in public employment, including teachers, were ineligible to stand for election.

Of the states with contested elections, Ondo state had as many as 49 per cent of councilors elected unopposed, and Bendel state as few as 12.5 per cent unopposed. Anambra state, which chose indirect election through a system of electoral colleges, returned 70 per cent unopposed.[21] There were also allegations of bribery in the electoral colleges. In the states created out of the Western Region, many senior politicians lost. These tended to be from the former parties that had become discredited after 1962 – the NCNC and the NNDP. The AG's senior politicians fared much better. Thus the local government elections of 1976 in Oyo state, Ondo state, Lagos state, Ogun state and all states carved out of the Western Region, gave some indication of voters' memories concerning interparty strife in the Yoruba-speaking areas.[22]

Some major politicians who had stayed loyal to the Action Group did lose, and some individuals who had been close to NNDP leaders won. Still, the toll was higher on former leaders of the NCNC in the west and from the NNDP. The view that the success or failure of a candidate depended on local factors has merit, but it must be modified by the losses incurred by such major figures from the past as Chief Mojeed Agbaje, S.A. Yerokun, Alhaji Saka Layonu and Chief Kolawole Balogun.[23] In the north, candidates were also viewed in terms of their membership in or association with former political parties, the NPC or NEPU.[24]

The local government elections provided the basis for a large share of the representation to the Constituent Assembly which was to debate the constitution drafted by the CDC. The Constituent Assembly was partially formed by elections conducted at the end of August 1977, with the local government councils acting as electoral colleges. Two hundred and three representatives were elected, and a further twenty were appointed by the Supreme Military Council. The chairman and deputy chairman were appointed later by the SMC.

Many of those elected to the local government councils had relatively little education and had not been prominent in politics, in part because public employees had not been allowed to stand, and in part because the arena was local and, especially in the system of indirect rule, the electoral process was a risky one. Many prominent people stood for Constituent Assembly election, however, including former members of the CDC, former federal commissioners, former federal permanent secretaries, prominent businessmen, academics and former important politicians, including Alhaji Shehu Shagari, Richard Akinjide, Joseph S. Tarka, Chief Fani Kayode, Jaja Wachukwu and Dr Kingsley Mbadiwe.[25]

Seventy-seven of the two hundred and three seats were uncontested, and a number of well-known candidates were disqualified by the electoral commissioners for either non-payment of taxes or alleged previous misconduct in office. The local government councils did look outside their own memberships for representatives to the Constituent Assembly.[26]

Thus, prior to the 1979 elections, Nigeria held elections for local government and then for Constituent Assembly, which once again thrust to the fore prominent former politicians. At the same time, academics, former ambassadors and civil servants were now in the Constituent Assembly, which gave them a forum for their views and a chance to become increasingly involved in the network of political links remaining from political life in Nigeria under military rule. Politicians had remained active in Nigeria from 1966 to 1977. They represented constituents at local levels, served as state and federal commissioners under military leaders and maintained and evolved their own networks of political relationships.[27] As the Constituent Assembly debated a new constitution, constitutional questions would become intertwined with political careers and with the question who would rule Nigeria under a civilian regime and through what vehicles?

The draft constitution put forward by the CDC was substantially the document given to the federal military government by the Constituent Assembly in June 1977.[28] There were important debates over the question of the creation of more states.[29] The issue of Sharia or Islamic courts was especially contentious and led to the walk-out of 93 members of the Constituent Assembly from the northern states.[30] Debates were very heated.[31]

The Constituent Assembly sent forward a constitution with an elected president as Head of State. The president was made Chief Executive and Commander and Chief of the Nigerian armed forces. The president appointed ministers, subject to the confirmation of an elected Senate. At least one minister had to be appointed from each state. He also appointed a chief justice, subject to Senate confirmation; other judges of the Federal High Court were appointed on advice of a Federal Judicial Commission whose members were appointed by the president. The president chaired the National Security Council, National Defense Council and the Council of State.[32]

The constitution also established an elected National Assembly, composed of a Senate and House of Representatives. The Senate had five elected representatives from each of the 19 states. The House was composed of 450 members based on population.[33] Bills originated in either house. The National Assembly had concurrent powers with the states for stipulated purposes and exclusive power for other purposes. Members of the National Assembly were guaranteed a four-year term.

The constitution that emerged from the Constituent Assembly at first was amended by the military government in minor ways. Its adoption was announced on 21 September 1978 to become effective on 1 October 1979. On 28 September 1979, however, one of the last acts of the military government was to amend the constitution.[34] The constitution has its own provisions for amendment (chapter I, part II, section 9) requiring special majorities in both Houses of the National Assembly and in two-thirds of the Houses of Assembly in the states. By decree the military government altered the provisions for elections of president and of governors of the states. The full effect of these changes and the reasons for them can best be understood in the context of analysis of the elections themselves.

PARTIES AND THE ELECTIONS OF 1979

The ban on politics was lifted on 21 September 1979. Although parties had been proscribed since January 1966, politics had not disappeared under the military regime and politicians had remained active in various forums. It is true that those military officers and civilian commissioners who wanted to engage in party politics were advised to resign their positions.[35] Within a week of the lifting of the ban, six political associations were announced including the Unity Party of Nigeria (UPN), the National Party of Nigeria (NPN) and the Nigerian Peoples Party (NPP). These three were to be major contestors throughout the elections. Other parties such as the Nigerian Advanced Party and the Nigerian Welfare Peoples Party were also formed. The speed of formation of parties substantiates the point that political networks had been developed prior to the repeal of prohibition of party politics. Indeed, many parties had as their precursors various social organizations such as the Committee of Friends which had members who became UPN founders.[36]

Given the rapid proliferation of parties, and the already large politicization of Nigerian life, a critical role was played by FEDECO. This body of 24 people appointed by the military government in May 1977, had the power to proscribe candidates (which it had already done for Constituent Assembly elections) and to regulate parties through audits, to disallow parties and to delimit constituencies. FEDECO was chaired by Chief Michael Ani, a former permanent secretary. Because the National Assembly had not yet come into being, and because the military wanted to distance itself from the political process during the transition, FEDECO became the arbiter of the elections until appeals were made to the judiciary for redress from its rulings. The police were given wide powers for regulating campaign activities through licensing of rallies, and a strong attempt was made to depoliticize the universities by refusing to allow university staff and full-time officers from taking part in active party politics. Lecturers, as public officers, had to resign from universities to enter partisan politics, and no party branches were allowed on campuses.[37] Election dates coincided with university vacations.

The elections themselves were contested by the National Party of Nigeria, the Unity Party of Nigeria, the Peoples Redemption Party (PRP) led by Alhaji Aminu Kano, the Nigerian Peoples Party, led by Nnamdi Azikiwe and the Great Nigerian Peoples Party (GNPP), which split off from the NPP and was led by Alhaji Waziri Ibrahim. Because all the parties that contested the elections were led by figures from the past some analysts said that the period of military rule had not permitted new political networks to grow up and that Nigeria was still dominated by the politics of ethnicity with each of the leaders of the major parties being the spokesman for a major ethnic community.

Awolowo had long been the leader of the Yorubas from the western states. Azikiwe had a similar position among Ibos in what had been the Eastern Region. Aminu Kano had been a president of the Northern Elements Progressive Union, which had been based in the Kano area and parts of the Middle Belt of northern Nigeria, and had struggled as a minority party with the Northern Peoples Congress for control of the Northern Region during the pre-military period. Waziri Ibrahim was a wealthy businessman with a strong political base among the Kanuri people of Borno state. He had been a minister in the Federal government before military rule. Alhaji Shehu Shagari had been Minister of Economic Development and Research and had held other ministerial posts in the civilian NPC-led government. Although he did not have the dominant position among the Hausa-Fulani that Awolowo had among the Yoruba or Azikiwe had among the Ibos, he was an important leader from the north, which had been dominated by the NPC.

It would not be completely accurate, however, to conclude that former political networks were in place again after an interregnum of almost 15 years. Major figures who had been Awolowo's associates in the past, such as Chief Anthony Enahoro from the midwest, Joseph Tarka, a leader of the Tiv, and S. G. Ikoku, did not join the UPN. The UPN was not able to recruit major leaders from the north to its banner. The UPN, like the other parties (except the Ibo-led NPP), elected an Ibo to be the vice presidential candidate.

The NPP was formed as a coalition of three social organizations: the National Council of Understanding, the Lagos Progressives and the Club of 19. This last comprised members of the Constituent Assembly who opposed Awolowo, opposed the Sharia courts and represented minorities, that is, they were not Hausa-Fulani, Ibo, or Yoruba.[38] Some prominent Yoruba opponents of Chief Awolowo were in the early NPP. This party split; one faction led by Waziri Ibrahim became the Great Nigerian Peoples Party, and the other faction was at first led by Chief Ogunsanya with supporters from the Lagos Progressives and the Club of 19.[39] It was this group that Nnamdi Azikiwe joined.

The NPN also had strong roots in the Constituent Assembly. A number of former military officers were involved in its early formation, including Major General Robert Adeyinka Adebayo who had been Military Governor of the Western State. Awolowo supporters had accused Adebayo of having sympathies with the NNDP. Major General Hassan Usman Katsina also supported the NPN. He was tied by blood to the ruling emirate in Katsina. A number of civilian commissioners under General Gowon were in the NPN too, including Enahoro, Chief Eke, Alhaji Shehu Shagari and Alhaji Shettima Ali Monguno. Thus the NPN seemed to have some NNDP Yoruba support (anti-Awolowo) and also support in the midwest and in the north. Ethnic representation within the NPN was fairly broadly based. Indeed, as Yahaya points out, the NPN tried to institutionalize diversity by allocating party positions to different areas of the country. Only members from the west (Yoruba) could contest for chairman of the party; the party's president had to come from the north. This was called 'zoning'.[40]

The PRP was led by Alhaji Aminu Kano and S. G. Ikoku, a former AG stalwart. The PRP was perceived as the most ideological of the parties, populist if not socialist, with support of trade union leaders such as Chief Michael Imodu. Parties were formed that were explicitly socialist, such as the Socialist Party of Workers, Farmers and Youths. This party, and more than 40 other associations, were not, however, registered by FEDECO as political parties. Indeed, only nineteen organizations applied for registration of FEDECO and only five were approved: NPP, GNPP, PRP, UPN and NPN.

FEDECO not only refused to register many political associations; it also disqualified many candidates for office at various levels. For a time, the issue of payment of taxes made questionable whether Aminu Kano and Nnamdi Azikiwe would be allowed to stand. Kano was disqualified and then reinstated. Over one-third of all candidates for governorships were disqualified, and nearly that many were disqualified for the Senate and House of Representatives.[41] Parties had to nominate new candidates.

It is true that former leaders dominated the new parties and that would-be new leaders frequently were not allowed to stand or their associations were barred. It is also true that each party had at its core a strong ethnic constituency, as the analysis of votes will show. The NPN, however, much more so than the old NPC, which had been a northern regional party in the First Republic, had representatives from different parts of Nigeria. New alliances had been made, which is not surprising given the fluid and personal nature of political relationships in Nigeria in the past and the injection of new elements from the military and the civil service as well as attrition of age and mortality.

How ideological were the parties that emerged? What was the nature of their support and program in class and ethnic terms? To answer these questions, we must examine an earlier period of Nigerian political life and analyze what class and ethnicity mean in contemporary Nigeria.

PARTIES, CLASS AND ETHNICITY IN NIGERIA

In the First Republic, political competition and economic strategies were not defined primarily in terms of income strata, class, or occupation.[42] The overt political struggles in Nigeria were largely defined in regional and ethnic terms.

An examination of the literature on the organization, operation and functioning of ruling political parties, their manifestos and the ideologies of party leaders in the 1950s and 1960s fails to demonstrate any translation from general statements to policies to deal with inequality. This is striking even when one examines populist leaders like Aminu Kano, Adegoke Adelabu and Chief Awolowo or when one looks at 'populist' parties operating in situations of structured inequality.

None of the major political parties that controlled national or regional governments in the 1950s and up to 1966 could be called socialist parties or parties strongly committed to equity issues. This statement covers the AG, the NNDP, the NCNC and the NPC. Even major opposition parties, some of which had distinctive social compositions — for example NEPU, which was officered by petty tradesmen, shopkeepers and craftsmen — were not organized on a class basis and did not structure their opposition primarily on a platform of redistribution.[43] NEPU can be considered a populist party.[44] The conservative NPC had a larger following among wage laborers than NEPU.[45] The NEPU party leadership was perceived as politicians who lived off politics.[46]

One of Nigeria's major political figures has been Chief Obafemi Awolowo. Chief Awolowo in his book, *The People's Republic*, criticizes capitalism.[47] The AG, which Chief Awolowo led, did not, however, function as a party of redistribution either in or out of power. The AG, more than any Nigerian political party, tried to organize the peasantry, but its backbone comprised men of the 'new class' and rising professionals, businessmen and traders.[48]

Along with Chief Awolowo, two other major leaders of parties defined themselves in populist and socialist terms: Aminu Kano and Adegoke Adelabu. Aminu Kano stressed equality of opportunity, extension of education and elimination of privilege; still, it is hard to find in Aminu Kano a translation from general goals and ideals to specific policies.[49] Aminu Kano was criticized for failing to have an effect on the military government he served as Commissioner for Health.[50]

Adegoke Adelabu was another leader who failed to translate general socialist ideas and relate them to specific Nigerian conditions.[51] He, perhaps more than any other Nigerian politician in the 1950s, focused on the need to redistribute wealth, but Adelabu's Ibadan party hardly functioned as a radical party.[52]

This civilian period of 'socialist' leaders without socialist parties can be explained by the need to appeal to conservative and traditional elements.[53] Also pursuit of personal advantage was not irrelevant to Nigerian politicians. Thus, the conditions were absent for a party politics based on class struggle at home. Some observers of Nigerian politics suggest that an elite was in the saddle during the civilian period that simply tried to mask its class interests.[54] Sklar calls it a political class.[55] But class issues did not dominate organized party politics and conservative and communal appeals were frequently successful.

So far, it has been difficult to see the development of strong, national, industrial working-class organizations. Nor have parties emerged in the 1979 elections that organized on the basis of class interests or occupational categories. Some additional survey data show why this pattern has not yet developed. Donald Morrison, analyzing a national survey of Nigerian adults carried out in 1974, argues that though the objective reality in Nigeria may be a slowing of social and occupational mobility, the openness of Nigeria's social mobility is still assumed by respondents.[56] Morrison shows, however, that there are marked and pervasive variations in perceptions of inequality among those residing in different states (and residence in a state is correlated with ethnic membership), as well as in the reality of those perceptions. He makes clear that there is an association between residence in a state and responses to views as to whether most people get a fair share in life, or whether ordinary people are better off since independence. At the same time, Morrison shows that there is little downward mobility in Nigeria and that there is a strong positive relationship between status and participation, between fathers' level of education and children's level of education and between occupation and education, so that mobility and opportunity are certainly related to starting points for individuals.

Earlier surveys had shown many of the same phenomena. Work on participation and political equality showed that Nigeria had high rates of associational membership similar to more developed societies. Membership in religious and ethnic associations was especially high, as was the percentage of those reporting political discussions in such associations.[57]

Even in urban areas, where political participation has tended to be higher than in rural areas, correcting for socioeconomic resource levels,[58] elites have found it easier to organize around communal cleavages, that is language, ethnic and neighborhood ties, than around occupational ones. Given the lack of class solidarity in Nigeria it is not surprising that strong appeals to working-class interests did not emerge in the 1979 elections. Moreover, since in Nigeria urban workers seek no alliance with the rural peasants or the urban unemployed, and trade unions protect the privileges of those who have jobs, it is difficult for urban-based workers' parties to extend their reach beyond the trade-unionized sectors.

It is true, of course, that parties that called themselves socialist, such as the Nigerian Workers' and Peasants' Vanguard Movement, either were not allowed to contest or never went through the final process before FEDECO in order to register. Thus, no explicitly workers' party contended. While elements within the UPN and the PRP saw their parties as socialist, it would be more accurate to see these parties as populist.

The PRP did call for the state to take the commanding heights of the economy, and its manifestos were more conventionally socialist than were those of the other parties, though many ideas in its programs remained highly general. It, like the other parties, avoided getting into details on the old vexing issue of revenue allocation between the states and between the Federal government and the states. The PRP tried to paint the NPN as a party committed to restoration of the powers of traditional leaders.[59]

Other issues surfaced during the campaign including specific promises to create more states, to increase defense spending and demobilization of the armed forces and to move the federal capital from Lagos to Abuja. As Panter-Brick has noted, however, the parties gave relatively little indication of their priorities.[60] Although there were programmatic distinctions between the parties, and though they campaigned all over Nigeria, their strengths were less that of programmatic appeal to economic strata than the appeals of personality and ethnic coalition building. Nonetheless, given the history of Nigeria's elections, it was no small thing that the parties tried to campaign nationally and that they were able to hold rallies and to operate outside their base areas.

ELECTORAL ANALYSES

Data. Data on the Nigerian elections of 1979 have been presented in a number of sources. The Nigerian press reported electoral results on release from FEDECO. Most of the reports in *West Africa*, the *Nigerian Tribune* and the *Daily Times* are consistent except for typo-graphical errors. FEDECO itself was required to report to the National Assembly on the elections, but the report of FEDECO provides little confidence in the statistical base or presentation of data. No overall figure for the registered electorate is provided. There are many clear errors in turnout and voting and many inconsistencies in the tabulations.[61] Indeed, the initial figures FEDECO gave for the registered electorate of 47.5 million voters seemed to many observers demographically suspect. And this figure establishes turnout rates. Of this total, 51.3 per cent were women.[62]

The analyst faced with the data problems for five different elections has many choices to make. I have tried to present summary results for the elections and to use percentage figures for presidential, gubernatorial and Senate elections to show stability, turnout and bandwagon effects. Also, the electoral data, with all their problems, allow us to see certain ethnic patterns. Without having a better sense of the relationship between census districts and constituencies, and in the absence of voter surveys, it would be extremely risky to relate voting to income and occupational patterns. The relative absence of class analysis in the pages that follow stem in large part from these difficulties. At best, the electoral analyses should be seen as tentative, though it is possible to reach conclusions on the basis of the data we have.

Turnout. Between 7 July and 11 August, Nigeria had five elections: for the Senate (7 July), for the House of Representatives (14 July), for state assemblies (21 July), for state governors (28 July) and for the president (11 August). Summary results of the elections are presented in tables 21 to 33. Seats won and percentages are given for presidential, Senate and gubernatorial elections. Only seats won are given for House of Representatives and state assembly elections since the data for those elections seem more dubious.

The staggering of elections made it possible for voters in later elections to take account of earlier tallies. Voters in the presidential elections knew what had occurred in the elections for the Senate and in subsequent elections for the House of Representatives, for state executives and for state legislators. This meant that switching votes and bargaining between parties was possible. Bandwagon effects, therefore, must be assessed.

TABLE 21: Presidential Election, August 11, 1979

State	Total Votes Cast	Waziri Ibrahim GNPP	%	Obafemi Awolowo UNP	%	Shehu Shagari NPN	%	Aminu Kano PRP	%	Nnamdi Azikiwe NPP	%
Anambra	1,209,038	20,228	(1.67)	9,063	(0.75)	163,164	(13.5)	14,500	(1.20)	1,002,083	(82.88)
Bauchi	996,683	154,218	(15.44)	29,960	(3.00)	632,989	(62.49)	143,202	(14.34)	47,314	(4.74)
Bendel	669,511	8,242	(1.23)	356,381	(53.23)	242,320	(36.2)	4,939	(0.7)	57,629	(8.6)
Benue	538,897	42,993	(7.97)	13,864	(2.57)	411,648	(76.39)	7,277	(1.35)	63,097	(11.7)
Borno	710,968	384,278	(54.04)	23,885	(3.35)	246,778	(34.71)	46,385	(6.52)	9,462	(1.35)
Cross-River	661,103	100,105	(15.41)	77,775	(11.76)	425,815	(64.40)	6,737	(1.01)	50,671	(7.66)
Gongola	639,138	217,914	(34.09)	138,561	(21.67)	227,057	(35.52)	27,750	(4.34)	27,856	(4.35)
Imo	1,153,355	34,616	(3.00)	7,335	(0.64)	101,516	(8.80)	10,252	(0.59)	999,636	(86.67)
Kaduna	1,382,642	190,936	(13.80)	92,382	(6.68)	596,302	(43.12)	437,771	(31.66)	65,321	(4.72)
Kano	1,220,691	18,482	(1.54)	14,873	(1.23)	243,423	(19.94)	932,803	(76.41)	11,082	(0.91)
Kwara	354,605	20,251	(5.71)	140,006	(39.48)	190,142	(53.62)	2,376	(0.67)	1,830	(0.52)
Lagos	828,414	3,943	(0.48)	681,762	(82.30)	59,515	(7.18)	3,874	(0.47)	79,320	(9.57)
Niger	383,347	63,273	(16.50)	14,155	(3.67)	287,072	(74.88)	14,555	(3.77)	4,292	(1.11)
Ogun	744,668	3,974	(0.53)	689,655	(92.61)	46,358	(6.23)	2,338	(0.31)	2,343	(0.32)
Ondo	1,369,849	3,561	(0.26)	1,294,666	(94.51)	57,361	(4.19)	2,509	(0.18)	11,752	(0.86)
Oyo	1,396,547	8,029	(0.57)	1,197,983	(85.78)	177,999	(12.75)	4,804	(0.32)	7,732	(0.55)
Plateau	548,405	37,400	(6.82)	29,029	(5.29)	190,458	(34.73)	21,852	(3.98)	269,666	(49.17)
Rivers	687,951	15,025	(2.18)	71,114	(12.33)	499,846	(72.65)	3,212	(0.46)	98,754	(14.35)
Sokoto	1,348,697	359,021	(26.61)	34,102	(2.52)	898,094	(66.58)	44,977	(3.33)	12,503	(0.92)
Totals	16,846,491	1,686,489	(10.0)	4,916,551	(29.2)	5,688,857	(33.8)	1,732,113	(10.3)	2,822,523	(16.8)

Source: Keith Panter-Brick, "Nigeria: The 1979 Elections," in _Afrika Spectrum_, vol. 3, 1979, p. 330.

TABLE 22:

Senate Seats Won by Each Party, by State, July 7, 1979

State	NPN	UPN	NPP	GNPP	PRP
Anambra	-	-	5	-	-
Bauchi	5	-	-	-	-
Bendel	1	4	-	-	-
Benue	5	-	-	-	-
Borno	1	-	-	4	-
Cross River	3	-	-	2	-
Gongola	1	2	-	2	-
Imo	-	-	5	-	-
Kaduna	3	-	-	-	2
Kano	-	-	-	-	5
Kwara	3	2	-	-	-
Lagos	-	5	-	-	-
Niger	5	-	-	-	-
Ogun	-	5	-	-	-
Ondo	-	5	-	-	-
Oyo	-	5	-	-	-
Plateau	1	-	4	-	-
Rivers	3	-	2	-	-
Sokoto	5	-	-	-	-
Total	36	28	16	8	7

Note: Dash (-) indicates no seats won.

Source: Compiled by Author.

TABLE 23:

Gubernatorial Offices Won by Each Party

State	Party
Anambra	NPP
Bauchi	NPN
Bendel	UPN
Benue	NPN
Borno	GNPP
Cross River	NPN
Gongola	GNPP
Imo	NPP
Kaduna	PRP
Kano	PRP
Kwara	NPN
Lagos	UPN
Niger	NPN
Ogun	UPN
Ondo	UPN
Oyo	UPN
Plateau	NPP
Rivers	NPN
Sokoto	NPN

Turnout did go up from 12 million, which was only about 25 per cent of the 47.5 million registered electorate, for the Senate elections of 7 July to 16.8 million voters for the presidential elections of 11 August. The 28 July gubernatorial elections had 15.5 million voters. The turnout for the 7 July Senate elections was poor. There were heavy rains over much of the southern part of the country, and the election occurred during the Ramadan. Also, many administrative problems beset the Senate elections. Although there were 125,000 voting places and 125,000 presiding officers (FEDECO employed 400,000 people), it was still hard for individuals to find their names on the register at their polling place, and polling places were sometimes closed or out of ballots.[63]

The list of registered voters may have been heavily inflated. Some estimates show as much as 20 per cent to 50 per cent inflation. The total of about 47.5 million registered voters struck some observers as demographically unlikely. The problem, however, is the lack of any reliable Nigerian census. The 1973 census held under General Gowon was set aside by General Mohammed. The 1963 census, which is the one used as a base by the Nigerian government for statistical purposes, is itself suspect. It was a rerun of the 1962 census which was clearly inaccurate. Moreover, people were registered for the 1979

TABLE 24:

Seats Won in the House of Represenatiives
by Each Party, by State, July 14, 1979

State	Number of seats	Party				
		GNPP	UPN	NPN	PRP	NPP
Anambra	30	-	-	3	-	27
Bauchi	20	1	-	18	-	1
Bendel	20	1	12	6	-	2
Benue	19	-	-	18	-	1
Borno	24	22	-	2	-	-
Cross River	28	4	2	22	-	-
Gongola	21	8	7	5	-	1
Imo	30	-	-	5	-	28
Kaduna	33	1	1	19	10	2
Kano	46	-	-	7	39	-
Kwara	14	1	5	8	-	-
Lagos	12	-	12	-	-	-
Niger	10	-	-	10	-	-
Ogun	12	-	12	-	-	-
Ondo	22	-	22	-	-	-
Oyo	42	-	38	4	-	-
Plateau	16	-	-	3	-	13
Rivers	14	-	-	10	-	4
Sokoto	37	6	0	31	-	-
Total	450	43	111	168	49	79
Percent		9.8	24.7	37.4	10.9	17.4

Source: West Africa, August 27, 1979, No. 3241, p. 1572.

Note: Dash (-) indicates no seats won.

State Assembly Results, by State, July 21, 1979

State	Number of seats	Party				
		GNPP	UPN	NPN	PRP	NPP
Anambra	87	1	-	13	-	73
Bauchi	60	9	-	45	2	4
Bendel	60	-	34	22	-	4
Benue	57	6	-	48	-	3
Borno	72	59	-	11	2	-
Cross River	84	16	7	58	-	3
Gongola	63	25	18	15	1	4
Imo	90	2	-	9	-	79
Kaduna	99	10	3	64	16	6
Kano	138	3	1	11	123	-
Kwara	42	2	15	25	-	-
Lagos	36	-	36	-	-	-
Niger	30	2	-	28	-	-
Ogun	36	-	36	-	-	-
Ondo	68	-	65	1	-	-
Oyo	125	-	117	9	-	-
Plateau	48	3	-	10	-	35
Rivers	42	-	1	26	-	15
Sokoto	111	19	-	92	-	-
Total	1,347	157	333	487	144	226
Percent		11.8	24.7	35.2	10.8	18.8

Source: West Africa, August 27, 1979, No. 3241, p. 1572.

Note: Dash (-) indicates no seat won.

TABLE 26:

Voter Participation by State in Senate, Gubernatorial and Presidential Elections

State	No. of Registered Voters	July 7 Total Vote	July 28 Total Vote	August 11 Total Vote	August 11 Participation %	July 7 - August 11 % Increase	July 28 - August 11 % Increase
Anambra	2,601,548	953,496	1,016,065	1,209,038	46.5	26.8	18.99
Bauchi	2,084,059	708,342	824,022	998,683	47.92	40.99	21.20
Bendel	2,376,410	668,103	707,957	669,511	28.17	0.21	-(5.43)
Benue	1,563,413	467,184	514,072	538,879	34.47	15.34	4.83
Borno	2,753,400	518,604	690,887	710,968	25.82	37.09	2.91
Cross River	2,442,227	622,096	710,431	661,103	27.07	6.27	-(6.94)
Gongola	2,284,500	600,836	650,725	639,138	27.98	6.37	-(1.78)
Imo	3,465,198	1,013,740	1,090,893	1,153,355	33.28	13.77	5.73
Kaduna	3,420,839	997,028	1,241,437	1,382,712	40.42	38.68	11.38
Kano	5,174,447	967,198	1,151,241	1,195,248	23.10	23.58	3.82
Kwara	1,085,163	314,068	362,643	354,605	32.68	12.85	-(2.22)
Lagos	1,811,973	534,077	707,666	825,364	45.72	55.10	17.06
Niger	1,040,753	269,301	335,202	383,347	36.83	42.35	14.36
Ogun	1,603,004	413,441	687,504	744,668	46.45	80.14	8.31
Ondo	2,422,714	562,456	1,062,951	1,369,849	56.54	143.55	28.87
Oyo	4,520,120	977,234	1,131,431	1,396,547	30.90	42.91	32.27
Plateau	1,618,378	455,398	585,568	548,405	33.89	20.42	-(6.35)
Rivers	1,409,472	306,676	805,330	687,951	48.81	124.33	-(14.58)
Sokoto	3,756,139	964,974	1,224,041	1,349,593	35.93	70.95	10.26
Total	47,433,757	12,314,252	15,550,016	16,821,964	35.46	36.61	8.53

Note: July 7, senatorial elections; July 28, gubernatorial elections; August 11, presidential elections

Source: Author's compilation from FEDECO Data.

TABLE 27:

Party Shares of the Vote, by State
(percent)

State	Leading Party	Share of vote in Gubernatorial Election	Share of vote in Senatorial Election	Share of vote in Presidential Election	Increase from Senate to Presidential Vote
Anambra	NPP	76.0	73.4	82.8	9.4
Bauchi	NPN	53.2	45.6	62.5	16.9
Bendel	UPN	54.6	46.0	53.2	7.2
Benue	NPN	78.7	70.9	76.4	5.5
Borno	GNPP	55.8	53.9	54.0	0.1
Cross River	NPN	60.3	50.2	64.4	14.2
Imo	NPP	80.8	74.0	86.7	12.7
Kaduna	NPN	44.4	38.4	43.1	4.7
	PRP	45.2			
Kano	PRP	79.0	70.6	76.4	5.8
Kwara	NPN	51.9	49.1	53.6	4.5
Lagos	UPN	79.0	80.2	82.3	2.1
Niger	NPN	74.1	65.2	74.9	9.7
Ogun	UPN	93.6	87.4	92.6	5.2
Ondo	UPN	94.8	89.2	94.5	5.3
Oyo	UPN	84.4	77.8	85.8	8.0
Plateau	NPP	62.1	48.4	49.2	0.8
Rivers	NPN	76.9	50.0	72.7	20.7
Sokoto	NPN	62.8	60.2	66.6	6.4
Gongola	GNPP	47.6	37.2	34.1	3.1

Source: _West Africa_, September 10, 1979, no. 3243, p. 1633. For senatorial and Presidential elections. For gubernatorial elections my own collection from FEDECO reports.

PCEN-F*

TABLE 28:

Percentage of Total Vote in Each State by Party

State	GNPP July 7	GNPP July 28	GNPP Aug. 11	NPN July 7	NPN July 28	NPN Aug. 11	NPP July 7	NPP July 28	NPP Aug. 11	PRP July 7	PRP July 28	PRP Aug. 11	UNP July 7	UNP July 28	UNP Aug. 11
Anambra	1	2.1	1.7	22	18.4	13.5	74	76	82.9	2	2.8	1.2	1	0.7	0.7
Bauchi	27	25.3	15.4	45	53.2	62.5	6	2.3	4.8	18	16.1	14.3	4	3.1	3.0
Bendel	6	-	1.3	38	36.4	36.2	9	8.2	8.6	a	0.8	0.7	47	54.6	53.2
Benue	10	-	8	71	78.7	76.4	16	17.2	11.7	a	1.8	1.3	3	2.3	2.6
Borno	54	55.8	54	36	35.5	34.7	a	-	1.4	6	3.9	6.5	4	2.8	3.4
Cross River	26	21.7	15.1	50	60.3	64.4	11	11.4	7.7	-	-	1	13	6.6	11.8
Gongola	37	47.6	34.1	34	34.6	35.5	3	4.1	4.4	5	2.4	4.3	21	11.2	21.7
Imo	10	5.4	3	14	11.2	8.8	74	80.8	86.7	1	1.9	0.9	1	0.7	0.6
Kaduna	23	10.4	13.8	34	44.4	43.1	6	-	4.7	28	45.2	31.7	9	-	6.7
Kano	3	1.3	1.5	24	19	20.4	-	-	0.9	71	79	75.9	2	0.7	1.3
Kwara	11	-	5.7	49	51.9	53.6	a	-	0.5	a	-	0.7	40	48.1	39.5
Lagos	3	-	0.5	7	6.8	7.2	10	13.6	9.6	a	0.6	0.5	80	79	82.3
Niger	27	19.6	16.5	65	74.1	74.9	a	-	1.1	3	3.1	3.8	5	3.1	3.7
Ogun	a	-	0.6	12	6.4	6.2	a	-	0.3	-	-	0.3	88	93.6	92.6
Ondo	1	-	0.3	9	4.6	4.2	1	0.6	0.8	-	0	0.2	89	94.8	94.5
Oyo	1	0.6	0.6	21	14.4	12.7	a	0.5	0.6	a	-	0.3	78	84.4	85.8
Plateau	9	3.3	6.8	34	29.8	34.7	49	62.1	49.2	4	3	4	4	0.8	5.3
Rivers	15	0.9	2.1	50	76.9	72.7	28	21.1	14.4	a	0.3	0.5	7	0.8	10.3
Sokoto	33	34.5	26.6	59	62.8	66.6	-	-	0.9	4	2.7	3.4	4	-	2.5
Total	14.7	11.6	10.0	33.1	34.7	33.8	17.4	16.6	16.7	10.2	11.6	10.3	24.2	25.5	29.2

Note: July 7, senatorial elections
July 28, gubernatorial elections
August 11, presidential elections
Dash (-) indicates less than .1   a indicates less than 0.5 percent.

TABLE 29:

Seats Won and Total Votes in Gubernatorial and Senatorial Elections, by Party

Party	Seats Won		Total Votes		Percentage of Total Vote		No. of States 25% of Vote	
	Sena-torial elections	Guber-natorial elections	Sena-torial elections	Guber-natorial elections	Sena-torial elections	Guber-natorial elections	Sena-torial elections	Guber-natorial elections
NPN	36	7	4,077,380	5,383,425	33.1	34.7	12	12
UPN	28	5	2,976,488	3,952,744	24.2	25.5	6	6
NPP	16	3	2,144,308	2,568,170	17.4	16.6	4	3
GNPP	8	2	1,861,326	1,805,257	14.7	11.6	6	4
PRP	7	2	1,254,790	1,790,420	10.2	11.6	2	2

Note: July 7, senatorial elections; July 28, gubernatorial elections.

Source: Complied by Author from FEDECO reports.

TABLE 30:

Distribution of Seats in Legislative and Gubernatorial Elections
and Votes in Presidential Elections
(percentage of totals)

	GNPP	UPN	NPN	PRP	NPP
Senate (seats)	8.4	29.5	37.9	7.4	16.0
House of Represenatitive (seats)	9.6	24.7	⁻37.4	10.9	17.6
State Assemblies (states)	11.7	24.7	36.2	10.7	16.8
State Governors (states)	10.5	26.3	36.8	10.5	15.8
President (vote)	10.0	29.2	33.8	10.3	16.8

Source: S. Keith Panter-Brick, table 4, Nigeria: The 1979 Elections, *Afrika Spectrum* (Hamburg) No. 3, January 14, 1979.

elections in places where they were 'ordinarily residents'. This was defined as the place where one usually sleeps or lives. People may have been registered both in their place of origin and in the place to which they had moved. No names or addresses were recorded on voter cards. People were allowed to vote even if not on the polling register, provided that identities and residence were established.

Voter interest also may simply have been less than had earlier been anticipated. An opinion poll conducted by Lagos University two

TABLE 31:

Increase in Turnout Related to Increase in Leading
Party's Vote from Senatorial to Presidential Elections, by State

State	Increase in Turnout	Increase in Leading party's vote
Anambra	256,442	302,926 (NPP)
Bauchi	290,116	300,597 (NPN)
Benue	69,179	78,681 (NPN)
Kano	234,170	249,536 (PRP)
Kwara	40,527	36,860 (NPN)
Lagos	294,337	253,189 (UPN)
Niger	114,046	111,475 (NPN)
Ogun	481,167	459,244 (UPN)
Ondo	807,193	793,144 (UPN)
Oyo	421,113	439,287 (UPN)
Rivers	381,238	346,492 (NPN)
Sokoto	402,393	326,532 (NPN)

Source: S. Keith Panter-Brick, Table 5, "Nigeria: The 1979 Elections,"
 Afrika Spectrum, January, 1979.

Note: These figures are slightly different from Panter-Brick's in Table 5,
 "Voter Participation by State," For Ogun State Panter-Brick has an
 initial turnout of only 263,501 or 16% and I use a figure of 413,441
 or 26%. Borno, Cross River, Gongola, Imo, Kaduna, and Plateau States
 have been excluded in this table.

months before the election revealed a low level of political awareness
and interest among three local government areas of the Lagos
metropolitan area, places where one could expect relatively high
interest and participation. Only 58 per cent of the registered voters
polled in Mushin, Shomolu and Lagos mainland indicated some
interest in electioneering; and 42 per cent indicated apathy. The same
42 per cent indicated ignorance concerning the five parties that were
campaigning. Interest was correlated with socioeconomic status.[64]

The improvement in turnout from the earlier to the later elections
may be partially attributed to better administration by FEDECO.
There was also better weather in the south, and the presidential

TABLE 32:

Results of Kaduna State Elections for Senate, House of Representatives, and State Governor, by Party

Election		GNPP	NPN	NPP	PRP	UPN
Senate:	Votes won	232,204[a]	339,409[a]	61,807	278,514	85,094
	% of vote	23.3	34.0	6.2	27.9	8.5
	Seats won	-	3	-	2	-
House of Represen- tatives[b]	Votes won	249,691	485,822	50,501	357,972	68,530
	% of vote	20.6	40.1	4.2	29.5	5.6
	Seats won	1	19	2	10	2
State Governor	Votes won	129,580	551,252	-	560,605	-
	% of vote	10.4	44.4	-	45.2	-

Note: Dash (-) indicates no seats won or below 10% of vote.

[a]Panter-Brick gives a GNPP vote of 233,824 and an NPN Senate vote of 410,888. I have used different figures from FEDECO sources.

[b]Vote totals based on 32 of 33 constituencies.

Source: S. Keith Panter-Brick, "Nigeria: The 1979 Elections," Afrika Spectrum (Hamburg) No. 3, January 14, 1979, Table 7.

elections attracted more attention. Deliberate inflation of votes in at least some locales is also possible. The NPN's huge increases in its vote from the Rivers state seem improbable, to cite only one case. Gubernatorial turnout was higher than presidential turnout in six of the nineteen states.

Bandwagon Effects. The NPN share of the vote remained almost constant between the Senate and the presidential elections, 33.1 per cent of the vote and 33.8 per cent respectively. The PRP and the NPP also stayed almost the same. The PRP received 10.2 per cent in the Senate and 10.3 per cent in the presidential elections. The NPP vote declined from 17.4 per cent to 16.7 per cent. The GNPP saw a real decline from 14.7 per cent to 10.0 per cent and the UPN vote increased from 24.2 per cent to 29.2 per cent, largely by increasing turnout in its core areas of the Yoruba-speaking states.[65] Although no national

TABLE 33:

Results of Gongola State Elections for President,
State Governor, and Senate, by Party

Election	GNPP	UPN	NPN	PRP	NPP	Total
President						
Votes won	217,914	138,561	227,057	27,750	27,856	639,138
% of vote	(34.1)	(21.7)	(35.6)	(4.3)	(4.3)	
State Governor						
Votes won	309,775	72,952	225,310	15,973	26,715	650,725
% of vote	(47.6)	(11.2)	(34.6)	(2.5)	(4.1)	
Senate						
Votes won	223,121	124,707	203,226	30,708	17,830	599,592
% of vote	(37.2)	(20.8)	(33.9)	(5.10)	(3.0)	

Source: Panter-Brick, table 8.

bandwagon effect was perceptible in the presidential election, regional and state bandwagons tended to increase the vote of the party that had emerged as dominant in a state.

Martin Dent has shown that in every state except Gongola, the party receiving the highest vote in the Senate election increased its share of the vote in the presidential election.[66]

The average swing toward the leading party in 18 states was 7.7 per cent. In Gongola, the NPN was close to the GNPP in the Senate elections, receiving 33.8 per cent to the GNPP's 37.2 per cent. In the presidential election, the GNPP won 34.1 per cent and the NPN won 35.6 per cent. Dent argues that the GNPP's small lead in the Senate elections was overcome by the national swing to the NPN in the presidential election in Gongola. The problem with this argument is that in the gubernatorial elections the GNPP won 47.6 per cent to the NPN's 34.6 per cent of the vote. A sizable increase from Senate to gubernatorial vote for the GNPP could not be held in the presidential election in Gongola state.

In 18 out of 19 states, the leading party in the Senate elections increased its vote in the gubernatorial elections. (In Lagos state the

UPN vote declined from 80.2 per cent to 79.0 per cent.) Thus, bandwagon effects occurred in moving from Senate to gubernatorial elections. Parties that were strong in a state increased their vote in the elections most important to the states, those for governors. This was even true in Kaduna state where the NPN increased its vote after the Senate elections though it narrowly lost the governor's race to the PRP. If we compare gubernatorial percentages with presidential ones, we find that the leading party increased its vote in nine states and decreased its vote in ten states. The movement was frequently a narrow one. The bandwagon, if there was one, was hardly cumulative. Indeed, the large movement seemed to go from Senate to gubernatorial races with a smaller movement in either direction to the presidential race.

Increases in votes for a party come from switching and from increased turnout. We have seen the general tendency for the leading party to increase its vote, especially from senatorial to gubernatorial and from senatorial to presidential elections, less so from gubernatorial to presidential. The additional votes seem to have come more from increased turnout than from switching.[67] In 11 states, the number of additional votes from senatorial to presidential elections given to the leading party was within 15 per cent, above or below, of the additional numbers of voters (see table 31).[68]

Competitiveness of Elections. There were very few highly competitive elections for the Senate. Of the 95 races, only seven were close, with the second candidate within 3 per cent of the winner. Although there were five parties running, not every party participated in every race. The PRP participated in about half the contests, and the NPP participated in 50 out of 95. One candidate received a majority of the total votes in 65 races. In 23 races, a candidate had no majority, but the races were not close. One party won 70 per cent or more of the votes in eight states. In eleven states, a single party swept all five races. In only one state, Gongola, did as many as three parties win seats.

In the gubernatorial races, the winning candidates won at least 74 per cent of the votes in 10 out of 19 contests. In seven other races, a candidate won a majority of the votes, though in Kwara state, where only two candidates ran, the winning candidate received 51.9 per cent. In Gongola state, the winning candidate won 47.6 per cent, and the runner-up received 34.6 per cent. In Kaduna state, a close and unexpected result occurred. Malam Balarabe Musa, from the left wing of the PRP, won 45.2 per cent, whereas Alhaji Lawal Kaita of the NPN won 44.4 per cent (see table 32). More than half of the PRP's nationwide half-million increase in votes after the senatorial elections came from Kaduna state. On the basis of previous elections, the NPN candidate had expected to win.

Although the NPN increased its total vote by over 200,000, the PRP's doubling of its votes resulted in its victory. The doubling of the PRP vote was accounted for in good part by the withdrawal of the UPN and NPP candidates. The Kaduna state victory for Musa led to a paralysis in state government since the NPN controlled Kaduna's state legislature with 64 out of 99 seats. The governor was unable to appoint a cabinet. Also, the PRP governors of Kaduna state and Kano state split with the national leaders of the PRP, Alhaji Aminu Kano and S. G. Ikoku, and started to make common cause with the UPN governors. The Kaduna state election turned out to be highly consequential for the country as well as from the north. For the most part, however, the gubernatorial elections were not close contests.

The other competitive state election was in Gongola state. Here the GNPP did much better in the gubernatorial race than it had done in the senatorial election or was to do in the presidential election (see table 33).

Regionalism and Ethnicity. Even a cursory glance at the electoral data shows how heavily dependent each party was on its core constituency. The UPN won 20 of its 28 Senate seats in the 4 states of the old Western Region – Ondo, Oyo, Ogun and Lagos. Each of these states is overwhelmingly Yoruba. The UPN won four more seats in Bendel state, parts of which have some Yoruba speakers, though non-Yoruba UPN candidates won in non-Yoruba areas. Old party alliances were more important than ethnicity in Bendel state. Yorubas won two seats in Kwara state which has a significant Yoruba population. The GNPP won half of its eight Senate seats in its home area, Borno, and two more in the contiguous Gongola state. Two GNPP Senate seats were won in Cross River, where there are no significant numbers of Kanuris, but where the GNPP state chairman was strong. The same pattern holds for NPP and PRP Senate seats. The PRP won five seats in its home Kano state and two more in contiguous Kaduna state. In both states old hostilities against the Sokoto emirate

FIGURE 2:
Distribution of Votes for Presidential Candidates and Party Affiliations
of State Governors

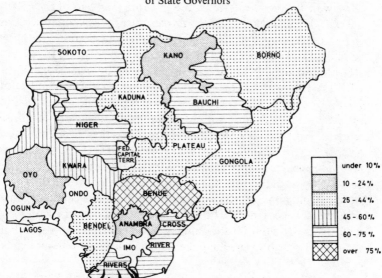

Map 1: Distribution of vote for Shehu Shagari (NPN).

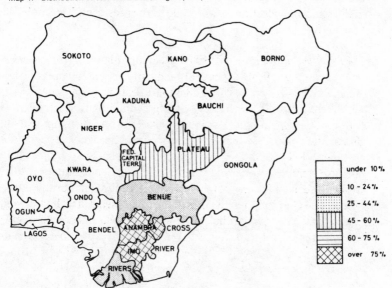

Map 2: Distribution of vote for Nnamdi Azikiwe (NPP).

FIGURE 2 (continued):

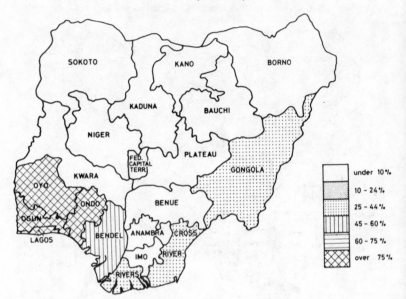

Map 3:   Distribution of vote for Obafemi Awolowo (UPN).

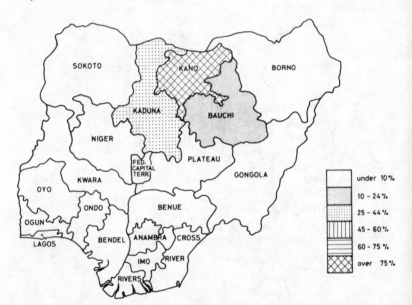

Map 4:   Distribution of vote for Aminu Kano (PRP).

FIGURE 2 (continued):

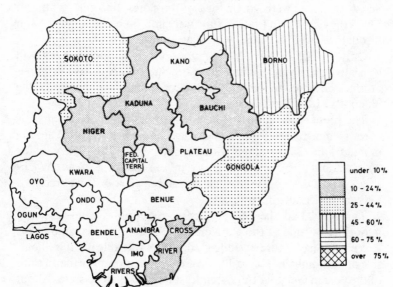

Map 5: Distribution of vote for Waziri Ibrahim (GNPP).

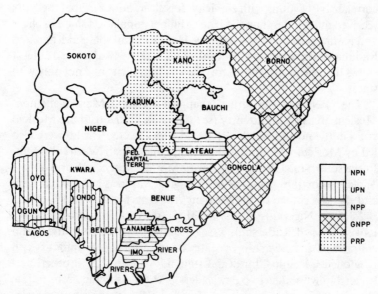

Map 6: Party affiliation of State Governors.

prevail, and the former NEPU was strong. Of the NPP's sixteen Senate seats, ten were won in the two Ibo states, Imo and Anambra. The NPP victories in Plateau state were not Ibo based but were won through electoral alliances with Plateau leaders.

Only the NPN showed strong support throughout the country in legislative elections, winning State Assembly seats in seventeen out of nineteen states and coming in first or second in all but six of the ninety-five races for the Senate.

The presidential results tell the same tale. Awolowo's vote was overwhelming in the Yoruba-speaking states. He also pulled heavily in Bendel and Kwara states with Yoruba populations. The vote for Azikiwe and the NPP was heavy in Ibo-speaking areas. Waziri Ibrahim's GNPP vote was widely spread but a majority was received only in the Kanuri Borno state.

The NPN had the broadest base of support, winning heavy majorities outside of the old Northern Region in Rivers and Cross River states (see figure 2). Indeed, the NPN was able to do well outside of the dominant Hausa-Fulani areas, by getting more than a third of the vote in Gongola state, Bendel state, and Plateau state. About one third of the population of Plateau state is Hausa-Fulani, and without knowing the constituency breakdown of the vote, I cannot correlate NPN voting with ethnicity. It is clear, however, that the NPN received more votes than the Hausa-Fulani population share in Niger and Kwara states and less than the Hausa-Fulani share in Kano and Kaduna states since the PRP took votes in those two states. Table 34 shows that the parties' votes correlate with ethnicity and not only with states.

The NPN was able to draw its support from both Moslem and non-Moslem areas of the country (see figure 3). It had to share Moslem votes in the north with the PRP and with the GNPP who were also led by Moslems, Mallam Aminu Kano and Alhaji Waziri Ibrahim. In the south, the UPN did well with Moslem voters in Yorubaland. Table 35 shows, by state, the percentage of Moslems in the population and the percentage of the Moslem vote won by each party.

Islam in Nigeria is not monolithic. In the north, Moslems have looked toward leaderships associated with the Sokoto and Kano emirates. The leadership of states is not always coterminous with religious leaderships, but Kano state has had Moslem brotherhood leadership with links to party leaders.[69] Moslems in the north follow Tijaniyya and Qadiriyya brotherhoods. In the southwest of Nigeria,

TABLE 34:

Major Ethnic Groups by Region and State
(percentages in parentheses)

States	Ethnic Groups
Pre-1967 Regions	
Lagos	Yoruba (80), Hausa (4), Ibo (5), Ibibio (4) Tiv (2), Bini (2)
Old Western Region	
Oyo	Yoruba (94), Ibo (2), Bini (2)
Ogun	Yoruba (96), Ibo (3)
Ondo	Yoruba (96), Bini (2)
Old Mid-Western Region	
Bendel	Etsako (44), Bini (25), Ibo (5), Itsekiri (2) Urhobo (20), Ijaw (1)
Old Eastern Region	
Imo	Ibo (99.5)
Anambra	Ibo (96), Bini (2), Yoruba (1.5)
Rivers	Ibibio (1), Ijaw (94), Yoruba (1.5)
Cross River	Ibibio (98)
Old Northern Region	
Kwara	Yoruba (67), Igala ( ), Igbira ( )
Plateau	Hausa (23), Fulani (9), Tiv (8), Ibo (2), Angas (9), Idoma (16), Yoruba (2), Warjara (4), Gwandara (9), Gbari (7), Kanuri (7)
Benue	Tiv (59), Idoma (34)
Gongola[a]	
Borno[b]	Hausa (46), Fulani (2), Kanuri (44)
Bauchi	Hausa (71), Fulani (26), Ibo (3)
Kano	Hausa (71), Fulani (13), Ibo (3), Kanuri (4)
Kaduna	Hausa (86), Fulani (5)
Niger	Hausa (31), Fulani (9), Gbari (18), Yoruba (14), Nupe (4), Tiv (4), Ibo (3), Igala (2)
Sokoto[a]	

[a] No data from sample

[b] The eastern half of Borno State, which is largely Kanuri, was not surveyed.

Source: Donald Morrison, "Inequalities and Social Rewards: Realities and Perceptions in Nigeria," in The Political Economy of Income Distribution in Nigeria, ed., Henry Bienen and Vremudia Diejomaoh (New York: Holmes and Meier, 1981).

among the Yoruba, there are sizable Moslem communities. The Ahmadiyya brotherhood is strong in addition to Tijaniyya and Qadiryya, though the Ahmadiyya has been banned as un-Islamic.

There has been conjecture whether Yoruba Moslems would become more northern oriented. In 1962 certain Yoruba factions thought it crucial to make alliance with the NPC and the north. Some who thought this were anti-Awolowo; some were Moslem. The NNDP leader Chief Akintola was Christian, and important leaders of the AG were Moslem, for example, Alhaji Adegbenro who was Premier of the Western Region. Some pro-NPC Yoruba were conservatives

FIGURE 3

Cross-tabulation of the Moslem Population with Votes for the NPN
in the Presidential Election, by State

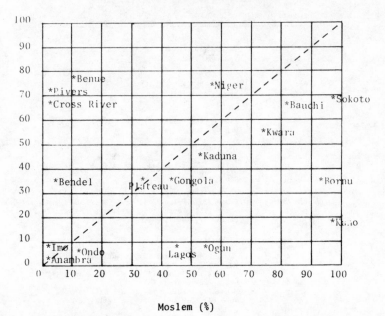

Moslem (%)

Source: John Paden, "Islam, Constitutional Change, and Politics
in Nigeria," draft paper, October, 1979.

who feared domination in the south by radical Ibo and Yoruba
groups. Still, the split between AG and NNDP did have a base in sub-
Yoruba ethnic distinctions, for Awolowo was supported by the
Yoruba of Ijebu, and Akintola drew support from the Yoruba of Oyo.
Oyo Yoruba and the people around the city of Ibadan tend to be more
heavily Moslem than in Ijebu areas. Many politicians who deserted
Awolowo in the early 1960s, however, were not Moslems.

In the 1979 elections, Awolowo did better in Ogun and Ondo states
than he did in Oyo state, but he still received 85 per cent of the vote
in the Oyo state presidential balloting. He received less in Lagos state,
but Lagos state has larger non-Yoruba populations than the other
Yoruba states. Awolowo was also able to carry Ibadan overwhelmingly,
where he had never done well before in competitive elections.

The Yoruba is the one large ethnic-language group comprising large

TABLE 35:

Percentage of Moslems in Each State and Votes, by Party

State	Moslems	% NPN	% GNPP	% PRP	% UPN	% NPP
Sokoto	97.6	66.5	26.1	3.3	2.5	0.9
Kano	97.4	19.9	1.5	76.4	1.2	0.9
Borno	93.1	34.7	54.0	6.5	3.4	1.4
Bauchi	80.6	62.5	15.4	14.3	3.0	4.7
Kwara	75.2	53.6	5.7	0.7	39.5	0.5
Oyo	62.4	12.8	0.6	0.3	85.8	0.6
Niger	59.7	74.9	16.5	4.0	3.7	1.1
Kaduna	56.4	43.1	13.8	31.7	6.7	4.7
Ogun	54.3	6.2	0.5	6.2	92.1	0.3
Lagos	44.3	7.2	0.5	0.5	82.3	9.6
Gongola	34.1	35.5	34.1	4.3	21.7	4.4
Plateau	25.7	34.7	6.8	4.0	5.3	49.2
Ondo	12.3	4.2	0.3	0.2	94.5	0.9
Benue	11.3	76.4	7.9	1.4	2.6	11.7
Bendel	7.4	36.2	1.2	0.7	53.2	8.6
Rivers	0.2	72.7	2.2	0.5	10.3	14.4
Cross River	0.1	64.4	15.1	1.0	11.8	7.7
Imo	0.1	8.8	3.0	0.9	0.6	86.7
Anambra	0.6	13.5	1.7	1.2	0.8	82.9

numbers of both Christian and Moslem voters. Without survey data correlating religion and ethnicity with voting among the Yoruba, it is not possible to parcel out religion and ethnicity.[70] Data do show, however, that Awolowo won overwhelmingly in areas of Yorubaland where there are large numbers of Moslems.

It would be difficult to parcel out religion from leadership, ethnicity and historic orientations in the vote for PRP, NPN and GNPP. The GNPP received support from Kanuris in Borno, but they are over-whelmingly Moslem, too. The PRP received support in the old NEPU strongholds in Kano and Kaduna states. The NPN had to split Moslem votes in the north with the PRP and GNPP. The NPN was also able to win in non-Moslem areas where minority peoples, especially in Rivers and Cross River states, feared their Ibo neighbors and wanted to make an alliance with a possible winner who was not physically close to them. The broad appeal of the NPN was in part a consequence of Ijaw and Ibibio aversion to their Ibo neighbors.

The Election of 1959 and 1979. There are important differences between the elections of 1959 and those of 1979.[71] One cannot simply regard the UPN as the reincarnation of the AG, the NPP as the revived NCNC, the PRP as NEPU 20 years later, and the NPN as the Hausa-Fulani NPC. The personal networks and factional alignments were different. Each party was, however, led by someone who had been either a leader or, in the case of Shagari, an important figure in the

TABLE 36:

Votes Won by Each Party in 1959 Parliamentary and
1979 Presidential Elections by Region

(percent)

Region	NPC (NPN)	AG (UPN)	NEPU/NCNC (PRP/NPP)
Eastern	-	23.1	64.6
Western	1.7	49.5	40.2
Lagos (city)	0.3	43.8	55.9
Northern	61.2	17.2	16.1

Region	1979 Election			
	NPN	UPN	PRP	NPP
Eastern	33.61	4.67	0.98	60.74
Western	14.91	83.78	0.63	0.68
Lagos (city)	7.22	82.69	0.47	9.6
Northern	55.46	12.51	23.92	8.11

Source: C. S. Whitaker, "Second Beginnings: The New Political Framework in Nigeria," testimony before the Subcommittee on Africa of the House Foreign Affairs Committee, U.S. House of Representatives, September 26, 1979.

Note: Dash (-) indicates less than .1%.

old party. The ethnic bases and appeals were retained, so let us assume that the new parties were lineal descendants from the old. Table 36 shows how the parties fared in the 1979 presidential and in the 1959 parliamentary elections.

The UPN in 1979 improved its share over 1959, since the old NCNC had had support in the Western Region, especially around Ibadan and Ife. There were probably more Ibos in Lagos as a share of the total population in 1959 than in 1979, as many Ibos migrated before and during the Civil War. The UPN vote improved over the AG vote in Lagos. Yoruba voters rallied around Awolowo in places where he did not have support in earlier elections. The UPN was less able to compete in the east and in the north than the AG had been able to do during the 1959 elections. Awolowo thought in 1959 that he could win enough votes in the north and east to form a government. Perhaps he thought this again in 1979, but he was even more incorrect in 1979 than in 1959.

The NEPU and the NCNC had been allies in 1959. In 1979, both

TABLE 37:

Seats Won by Each Party in Elections to the House of Representatives, 1959 and 1979
(percent)

1959 Election

Region	NPC (NPN)	AG (UPN)	NEPU/NCNC (PRP/NPP)		
Eastern	-	19.44	80.56		
Western	-	61.11	38.89		
Lagos (city)	-	33.33	66.67		
Northern	80.24	14.97	4.79		

1979 Elections Excluding the GNPP

Region	NPN	UPN	PRP/NPP	PRP	NPP
Eastern	38.14	2.06	59.79	-	59.79
Western	16.28	83.72	-	-	-
Lagos (city)	-	100	-	-	-
Northern	55.45	11.85	32.70	23.22	9.48

1979 Elections Including the GNPP

Region	NPN	UPN	PRP	NPP	GNPP
Eastern	36.63	1.98	-	57.43	3.96
Western	16.28	83.72	-	-	-
Lagos (city)	-	100	-	-	-
Northern	46.8	6	19.6	8	15.6

Note: Dash (-) indicates less than 1%.
Source: Whitaker, "Second Beginnings."

parties were thrown back on their core areas, though the NPP was able to do well in parts of the Middle Belt areas, especially in Plateau state. The NPP share of the vote declined in the non-Ibo areas of the old Eastern Region. The NPP did not do well in Rivers or Cross River states, in part because Ibos have migrated out of those areas too, having fled Port Harcourt and Calabar during the Civil War. Ibo influence clearly declined. Indeed, minorities wanted their own states to get away from dominant ethnic groups in all regions. The NPP did poorly in Bendel state, too. In Gongola state, which is not contiguous to the Ibo core states of Imo and Anambra, the NPP did well. The UPN did better in states contiguous to its core Yoruba areas, Kwara and Bendel, but this is also because there are Yoruba speakers there, especially in Kwara. The NPP had become a more ethnic party than the old NCNC. The PRP also could not move out beyond its core areas, though it did better in Kano and Kaduna states than the old NEPU had done.

Only the NPN can be said to have moved beyond the base areas of its old party. It increased its share of the vote in the old Eastern Region and even won votes in the Ibo heartland states. It suffered a decline in the percentage of the vote in the old Northern Region, losing votes to the GNPP and the PRP, but it won about one-third of its presidential, senatorial and gubernatorial votes outside of the old north.

Table 37 compares seats won in the 1959 and 1979 elections to the House of Representatives. The NPN was able to compete outside the north in a way that had been impossible for the NPC. The UPN was less competitive than the AG in the east, and the NPP won fewer votes than the NCNC had in the east and west.

CONCLUSION

The results are mixed, then, as we consider how ethnically determined were the 1979 elections. No party won every elected position within its core area, but parties did dominate these core areas. Many elections were not competitive, though the old categories, familiar in the 1950s and 1960s, of 'unopposed' and 'lost deposit' disappeared. Parties were able to win at least some votes outside their areas. The PRP was the most geographically bound of all the parties, drawing its support from Kano and Kaduna states.

The system was able to provide enough winners to keep parties going if they could maintain their own internal cohesion. Each party controlled at least two state executives, with the GNPP and the PRP each winning two, the NPP three, the UPN five and the NPN seven. Each party won at least seven Senate seats, and each at least nearly 10 per cent seats in the House of Representatives. Thus, parties were not frozen out. The multiple elections and layered federal system provided space for opposition parties at different levels. No party, including the NPN, dominated the subpresidential elected offices.

The spread of the votes led to a failure of the NPN to win a majority in the Federal Legislature. A coalition of parties was required, and one was put together between the NPN and the NPP. The NPP received critical ministries, junior ministries and the Speaker of the House of Representatives. Before the coalition was established, however, there was a crucial testing of the presidential election itself.

The constitution under which the elections took place called for a winning presidential candidate to have a plurality of votes and at least one-quarter of the votes in two-thirds of the states. Shehu Shagari had 5.7 million votes, and the runner-up, Chief Awolowo, had 4.9 million. Although Shagari had 25 per cent of the votes in 12 states, he won only a little more than 20 per cent of the votes in Kano state, which would have made his thirteenth state. The chief legal adviser of the NPN, Richard Akinjide, argued that this satisfied the constitutional requirements since two-thirds of 19 (states) is 12 and two-thirds. Thus, only one-sixth of the vote was required in the thirteenth state. FEDECO agreed with this interpretation. Chief Awolowo appealed this decision to the Special Elections Tribunal which upheld FEDECO's decision.[72] He then appealed the tribunal decision to the Nigerian Supreme Court, which by a 5–2 decision also upheld FEDECO.

The new president of Nigeria was, therefore, elected under a cloud. There were serious doubts that the proper procedures had been followed. If the election had gone to a run-off between Shagari and Awolowo, it would have been decided in an electoral college composed of those elected to the Federal Legislature and to the state assemblies. In the electoral college, no party would have had near a majority: the NPN would have had 691; the UPN, 472; the NPP, 320; the GNPP, 208; the PRP, 200. The NPN–NPP would have prevailed. Awolowo and the UPN would have needed the support of the NPP and either the GNPP or the PRP.

The aforementioned amendments to the constitution carried out as the last acts of the military government by decree eliminated the electoral college if a candidate did not win in the first direct election.

The amendments provided for a direct run-off with one-quarter of the votes still needed in two-thirds of the states. A third election was mandated if no winner emerged in the second. In the final run-off, the winner would have to have a majority of the votes. The last act of the 1979 election was an amendment not to change the rules. The consequences of this act, however, remained with Nigeria for many years. The legitimacy of the election was tainted. Nonetheless, Nigeria did carry out elections in a complex federal system and the civilian regime was maintained until the end of 1983. New elections were held in 1983 with even greater controversies over procedures and outcomes. However, President Shagari, elected for a second term, served only a few months in office before the military once again took over. The 1983 elections and the new coup are related, but different, stories.

NOTES

1. The history of this period and accounts of various elections can be found in James Coleman, *Nigeria: Background to Nationalism*, Berkeley, University of California Press, 1964; Richard Sklar, *Nigerian Political Parties*, Princeton, Princeton University Press, 1966; and Oyeleye Oyediran, 'Background to Military Rule', in Oyeleye Oyediran (ed.), *Nigerian Government and Politics Under Military Rule, 1966–79*, New York, St Martin's Press, 1979, pp. 1–24; S. Keith Panter-Brick (ed.), *Nigerian Politics and Military Rule: Prelude to Civil War*, London, Athlone Press, 1970; Billy J. Dudley, *Instability and Political Order: Politics and Crises in Nigeria*, Ibadan, University of Ibadan Press, 1973; John Mackintosh, *Nigerian Government and Politics*, Evanston Ill., Northwestern University Press, 1966.
2. For accounts and analysis of the crisis in the west see, Richard Sklar, 'Nigerian Politics: The Ordeal of Chief Awolowo, 1960–65', in Gwendolen Carter (ed.), *Politics in Africa: Seven Cases*, New York, Harcourt Brace and World, Inc., 1966, pp. 119–66; Billy J. Dudley, 'Western Nigeria and the Nigerian Crisis', Panter-Brick, *Nigerian Politics and Military Rule*, pp. 94–110; Oyeleye Oyediran, 'Crisis in an Organization: A Case Study of Pluralism in Nigeria', *Plural Societies*, vol. 5, no. 2, summer 1971, pp. 43–54; F. A. Baptiste, 'The Relations Between the Western Region and the Federal Government of Nigeria: A Study of the 1962 Emergency', MA thesis, Manchester University, 1966.
3. See Henry Bienen, *Armies and Parties in Africa*, New York, Holmes and Meier, 1978, pp. 186–251.
4. Among the surveys that do exist, see Margaret Peil, 'A Civilian Appraisal of Military Rule in Nigeria', *Armed Forces and Society*, vol. 2, no. 1, Fall 1975. Peil's sample was 830 people, half of whom lived in Lagos. Also see Leo Dare, 'Military Leadership and Political Development in the Western State of Nigeria', Ph.D. thesis, Carleton University, 1972.
5. In 1972–3, I carried out interviews with former members of the prorogued Western House of Assembly. Out of a possible 128 living members of the House of Assembly, 54 were interviewed. They were asked: 'Will there be civilian rule in 1976?' 8 (14.8 per cent) said 'yes'; 23 (42.6 per cent) said 'no'; 12 (22.2 per cent) said 'don't know'; 5 (9.3 per cent) responded that the military 'could not be forced

to go'; 4 (7.4 per cent) said that 'the military doesn't want to go but it will be forced to do so'; and 2 (3.7 per cent) did not answer. The politicians in the western state were not representative of Nigerian politicians, or of all Nigerians, but the interviews do suggest a suspicion of the military's intentions during this period.

6. See Robin Luckham, *The Nigerian Military*, Cambridge, Cambridge University Press, 1971.

7. J. Bayo Adekson, 'Dilemma of Military Disengagement', in Oyediran, *Nigerian Government and Politics*, p. 221.

8. In our interviews with former members of the Western House of Assembly in 1972–3, 29 (or 35.7 per cent) thought unequivocally that military men would stand for election; 10 of whom said they would not do well and 10 of whom thought only a few officers would win; 7 (13 per cent) were noncommittal, saying soldiers had the right to stand; 11 (20.4 per cent) did not answer; 4 (7.4 per cent) thought that they would not stand for election.

9. Azikiwe proposed this in a set of lectures reproduced in the *Sunday Times* 19 October 1972, and in the *Daily Times* 28 october 1972. See Bienen, *Armies and Parties in Africa*, pp. 257–60.

10. Murtala Mohammed put forward his program for military withdrawal on 1 October 1975. See *Daily Times* (Lagos) 1 October 1975. The program is described in Adekson, 'Dilemma of Military Disengagements'.

11. Important discussions are Adekson, 'Dilemma of Military Disengagements'; Alex E. Gboyega, 'The Making of the Nigerian Constitution', in Oyediran, *Nigerian Government and Politics*, pp. 235–58; Ali D. Yahaya, 'The Struggle for Power in Nigeria 1966–79', in Oyediran, *Nigerian Government and Politics*, pp. 259–75; Claude S. Phillips, 'Nigeria's New Political Institutions', *Journal of Modern African Studies*, vol. 18 no. 1, March 1980, pp. 1–22; S. Keith Panter-Brick, 'The Constitutional Drafting Committee', in Panter-Brick (ed.), *Soldiers and Oil: The Transformation of Nigerian Politics*, London, Frank Cass and Company, 1978, pp. 291–352. I have also benefited from Alaba Ogunsanwo's unpublished work on the Constituent Assembly and the constitution, done at Princeton, 1979–80, titled *The Public Debate on Nigeria's Constitution: October 1976 – September 1977*.

12. Phillips, 'Nigeria's New Political Institution's', p. 3, and Panter-Brick, 'The Constitutional Drafting Committee', p. 347. Chief Awolowo refused to serve; thus the CDC had 49 members.

13. The recommendations of subcommittees and the plenary committee can be found in *Report of Constitutional Drafting Committee Containing the Draft Constitution*, vols I and II, Lagos, Federal Ministry of Information, 1976. Of the 28 memorandums received by the CDC that referred specifically to party, only one favored a one-party system and five favored a no-party system. The rest supported two or more parties. See Panter-Brick, 'The Constitutional Drafting Committee', p. 307. In the interviews we carried out with politicians in 1972–3, only one person was in favor of a one-party state, 33 were against, one said it was up to the people to decide, and 19 did not answer that question.

14. There were four political scientists on the CDC, including the late Billy Dudley who was an influential member. Professor Dudley had written extensively of the need to create rules of the game in which bargaining could go on between many players. He believed that the three- and then four-region system of the First Republic had been intrinsically unstable and utilized game theory models to argue his case. See Billy J. Dudley, *Instability and Political Order*.

15. Henry Bienen, 'One-Party Systems in Africa', in *Armies and Parties in Africa*, pp. 44–5; Sklar, *Nigerian Political Parties*; Billy J. Dudley, *Parties and Politics in Northern Nigeria*, London, Frank Cass and Company, 1968.

16. Phillips, 'Nigeria's New Political Institutions', pp. 7–8.
17. See *Federal Military Government Views on the Report of the Panel on Creation of States*, Lagos, Federal Ministry of Information, 1976; also see Ali D. Yahaya, 'The Creation of States', in Panter-Brick, *Soldiers and Oil*, pp. 201–3.
18. Adekson, 'Dilemma of Military Disengagements', p. 221.
19. See *Suggested Framework for a National System of Local Government*, Lagos, Federal Ministry of Information, 1976; *Guidelines for Local Government Reform*, Lagos, Federal Ministry of Information, 1976.
20. For the local government reorganizations and elections see S. Keith Panter-Brick, 'Introduction', in Panter-Brick, *Soldiers and Oil*, pp. 253–6; A. E. Gboyega and Oyeleye Oyediran, 'A View from Ibadan', in ibid., pp. 257–69; Abubakar Yaya Aliyu, 'As Seen in Kaduna', in ibid., pp. 270–87.
21. Panter-Brick, *Soldiers and Oil*, p. 256. States could allow up to 25 per cent of the councilors to be chosen as nominated members, ibid., p. 267. In systems where indirect election prevailed, local government areas were broken into primary units, and these were grouped into electoral colleges from which councilors would subsequently be elected. In Kaduna state, electoral colleges were formed as single member constituencies.
22. Parts of Kwara state and Bendel state also have large numbers of Yoruba.
23. I have not looked systematically at all losses and victories and correlated them with past party identification. Looking at major figures who stood leads me to believe that Action Group stalwarts did considerably better on the whole than former NNDP or NCNC figures.
24. Aliyu, 'As Seen in Kaduna', p. 279, also notes that identification with rival villages or communities was important for voters' choices. 'In areas where electoral colleges were composed of members from different villages, it was generally the candidate from the village with the larger number of voters in the college who won the election'. ibid., p. 280.
25. For a rundown on candidates, see *West Africa*, no. 3132, 18 July 1977, pp. 1455–6. Also see *West Africa*, no. 3136, 15 August 1977, pp. 1659, 1661.
26. The elected members to the Constituent Assembly are listed in *West Africa*, no. 3140, 12 September 1977, pp. 1855, 1857, 1859.
27. See Henry Bienen, 'Politicians Under Military Rule', in *Armies and Parties in Africa*, pp. 211–32.
28. Phillips, 'Nigeria's New Political Institutions', p. 10.
29. The debates can be followed in Federal Republic of Nigeria, *Proceedings of the Constituent Assembly*, Lagos, Federal Ministry of Information, 1977. The public debates are detailed in a forthcoming work by Alaba Ogunsanwo, *The Public Debate on Nigeria's Constitution: October 1976 – September 1977*, Princeton, NJ, Center of International Studies, Princeton University, 1980. Various issues of *West Africa* followed the debates, as did Nigerian newspapers such as the *New Nigerian* (Lagos and Kaduna) and the *Daily Times* (Lagos).
30. The northern states of Nigeria have had a dual system of law, having secular and Islamic law with Sharia courts. These courts have heard the overwhelming majority of cases. The issue in the Constituent Assembly was whether Nigeria should have a Sharia Court of Appeals at the highest level. Opponents prevailed who argued that this would violate the separation between church and state.
31. Gboyega, 'The Making of the Nigerian Constitution', p. 246, suggests that the proceedings of the Constituent Assembly were more controversial than those of the CDC because individuals felt that they had a mandate, as elected representatives, and because of a sense of the finality of decisions reached in the assembly.
32. The Council of State is advisory body to the president comprising the president as chairman, the vice president, former presidents and heads of government, the

president of the Senate, the president of the House of Representatives, former chief justices, the attorney general, governors of the states and a person appointed by a council of chiefs from each state.

33. The constitution is published as *The Constitution of the Federal Republic of Nigeria, 1979*, Lagos, Federal Ministry of Information, 1979,

34. The amendments to the constitution, published as Decree numbers 104 and 105, can be found in the *New Nigerian*, 27 December 1979.

35. A number of military officers had left the military before the fall of 1978. Some of these were to be quite active in partisan politics, either standing for party or government office or serving in appointed party positions. Among such officers were Major Generals Robert Adeyinka Adebayo, Hassan Usman Katsina and Olufemi Olutoye, Inspector-General of Police Sam Kalem, and Deputy Inspector General of Police T. A. Fagbola.

36. Yahaya, 'The Struggle for Power in Nigeria, 1966–79', p. 269.

37. Phillips, 'Nigeria's New Political Institutions', p. 17.

38. Yahaya, 'The Struggle for Power in Nigeria. 1966–79', p. 270.

39. Ibid. A Yoruba, Chief Akinfosile, became the chairman of the NPP.

40. Ibid., p. 274.

41. Phillips, 'Nigeria's New Political Institutions', p. 20.

42. See chapter three.

43. The class struggle that NEPU saw was a dichotomous one between members of the native administrations and ordinary *talakawa* or commoners, see Dudley, *Parties and Politics in Northern Nigeria*, p. 169.

44. Coleman, *Nigeria: Background to Nationalism*, p. 365.

45. Sklar, *Nigerian Political Parties*, pp. 335–7.

46. Dudley, *Parties and Politics in Northern Nigeria*, pp. 179–80.

47. This book was published in 1968, Ibadan, Oxford University Press.

48. Sklar, *Nigerian Political Parties*, p. 256.

49. For a biography of Aminu Kano see Alan Feinstein, *African Revolutionary: The Life and Times of Nigeria's Aminu Kano*, New York, Quadrangle, 1973.

50. Chief Awolowo did resign after two years as commissioner. Aminu Kano held a commissionership for almost a decade.

51. Ken Post and George Jenkins, *The Price of Liberty: Personality and Politics in Colonial Nigeria*, Cambridge, Cambridge University Press, 1973, p. 134.

52. Ibid., pp. 134–5.

53. Sklar, *Nigerian Political Parties*, p. 294.

54. Sayre O. Schatz, *Nigerian Capitalism*, Berkeley, University of California Press, 1977, p. 156.

55. Richard Sklar, 'Contradictions in the Nigerian Political System', *Journal of Modern African Studies*, vol. 3, no. 2, 1965, p. 204.

56. The data reported in Morrison's work are from a survey (N-3755) carried out in the summer of 1974. Gongola and Sokoto states and the eastern half of Borno state are not represented in the sample. About 14 per cent of the population is thus missing. See Donald Morrison, 'Inequalities of Social Rewards: Realities and Perceptions in Nigeria', in Bienen and Diejomaoh (eds), *The Political Economy of Income Distribution in Nigeria*, New York, Holmes and Meier, 1981, pp. 173–92.

57. Sidney Verba, Norman H. Nie and Jae-On Kim, *Participation and Political Equality: A Seven Nation Comparison*, Cambridge, Cambridge University Press, 1978, p. 103, table 6-1. Fieldwork in Nigeria was actually carried out in this study in 1966. Margaret Peil's work, carried out in Nigerian cities in 1970–1 also found high rates of membership in organizations. See *The Nigerian Government: The People's View*, London, Cassell, 1976.

58. Verba, Nie and Kim, *Participation and Political Equality*, p. 270.
59. S. Keith Panter-Brick, 'Nigeria: The 1979 Elections', *Afrika Spectrum*, vol. 3, January 1979, p. 328.
60. Ibid., pp. 329–30.
61. For a critique of the electoral data in FEDECO Report on the 1979 elections see S. Keith Panter-Brick, 'Scandal of FEDECO's Inaccuracies', *West Africa*, no. 3319, 9 March 1981, pp. 477–81.
62. Panter-Brick, 'Nigeria: The 1979 Elections', p. 320. It has been reported that conservative Moslems in the north gave approval to women voting and 'led the Purdah women of their own households to vote.' See 'Sidelights of Nigeria's Six Elections', *West Africa*, no. 3242, 3 September 1979, pp. 1592–5.
63. Details on voting procedures can be found in Panter-Brick, 'Nigeria: The 1979 Elections'.
64. This poll was reported in the *Punch* newspaper and in *Agence France Press*, no. 2585, 18 May 1979.
65. Martin Dent, 'Mystery of the Missing Bandwagon', no. 3243, *West Africa*, 10 September 1978, pp. 1633–4, gives slightly different figures for party percentages of the vote.
66. Ibid., p. 1633. Dent's figures, as noted, are slightly different from those cited in table 30.
67. As Panter-Brick argues, 'Nigeria: The 1979 Elections'.
68. Ibid.
69. See John Paden, *Religion and Political Culture in Kano*, Berkeley, University of California Press, 1973; and Paden's 'Islam, Constitutional Change, and Politics in Nigeria', draft paper, October 1979.
70. District breakdowns would not give us good information of Yoruba Moslem voting in any case; that could be done only through surveys since geographic distributions would not indicate religious preference very well.
71. It is more useful to compare 1979 with 1959 because the 1964 and 1965 elections were so tainted with thuggery, ballot stuffing and boycotts.
72. Many state elections were appealed to special election tribunals also. For example, the deputy governor of Imo State was disqualified. Charges were brought against individuals after elections on the grounds that they had not met electoral requirements.